LABORATORIES AGAINST DEMOCRACY

PRINCETON STUDIES IN
AMERICAN POLITICS

Historical, International, and Comparative Perspectives

*Suzanne Mettler, Eric Schickler, and
Theda Skocpol, Series Editors*

*Ira Katznelson, Martin Shefter, Founding
Series Editors (Emeritus)*

A list of titles in this series appears in the back of the book.

Laboratories against Democracy

HOW NATIONAL PARTIES TRANSFORMED STATE POLITICS

JACOB M. GRUMBACH

PRINCETON UNIVERSITY PRESS

PRINCETON & OXFORD

Requests for permission to reproduce material from this work
should be sent to permissions@press.princeton.edu

Published by Princeton University Press
41 William Street, Princeton, New Jersey 08540
99 Banbury Road, Oxford OX2 6JX

press.princeton.edu

First paperback printing, 2023
Paper ISBN 978-0-691-21846-5

The Library of Congress has cataloged the cloth edition as follows:

Names: Grumbach, Jacob M., 1987– author.
Title: Laboratories against democracy : how national parties transformed state
    politics / Jacob M. Grumbach.
Description: Princeton, New Jersey : Princeton University Press, 2022. | Series:
    Princeton studies in American politics | Includes bibliographical references and
    index.
Identifiers: LCCN 2021040301 (print) | LCCN 2021040302 (ebook) |
    ISBN 9780691218458 (hardback) | ISBN 9780691218472 (ebook)
Subjects: LCSH: U.S. states—Politics and government. | Political parties—
    United States. | Political parties—United States—States. | Federal government—
    United States. | State governments—United States. | Polarization (Social sciences)—
    Political aspects—United States. | BISAC: POLITICAL SCIENCE / Political
    Ideologies / Democracy | POLITICAL SCIENCE / Political Process / General
    Classification: LCC JK2408 .G77 2022 (print) | LCC JK2408 (ebook) |
    DDC 320.973—dc23
LC record available at https://lccn.loc.gov/2021040301
LC ebook record available at https://lccn.loc.gov/2021040302

British Library Cataloging-in-Publication Data is available

Editorial: Bridget Flannery-McCoy and Alena Chekanov
Production Editorial: Sara Lerner
Jacket/Cover Design: Karl Spurzem
Production: Erin Suydam
Publicity: James Schneider and Kathryn Stevens

This book has been composed in Arno

CONTENTS

LIST OF FIGURES AND TABLES

Figures

Tables

PREFACE

IT WAS A DIFFERENT era of social science when I began my dissertation in 2015. It is not that scholars in my discipline of political science, or adjacent ones like economics and sociology, were avoiding addressing pressing research questions. But there was less of a sense of urgency.

In these "before times," I was motivated to explain the wave of major state-level policies implemented in the 2000s and 2010s, especially those that resulted from the Republican electoral wave that swept across the Midwest and Southeast in 2010. New Republican governors like Scott Walker of Wisconsin and Rick Snyder of Michigan passed a series of major policies that restricted labor unions, cut taxes on the wealthy, and made it harder for women to get an abortion. Just as important, many of these Republican state governments rejected the Medicaid expansion authorized by the Affordable Care Act—an unprecedented refusal of free money from the national government to provide health care to their own residents.

Democratic states implemented major policy changes, too. They created new fuel efficiency standards and subsidies for renewable energy. They increased their state minimum wages. Many raised taxes on their wealthiest residents.

The challenge, as I saw it, was to explain these rapid policy changes that had occurred without much corresponding movement in the prevailing public opinion among residents in these states. For the most part, the average voter in each state hadn't much changed their attitudes on abortion, teachers unions, the minimum wage, and the like. You can't explain change in a Y variable with an unchanging X variable, and you definitely can't explain it with an X variable moving in the opposite direction.

My interest in state-level policy reflects my coming-of-age in a political era of impasse at the federal level. I was first eligible to vote in 2006, and the subsequent decade was essentially one long stint of divided national governance, with one party in control of Congress and the other the presidency. Gridlock was intense. Despite ongoing wars and a financial crisis, major legislative action was frequently preempted by threats of a Senate filibuster. In this context, the major policy action was occurring in the states, most of which were controlled by a single political party.

But as time went on, I became increasingly concerned that state politics wasn't the whole story. I had written about how federalism could serve as a "safety valve" for policy demanders who were out of power in Washington, D.C., and described the clear consequences of a persistently gridlocked national government for policy across the fifty states. Yet policy activity doesn't just flow naturally from D.C. to the states, and national and state governance are not exchangeable substitutes. If you, an environmental activist, are out of power in Washington, D.C., passing a climate policy in California does not neatly translate to half a loaf or a second-best option. And if you, a wealthy individual, wish to make it more difficult for people to vote, your action at the state level reverberates across the entire American political system. In sum, the adage "think globally, act locally" doesn't quite capture profound transformation of politics in the fifty states.

Above all, it was the Trump era that gave me a new respect for the importance of federalism in explaining the ups and downs of the roller coaster of American politics. Among pundits and many scholars, the Trump presidency was federalism's time to shine. "Aren't you glad to have federalism now that the Trump coalition is in power in Washington?" they asked, not infrequently. They pointed to state governments that were using policy and bureaucracy to fight against the Trump coalition on immigration enforcement, environmental regulation, and much more. At the time, I mostly agreed.

But my research on the states was giving me a nagging feeling. Ominously, many of the trends connected to both the ascendance and realization of Trumpism—authoritarianism, inequality, and the narrowing of democracy—were coming from the state level. Racial authoritarianism in policing, longstanding but increasingly visible in recent years, was a state and local affair. Inequality in political voice, in which narrow and wealthy interests set the policy agenda, was especially extreme at the state level. And the steady chipping away at democratic institutions through voter suppression, gerrymandering, and corruption was spreading across states. Trump has been characterized as an aberrant wrecking ball that disrupted American politics. But it was the states that were the wrecking ball, clearing a path for Trumpism throughout the American political system.

That is why this book is only very loosely connected to my dissertation. Here I try to take stock of how federalism shapes modern American politics. Doing justice to this task requires breadth in analytical lens. It is not enough to just study voters, or organizations, or institutional rules, or public policy and political economy; it takes the wisdom of research in all of these areas to shed light on how American politics works in the twenty-first century—and how we can change it.

ACKNOWLEDGMENTS

I HAVE BEEN LUCKY to have received guidance, feedback, and support from an incredible group of scholars and organizations. I hope the reader believes me when I say that this book would not have been possible without them.

Portions of chapter 3 have been developed from my article "From Backwaters to Major Policymakers: Policy Polarization in the States, 1970–2014," *Perspectives on Politics* 16, no. 2 (2018): 416–35; portions of chapter 5 have been developed from my article "Interest Group Activists, Party Insiders, and the Polarization of State Legislatures," *Legislative Studies Quarterly* 45, no. 1 (2020): 5–34.

This book is based (loosely) on my dissertation, "Polarized Federalism," which was advised by an extraordinary committee at UC Berkeley, including co-chairs Paul Pierson and Eric Schickler, as well as Sarah Anzia, Sean Gailmard, and Amy Lerman. At conferences, over email, and on Zoom, these and other graduate school advisors of mine continued to provide mentorship and feedback on this project long after my graduation.

This book, I hope, also represents the wisdom of my cherished community of scholarly colleagues, mentors, and friends across the country. My University of Washington colleagues, especially Megan Francis, Chris Parker, and Sophia Jordán Wallace, as well as my department chair John Wilkerson, were instrumental. My team of democracy scholars, Adam Bonica, Charlotte Hill, and Hakeem Jefferson, kept my eyes on the prize. My labor politics colleague Paul Frymer and my undergraduate advisor, Dorian Warren, got me in the game and kept me from falling through the cracks. I drew heavily on the research and feedback of many other social scientist colleagues and friends: Abhay Aneja, Andrew Baker, David Bateman, Jessica Bulman-Pozen, Nick Carnes, Ruth Collier, Justin de Benedictis-Kessner, E. J. Dionne, Michele Epstein, Bernard Fraga, Jacob Hacker, Zoli Hajnal, Hahrie Han, Alex Hertel-Fernandez, Matt Grossmann, Christian Hosam, Destin Jenkins, Taeku Lee, Gabe Lenz, Trevon Logan, Neil Malhotra, Tom Mann, Andrew McCall, Nolan McCarty,

Suzanne Mettler, Jamila Michener, Rob Mickey, Lisa Miller, Quinn Mulroy, Neil O'Brian, Tom Ogorzalek, Norm Ornstein, Phil Rocco, Alexander Sahn, David Schleicher, David Shor, Theda Skocpol, Joe Soss, Lester Spence, Nick Stephanopoulos, LaFleur Stephens-Dougan, Leah Stokes, Sidney Tarrow, Michael Tesler, Kathy Thelen, Chloe Thurston, Sam Trachtman, Shad Turney, Chris Warshaw, Vesla Weaver, Chris Zepeda-Millán, Dan Ziblatt, and many others. I also have to give a shout-out to my academic Twitter friends, who are too numerous to mention but whose wit and wisdom have influenced my thinking.

Seminar participants at UW, including at the Washington Institute for the Study of Inequality and Race (WISIR), Center for Statistics and the Social Sciences (CSSS), and Bridges Center for Labor Studies, were amazingly helpful. I also received insightful feedback on parts of the manuscript at American politics and political economy seminars across the country (they were on Zoom, but it felt like I was there in person). I thank seminar attendees at Johns Hopkins, Princeton, the University of Minnesota, the University of Oregon, UCLA, UCSD, and Vanderbilt.

I want to thank the three anonymous scholars who peer reviewed this manuscript for Princeton University Press. Their outstandingly helpful feedback sharpened my argument and, in many ways, made this book what it is. I also owe a major debt of gratitude to Princeton University Press editor Bridget Flannery-McCoy, as well as editorial associate Alena Chekanov, production editor Sara Lerner, and copyeditor Jenn Backer. Their gracious commitment and meticulous reading shepherded this project from start to finish. I counted on outstanding research assistance from Jeffrey Grove, Dennis Young, and Abhi Desai.

For countless ideas and for helping to publicize the research findings in this book, I thank an amazing set of journalists and news editors: Perry Bacon, Zack Bauchamp, Jamelle Bouie, Brooke Gladstone, G. Elliott Morris, and Paul Rosenberg. In terms of data, I stand on the shoulders of giants, relying on painstakingly collected data sets from the Correlates of State Policy Project, the MIT Election Lab, and Devin Caughey and Chris Warshaw.

Most importantly, I want to thank my family, who kept me going every step of the way. To my wonderful mom and dad, Lisa and Kevin, thank you for your dedication to your kids. To my sister Aimee and brother Matty, thank you for the solidarity in good times and bad (and especially for the dancing). My big cousin Chris, my uncle Anthony, and so many in my chosen family, including

Nick Borelli, Talya Courtney, Destin Jenkins, and the Kline brothers, have each spent untold hours talking politics with me. Finally, I wouldn't be who I am (and this book wouldn't be what it is) without my late grandparents Gertrude, Louis, Madeleine, and Mel. Each passing year makes me more grateful to be a part of this family. Thanks for everything.

THE CRISES OF 2020

THREE MONUMENTAL crises in 2020 revealed an American political system that lacked the capacity to solve fundamental challenges. The American response to the Covid-19 pandemic has been plagued by coordination problems, negative spillovers, and decentralized accountability. The police murder of George Floyd, once again highlighting racial authoritarianism long endemic to American policing, galvanized an unprecedented protest movement throughout the country. And, in the midst of all of this, American electoral democracy hung in the balance as President Donald Trump attempted to delegitimize mail voting and encouraged his supporters to engage in voter intimidation at urban polling places.

In its Covid-19 response, its policing, and its democratic performance, the United States was lagging behind other wealthy countries. Despite not being hit by an early pandemic wave, by the end of 2020, nearly 300,000 Americans had died from Covid, one of the world's highest death rates per capita. In its criminal justice system, the videos of officers brutalizing Black Americans with near impunity are only the most visible feature of American police forces that arrest and commit violence against citizens at rates far beyond those of any other country (Picheta and Pettersson 2020). In terms of its democratic performance, U.S. political institutions were increasingly under entrenched minority rule.

These crises—Covid-19, policing, and democracy—did not just implicate the usual suspects, such as America's legacy of institutional racism and its porous welfare state. Crucially, the crises also thrust American *federalism*—the broad authority given to state and local governments—into the spotlight. The Covid-19 pandemic exposed problems in coordinating state governments' procurement of personal protective equipment (PPE) for essential workers, maintaining safety net programs, distributing vaccines, and holding leaders accountable for their performance. State and local responses to calls for police and criminal justice reform have shown these governments to be fearful of or captured by powerfully concentrated police interests. And state governments have innovated new ways to suppress votes and gerrymander districts, and have lacked the capacity and, at times, the will to administer mail voting during a pandemic.

Like Germany, India, and Mexico, the United States has a political system with a multilevel federal structure, but the American version of federalism is an especially decentralized one. It endows state (and, by extension, local) governments with broad authority. This is true of public health policy, where pandemic responses were lacking, and even more so of policing, education, and housing policy. Much of American social policy, such as Medicaid and anti-poverty programs, is administered by the states. State authorities administer and certify elections—all of them, for every public office from dog catcher to U.S. president.

These and other policy failures were not just the product of dysfunction in the White House. They are not solely the result of the widening political polarization over the past generation, or even the asymmetric rightward movement of the Republican Party. Instead, the challenges facing the United States—from rising inequality to weak crisis management to democratic backsliding—are the result of a distinctly modern phenomenon: the combination of nationally coordinated political parties and the decentralized institutional structure of American federalism.[1]

The powerful role of state governments in the American political system is central to understanding the modern policy and political economy landscapes of the United States. But a focus on these institutions, the rules of the game, is incomplete without an analysis of the players on the field. The general form of American federalism has persisted for hundreds of years, but in recent decades this decentralized institutional structure has collided with nationalized party coalitions, supported by highly coordinated networks of political organizations, national media, and a racially sorted electorate.

---

1. Recent examples abound of states' role in modern American political problems. Budget-constrained states refuse free federal money for Medicaid expansion, causing thousands of preventable deaths and leaving American health care far behind that of other wealthy countries. State unemployment administrators are backlogged and hamstrung, in contrast to the Federal Reserve's rapid provision of free credit to large firms and the financial industry in the 2008 financial crisis and Covid-19 recession. State election administrators act in concert with national Republican interests to innovate new ways to suppress votes, constrain the other side's political organizations, and otherwise expand minority rule.

Facing a polarized and frequently divided national government, partisan coalitions of donors, activists, and organizations shifted their focus downward to state governments. State governments became the main sites of policy action in the American political system, as they had been before the 1930s. This shift to the state level did more than just shift the location of political activity. It fundamentally changed the playing field of American politics. It gave greater voice to groups that could effectively move their political and economic resources across state borders and benefited those who could marshal information to set policy agendas and influence state-level politicians. And as under Jim Crow, a coalition used state governments to weaken American democracy.

PART I

Federalism and the Resurgence of the States

1

Introduction

"I GUARANTEE YOU we can draw four Republican congressional maps," Republican Kansas State Senate leader Susan Wagle told donors at a closed-door fundraiser in 2020. "That takes out [Democratic U.S. House Representative] Sharice Davids. . . . But we can't do it unless we have a two-thirds majority in the Kansas Senate and House."[1]

Such an appeal might have sounded strange a generation ago. Here was a legislative leader in Kansas *state* government outlining a *national* strategy for the Republican Party. Wagle's appeal to contribute money to state-level Republicans was light on the Kansas-specific issues, but it emphasized how state government could play a role in the national tug-of-war over American politics and policy. It outlined a strategy of gerrymandering—a way for this coalition to tilt the rules of democracy in its favor.

The United States has a unique constitutional system. Many of its distinctive institutional features have come under fire in recent years. The Electoral College has been criticized for installing presidents who do not win the popular vote, Senate apportionment for granting equal influence to Wyoming's 573,000 residents as California's 40 million, and even the unitary executive for granting too much authority to presidents. But Wagle was describing a way to take advantage of a less often discussed but critically important feature of the U.S. political system: *American federalism*, a system in which authority is dispersed across multiple levels of government.

---

1. Sherman Smith, "Kansas Senate President Pushes Redistricting Plan That 'Takes Out Sharice Davids,'" *Shawnee Mission Post*, October 10, 2020, https://shawneemissionpost.com /2020/10/10/kansas-senate-president-pushes-redistricting-plan-that-takes-out-sharice-davids -103243/.

While institutional authority is highly decentralized, American political parties no longer are. Over the past half century, the Democratic and Republican parties have transformed from loose networks into more tightly knit partisan teams of activists, organizations, and candidates. Like Wagle at the Kansas fundraiser, these partisan teams coordinate across the many decentralized institutional venues of American federalism to pursue their increasingly national political visions.

Federalism expands the number of institutional venues in which American politics is fought, and it puts the main levers of democracy, such as legislative districting and election administration, at the state level. American federalism has existed in one way or another for well over two centuries—but nationally coordinated and polarized political parties have not. As the Kansas example shows, national political coalitions have developed new strategies to exploit the decentralized institutional features of American federalism.

What happens when today's *national* Democratic and Republican parties collide with the critically important *subnational* institutions of American federalism? That is the subject of this book. Classic theories of federalism often lead us to expect that institutional decentralization is a "safety valve" in times of political crisis, and such an attitude is commonplace in contemporary political discourse. CNN analyst Asha Rangappa and political scientist Michael McFaul each separately tweeted that they were "thankful for federalism"; legal scholar Erin Ryan proclaimed that "I've never been more grateful for federalism than I am right now." For many, the era of national partisan polarization makes the decentralized institutions of federalism all the more appealing, a harkening back to a time when "all politics [was] local."

But today's nationally coordinated parties have fundamentally changed the way that American federalism operates. State governments do not serve as a safety valve for national politics. Instead, they exacerbate national challenges, including unequal political influence and declining accountability—leaving American democracy at risk of backsliding. Indeed, contrary to the hopes of James Madison, a large federal republic may not help contain factions but empower them. And contrary to the hopes of Louis Brandeis, state governments may not be "laboratories of democracy" but laboratories *against* democracy.

I argue, in brief, that the nationalization of the Democratic and Republican parties—the increased national coordination among activists, groups, and candidates in each party coalition—has produced three consequences: a resurgence of state governments as the center of American policymaking, reduced policy learning between states controlled by opposing parties, and democratic backsliding in states controlled by the Republican Party.

These three consequences lead me to take a fresh look at two prominent theories of American federalism. The first is that state governments are efficient and effective laboratories of democracy, learning from and emulating successful policy experiments from other states and rejecting the failed ones. The second is that the decentralization of power in federalism improves the relationship between the governing and the governed, fostering representation, responsiveness, and democratic inclusion. These theories enjoy wide appeal among scholars and pundits across the ideological spectrum.

These ideas are alluring—and deeply embedded in the American ethos. But this book provides new arguments and evidence that they no longer accurately describe the functioning of federalism. Instead of emulating successful policy experiments from other states and rejecting failed ones, laboratories of democracy exist in separate partisan "scientific" communities. And instead of safeguarding democracy, some state governments have become laboratories *against* democracy—innovating new ways to restrict the franchise, gerrymander districts, exploit campaign finance loopholes, and circumvent civil rights in the criminal justice system.

Federalism or State Politics?

The U.S. Constitution occupies a position of admiration in popular culture, "remain[ing] an object of reverence for nearly all Americans," in the words of former U.S. attorney general Ed Meese.[2] Scholars go so far as to call it "the Bible" of "American civil religion" (Lerner 1937, 1294; see also Levinson 2011; Franks 2019).[3] But the tone of discourse about American institutions has shifted quickly and dramatically since 2016. Scholars, journalists, and observers increasingly worry about the erosion of norms in American politics—and the apparent inability of the rules of the Constitution to contain the erosion. Support for the Electoral College, the Supreme Court, and the U.S. Senate has polarized and declined. Federalism, however, has remained popular across partisanship and among scholars, pundits, and the public alike.

2. https://www.heritage.org/political-process/report/the-meaning-the-constitution.

3. As recently as 2015, Matthew Yglesias observed that "the idea that America's constitutional system might be fundamentally flawed cuts deeply against the grain of our political culture."

This is not to say that there has not been some prominent scholarly skepticism toward American federalism. Progressive Era thinkers worried that state governments were woefully amateurish and easily captured by the powerful. Historians highlight the triumphs of national state building to take on the challenges of the Depression and World War II (e.g., Smith 2006). Economists have emphasized the gains from scale to be obtained by greater national investment and standardization (e.g., Konczal 2016). And, profoundly, historical scholars of race and democracy would note that state governments were the institutional enemy of abolitionists, anti-lynching activists, and civil rights pioneers.

More recently, historical institutionalist scholars in political science have engaged in critical studies of federalism. In *Fragmented Democracy* (2018), Jamila Michener uses the case of Medicaid administration to investigate how federalism creates inequality in access to political resources and how this affects democratic inclusion. Lisa Miller's *The Perils of Federalism* (2008) points to the potential for a greater decentralization and numerosity of political venues to disincentivize ordinary people's political participation. Rob Mickey's *Paths Out of Dixie* (2015) investigates the "authoritarian enclaves" of the Jim Crow South and their implications for democracy in a federal republic. Although this book uses mostly quantitative empirical methods, I draw on theories from this and other qualitative critical federalism scholarship (e.g., King 2017).

I also draw on a related literature that conceptualizes parties as networks of groups and politics as "organized combat" between them over their policy goals (e.g., Karol 2009; Hacker and Pierson 2010; Bawn et al. 2012). Recent books, such as *State Capture* by Alexander Hertel-Fernandez and *Short Circuiting Policy* by Leah Stokes, speak to the importance of groups, such as green energy firms or conservative organizations like the American Legislative Exchange Council (ALEC), in state politics and throughout the American federal system. Understanding the group-based structure of party coalitions is crucial for understanding how their nationalization transformed American federalism.

These critical federalism studies, however, have remained mostly outside of the political science mainstream (at least in the American politics subfield).[4] By contrast, there has been something of a resurgence of research in the American

4. Weissert (2011, 965–71) notes that when it comes to American and comparative scholarship on federalism, there is little "cross-fertilization of research across the two worlds." Further, the comparative politics scholarship tends to be more focused on the relationship between federalism and democracy—and generally more critical of federalism.

politics subfield of *state and local politics*. Scholars of American politics have long used variation across states as a way to test theories of legislative rules, public opinion, and other political forces.[5] To understand whether term limits decrease polarization, for instance, a scholar might compare trends in states that have term limits to those that do not, drawing conclusions about how term limits are likely to work in legislative institutions in general. These studies matured from investigating cross-sectional variation—a very difficult way to produce causal evidence given the vast differences between states on so many observed and unobserved characteristics—to highly sophisticated investigations into the measurement of and causal relationships between state public opinion, policy, and socioeconomic outcomes. Many of these studies have uncovered troubling issues in state and local politics, including unequal political influence (Rigby and Wright 2013), racial conflict (Duxbury 2021), unresponsive policy outcomes (Lax and Phillips 2012), and minimal electoral accountability for "out-of-step" legislators (Rogers 2017). Others, such as the classic *Statehouse Democracy* (Erikson, Wright, and McIver 1993) and Devin Caughey and Christopher Warshaw's *Dynamic Democracy* (forthcoming), find evidence that state policy is responsive to public opinion and paint a more optimistic picture of democracy in the states. This book builds on this state and local politics research.

For the most part, however, state and local politics research has treated the states as fifty separate polities, in which theories of "American politics" writ large are transplanted onto the states. As a political science professor of mine, Paul Pierson, would joke, quantitative Americanists tend to study the states primarily as a way to increase one's N to 50—to increase the "sample size" of governments as one might increase the number of rat cages for a lab experiment.[6] While this kind of research strategy might help scholars "address a domain of questions with greater statistical rigor because of the large number of states" (Brace and Jewett 1995, 655), it misses how political groups use state-level authority in ways that are inextricably tied to the politics of other states

5. This is closely related to the "subnational comparative method" in comparative politics scholarship.

6. Researchers have used the state level as a way to increase their N to 50 in cross-sectional studies of the roles of public opinion (Erikson, Wright, and McIver 1993; Lascher, Hagen, and Rochlin 1996), interest groups (Gray and Lowery 1988), descriptive representation (Bratton and Haynie 1999; Sanbonmatsu 2002), or institutional rules and legislative organization (Chubb 1988; Poterba 1995; Carey, Niemi, and Powell 1998; Barrilleaux and Berkman 2003; Overby, Kazee, and Prince 2004).

and, more importantly, to national politics. Although I am a quantitative Americanist, I take a slightly untraditional path in investigating how the use of state authority under federalism has changed as the political parties have become more nationally coordinated.

The Nationalization of the Parties

Decentralized federal institutions have existed throughout American political history, but nationalized parties have not. By nationalized parties, I mean political parties in which aligned groups, activists, candidates, and incumbents—in all offices at all levels of government—share similar policy agendas and see themselves engaged in broader political conflict with the other national party. Nationalized parties are polarized, with a growing distance between the policy goals of the average Democrat and average Republican, but this is not the whole story. Nationalized parties are polarized *and* nationally coordinated.

Although intraparty conflict continues, such as in contentious primary elections between "establishment" and "outsider" candidates, no longer do the parties mobilize predominantly around parochial issues or have distinct regional subcultures. Instead, they battle in the national arena, as the Republican government of Texas did in attempting to sue states who gave their Electoral College votes to Joe Biden,[7] or the Arizona state GOP did in calling on citizens to give their lives to overturn the results of the 2020 presidential election.[8] "There is one national Republican Party, just as there is one national Democratic Party," in the words of Lee Drutman (2018a).

Today's national Democratic and Republican parties are consolidated in new and important ways. Major organizations in each "extended party network," such as the National Rifle Association for Republicans or MoveOn .org for Democrats, are national in scope and yet highly mobile, able to shift political resources across geography and levels of government in search of advantageous terrain or to respond to political threats. Elites, activists, and

---

7. *State of Texas v. Commonwealth of Pennsylvania, State of Georgia, State of Michigan, and State of Wisconsin* (2020), https://www.texasattorneygeneral.gov/sites/default/files/images /admin/2020/Press/SCOTUSFiling.pdf.

8. John Bowden, "Arizona GOP Asks If Followers Willing to Give Their Lives to 'Stop the Steal,'" *The Hill*, December 8, 2020, https://thehill.com/homenews/news/529195-arizona-gop -asks-if-followers-willing-to-give-their-life-to-stop-the-steal.

voters are coordinated by the internet and powerful national media apparatuses. State and local parties, on the other hand, once central forces in American politics, are increasingly "pawns" in national politics (Schlozman and Rosenfeld 2019, 166).[9]

The old phrase "all politics is local" no longer applies to the political parties—but it does apply to American political institutions. What happens when you mix nationalized party coalitions with America's highly decentralized federal institutions? As the parties polarize, gridlock in Congress becomes more likely, and policy action moves down to the state level, with profound consequences. The shift to the state level does not simply change the location of political battles. It fundamentally changes the terrain of American politics, providing new advantages to groups who have the informational capacity to monitor politicians at lower levels of government and groups that can move political and economic resources across borders. And it opens up new opportunities for groups to tilt election administration and institutional rules in their favor, posing new challenges for American democracy.

National Parties in Subnational Politics

The collision of national parties and American federalism has had a series of profound consequences across the states. Table 1.1 outlines these consequences: a resurgence of state policy, the polarization of state policy learning, and, in some states, democratic backsliding.

9. The causes of party nationalization are multifaceted. They include shifts in technology and the media environment, in the strategies of activist organizations, in the decline of labor unions and the rise of economic inequality, and in elite electoral strategies around race and cultural conflict. This large-scale investigation of the transformation of the Democratic and Republican parties since the "textbook Congress" of the 1970s has yielded some of the most important political science research of the past two decades. The political consequences of party nationalization are also broad. National parties have fundamentally different incentives in federal systems than do decentralized parties with distinct regional group networks and cultures. Much of this ground has been covered by scholars of polarization. In an environment of polarized national parties, individual electoral candidates understand that, no matter where they are running, or for what level of government, their fates are tied to the national party brand. Ordinary Americans feel increased antipathy toward the opposing party, and their sociocultural identities grow more interwoven with their partisan identities. Parties in government engage in more procedural brinkmanship in legislatures, courts, and agencies in order to thwart their opponents.

TABLE 1.1. Consequences of the Collision of National Parties and American Federalism

State Policy Resurgence
Increased policy variation across states
Policy polarization between blue states and red states
Advantages for concentrated and well-resourced groups
Examples: Health policy outcomes increasingly tied to state of residence

Polarized Laboratories of Democracy
Separate partisan networks of legislative subsidizers
Decreased policy emulation between red and blue states
Little relationship between policy success and diffusion
Examples: Coordination of interest group activists; ALEC model bills

Laboratories of Democratic Backsliding
Increased use of state authority to shape democratic performance
Declining democratic performance in Republican-controlled states
Examples: Voter suppression; gerrymandering; repression of protest

State Policy Resurgence

The collision of national parties and federalism has transformed the American political economy. The first consequence of the collision is *state policy resurgence*. As the federal government became increasingly polarized and divided government more likely, policy-demanding groups had greater incentive to follow the adage "think globally, act locally" by shifting political resources to the state and local levels. As in earlier periods when subnational coalitions were unable to achieve their goals at the national level, this massive influx of political resources and efforts in the states has generated a simple result: important state policy changes. These major policy changes, such as vehicle fuel efficiency standards, tax cuts for high earners, or refusing expanded Medicaid, have put state governments at the center of American public policy. State policies have become increasingly varied, and this variation is increasingly driven by the party that controls the state government. Americans' tax rates, gun laws, health insurance subsidies, and ability to obtain a legal abortion are now determined by one's state of residence to an extent not seen since before the civil rights revolution of the mid-twentieth century.

But not all political actors have the ability to efficiently *venue shift*—to shop for the most advantageous political terrain among the multitude of governments contained in the American federal system. Groups with coordinated and mobile political resources—who do not face the same information, time, and mobility constraints as ordinary voters—are better able to strategically locate and shift resources toward the most favorable political venues, both vertically from the national to the state level and horizontally across states. Activist groups on issues like abortion and the environment funneled money into state legislative campaigns. Organizations like the American Legislative Exchange Council (ALEC) spread model bills across the states, providing an easy way for conservative state politicians to introduce legislation. Ordinary voters, on the other hand, are geographically constrained and, as Daniel Hopkins (2018) shows in *The Increasingly United States*, increasingly inattentive to state and local politics.

Whereas many theorized that federalism would incentivize state governments to customize policy to local preferences, the state level is increasingly dominated by national groups who exploit the low-information environments of amateurish and resource-constrained legislatures, declining local news media, and identity-focused voters. Local constituents can still influence state politics, but only with a blunt tool: choosing whether the national Democratic Party or national Republican Party should control their state.

Partisan Laboratories of Democracy

The second consequence is the transformation of states to *polarized laboratories of democracy*. Louis Brandeis posited that states can learn from each other's policy experiments, emulating successful policies and rejecting the ones that fail. But I argue that two features of modern polarization act as wrenches in the gears of Brandeis's theory. First, facing heavy constraints on policymaking resources, state governments have long counted on outside experts and interest groups to help them produce laws. Today, however, interest groups and expert organizations are much more likely to be aligned with one party or the other. In the language of Brandeis's laboratories metaphor, the "scientific" communities behind state-level policymaking are increasingly separated by party. Second, partisanship incentivizes politicians to avoid emulating successful policies from the opposite party, because it would provide evidence that the other party has good policy ideas.

I draw on advances in the policy diffusion literature to test whether state governments emulate efficient and successful policies from other states—or only do so from copartisan governments. The hopeful idea of laboratories of democracy predicts that states will copy policies that produce economic success, such as reduced unemployment, or political success, such as electoral victories for the governors who implemented the policies. But I show that, while this may have been true in the past, it has not been true in recent decades. After the 2008 financial crisis, Democratically controlled Minnesota improved its economy by increasing public investments in education and infrastructure, but Republican-controlled Wisconsin to the east ignored its neighbor's success, instead opting for steep tax cuts for high earners. There is little evidence that the kind of policy success experienced in Minnesota led to greater emulation from other states—and to the extent that success matters, it only does for states controlled by the same political party.

Democratic Backsliding in the States

The third consequence is the return of states as *laboratories of democratic backsliding*, where the national Republican Party coalition in particular has innovated new ways to make American democracy narrower and more restrictive. I say "return," because much of American history involves civil rights activists calling on the federal government to take action against racially authoritarian state governments. Yet while the politics of race and democracy in America are still topics of intense discussion, there has been less systematic inquiry recently on how federalism's prominent role for state government relates to it.

Indeed, federalism and democracy are still deeply interwoven today. By endowing states with authority over election administration and other key levers of democracy, national parties can use the states that they control to rig the game in their favor by limiting the ability of their political enemies to participate.

I investigate whether state governments have been democratic champions or democratic villains over the past two decades. I develop a new set of publicly available measures of state democratic performance, which I call the *State Democracy Index*, based on dozens of measures of state performance in elections, legislative districting, civil liberties, and other components of democracy. The measure allows me to test long-standing theories of how democracy expands and contracts, such as changes in party competition, polarization, racial demographics, and the coalitions in control of state government.

When it comes to democratic backsliding in the states, the results couldn't be clearer: over the past two decades, the Republican Party has eroded democracy in states under its control. Republican governments have gerrymandered districts, made it more difficult to vote, and restricted civil liberties to a degree unprecedented since the civil rights era. It is not local changes in state-level polarization, competition, or demographics driving these major changes to the rules of American democracy. Instead, it is the groups that make up the *national* coalition of the modern GOP—the very wealthy on the one hand, and those motivated by white identity politics and cultural resentment on the other.

Methodological Approach

I classify the methodology in this book in different ways. The quantitative methods and data analysis of variables that change over time will be familiar to those interested in the budding area of quantitative American political development (APD), as well as American political economy (APE). Perhaps the greatest common thread between these scholarly communities is a focus on *big questions* that are not always amenable to traditional research designs that aim to uncover unbiased estimates of *causal* relationships. Many interlocking processes, in which causes and consequences feed back into each other, have caused the changes in American democracy that I chronicle in this book.

The challenge of answering these big questions has led me to embrace methodological pluralism. This book is mostly quantitative. A lot of the quantitative work I do is in building new quantitative *measures* of concepts that we typically speak about qualitatively, such as how conservative a state's abortion policy is, or whether the quality of a state's electoral democracy has risen or fallen. Importantly, the measures I create in this book will be helpful for other researchers who want to dig into state politics and policy. I am especially eager for other scholars, think tanks, and political observers to use my State Democracy Index to further delve into the causes and consequences of democratic backsliding in the states. When it comes to understanding the threats to American democracy and how to fight them, it takes a village.

In addition to creating new measures, I use more traditional quantitative analysis to test hypotheses about causes and effects. My workhorse here is the *difference-in-differences* design, which, rather than "controlling" for state characteristics and comparing otherwise similar states, looks at whether a change *within* a state produces a change within that same state.

Still, I draw heavily on qualitative knowledge. The theories I propose and test are informed by historical and qualitative scholarship. It is also critical to qualitatively interrogate quantitative measures that attempt to capture broad concepts like democracy and policy liberalism. Moreover, I use qualitative cases not only to illustrate the statistical results but also to provide additional evidence about the causes and consequences of the collision of national parties and federalism when using quantitative measures and methods is not feasible.

Another important methodological choice is this book's focus on the U.S. case rather than comparisons across countries. It may seem at first that it is impossible to learn about the role of federalism this way. Federalism has been a constant throughout American history; there is no variation in this "treatment" variable. But I argue that we can actually learn a great deal from a U.S.-specific focus. First, we can test whether the patterns in real-world data match the long-standing theories of American federalism. This is what I do, for instance, in the "Partisan Laboratories of Democracy" chapter. I take on the traditional idea that states are laboratories of democracy that emulate effective policies in ways that produce better governance and show that this doesn't appear to have happened much in recent years. Second, we gain tremendous insight by looking at change over time. In the "Laboratories of Democratic Backsliding" chapter, I test whether a rise in polarization, political competition, or Republican control of state government leads to changes in democratic performance.

The major crises in modern American politics are not just the result of institutional racism, plutocratic influence, or partisan polarization. They are a product of these forces flowing in a *federal institutional system* of government. Federalism provides numerous political *venues* for *national*, not just parochial, political actors to battle. The structure and multiplicity of these venues make it more difficult for ordinary Americans to hold politicians accountable in elections. This structure is advantageous to well-resourced interests, who can move their political money and influence across venues in highly strategic ways. Federalism makes it easier for political actors to tilt the rules of American democracy, itself, to their advantage. Antidemocratic interests need only to take control of a *state* government for a short period of time to implement changes that make it harder for their opponents to participate in politics *at all levels*—local, state, and national.

This book combines institutional analysis with a historical focus on political parties and organizations. The institutional analysis, whether based in game theory or qualitative argumentation, teaches us about how the rules of American politics shape the incentives of politicians, organizations, and voters. The historical and behavioral analysis teaches us about what these political actors want out of politics. Understanding the nationalization of American politics, where the Democratic and Republican parties compete as coordinated teams at every level, requires knowledge of institutional incentives, the connections between politics and the economy, the politics of geography, the behavior and attitudes of the broader public, and the historical development of American politics. Gone are the days when a single research framework could explain major political transformations.

I develop new tests of classic theories of American federalism, such as whether states act as effective laboratories of democracy, or about how states expand or contract democracy. But before presenting the results of these tests, I delve into the traditional, hopeful understanding of American federalism. In the conventional view, federalism is not only functional and efficient but deeply embedded in American national identity. This mythos stretches back to the Founding but has seen a resurgence over the past generation. This mythos, however, has conspicuously neglected a major research tradition that has long called into question the utility of federalism: scholarship on race and civil rights.

I am frequently asked the question, "Weren't you relieved to have federalism once Donald Trump became president?" This line of thought is alluring. Certainly, at a given moment in time when one opposes the national government, it is helpful to have state governments that can govern differently. State governments have pushed back against Trump administration initiatives in areas like immigration, environmental policy, and reproductive rights, with some success. But this is not the right question because, absent federalism, there is a good chance Trump would not have become president in the first place. The collision of federalism and nationally polarized parties helped create fertile ground for Trumpian politics.

Preview of the Book

In the next chapter, I outline existing theories of federalism—and contrast them with my argument about the role of national parties. Three groups of scholars proposed important theories of how politics works within the decentralized institutions of American federalism. Whether they argued that it reduces national polarization, incentivizes policy experimentation and learning, increases efficiency, or protects against tyranny, dominant theories were optimistic about the role of American federalism in mitigating political challenges. This chapter describes in detail how today's national parties render the mechanisms of these theories inoperable. In particular, I draw on political economy and historical institutionalist literatures to argue that the increased coordination of groups and organizations in national party coalitions has increased inequality of influence in state politics, reduced policy learning, and made the United States more vulnerable to democratic backsliding.

Chapter 3 argues that the nationalization and polarization of the parties in a federal system have had the paradoxical effect of increasing the importance of the state level in policymaking. As Congress polarized and divided government became more common in Washington, D.C., activists and organizations in the national Democratic and Republican coalitions set their sights on the states, passing significant policies in the states controlled by their party. After a half century in which national civil rights and economic policy had made governance more *similar* across states, state policy once again diverged, with policies in the areas of taxation, health care, the environment, gun control, abortion rights, and labor polarizing between red and blue states. In the areas of education and especially criminal justice, however, state policies did not diverge.

In part 2, I turn to the question of *who governs* the resurgence of state policy and argue that activists and organizations, not ordinary voters, have been in the driver's seat. Chapter 4 shows that while policy has shifted dramatically, public opinion in the states has been mostly static over the past generation. In the process, I also review literature and present new evidence that even compared to national politics in the United States, state and local politics are especially unequal by income, race, and age.

Groups with time, information, and mobile political resources—especially money—are particularly advantaged in state politics. Chapter 5 shows how activist groups have set policy agendas and polarized legislatures in the states. Over the previous two decades, activist networks, such as gun rights activists affiliated with the NRA, used campaign contributions, primary election endorsements, online organizing, and similar tactics to get candidates for state-level offices aligned with the goals of the national coalition.

Chapter 6 investigates whether Louis Brandeis's theory of states as policy laboratories operates in the era of national parties. Do states learn from each other, emulating successful policy experiments and rejecting failed ones? Or does the nationalization of the Democratic and Republican parties mean that state governments live in separate partisan "scientific" communities? I find that states are more likely to emulate electorally successful policies from other states—but only when those states are controlled by the same political party.

Part 3 investigates what might become the most important consequence of party nationalization: democratic backsliding. American federalism gives state governments authority over critical democratic institutions, especially election administration and legislative districting. Chapters 7 and 8 provide new evidence that the quality of democracy is diverging between states—with states like North Carolina and Wisconsin experiencing dramatic democratic backsliding over the past decade. Specifically, chapter 7 develops a systematic quantitative measure of democratic performance in the fifty states, the State Democracy Index.

Chapter 8 uses the State Democracy Index to investigate the cause of democratic changes in the states. States' levels of polarization, partisan competition, and demographic change have little relationship to their democratic performance. In the era of national parties, it is party control of government that drives democratic backsliding. Specifically, control by the Republican Party—a national coalition that combines the very wealthy with an electoral base motivated by racial and cultural conflict—dramatically reduces democratic performance.

In the conclusion I discuss the implications of this research for our understanding of federalism, the Democratic and Republican parties, and American politics more broadly. I discuss how different kinds of political groups and organizations might engage with policy feedbacks—how policy can affect future politics—in the context of national parties and decentralized institutions. Considering the transformation of American federalism over the past generation, I point to areas of further research into the roles of institutions, organizations, public opinion, elections, and democracy. Most importantly, I consider how policy and institutional reform can protect American democracy from threats that arise from Washington, D.C., as well as the states.

2

The Mythos of American Federalism

This means making the best use of the incredible tool of federalism our founders gave us. During the 20th century, we dialed up the power of the federal government, ending up with the heavy hand of the modern administrative state and imperial presidency. It is now time to shift power back.

—RICHARD FLORIDA, "SHIFT POWER BACK TO THE LOCAL LEVEL"

This federalist structure of joint sovereigns preserves to the people numerous advantages. It assures a decentralized government that will be more sensitive to the diverse needs of a heterogeneous society; it increases opportunity for citizen involvement in democratic processes; it allows for more innovation and experimentation in government; and it makes government more responsive by putting the States in competition for a mobile citizenry.

—SUPREME COURT JUSTICE SANDRA DAY O'CONNOR, MAJORITY OPINION IN *GREGORY V. ASHCROFT* (1991)

THINKERS IN THE AGE of Trump are increasingly critical of the U.S. Constitution—for good reason. The institutional rules of the game, from Senate apportionment to the Electoral College to presidential privilege, are clashing with the realities of partisanship and geography. "The Constitution is broken," writes legal scholar Michael Gerhardt (2020) in the *Atlantic*. Single-member congressional districts generate "a deep unfairness here that increasingly undermines democratic legitimacy," in the words of Lee Drutman (2018b). E. J. Dionne, Norman Ornstein, and Thomas Mann (2017) point to the geographic clustering of Democratic voters in populous cities and states that bumps up against electoral boundaries to create "a long-term trend in Americans toward minority rule" (see also Rodden 2019). Ryan Cooper (2017) sums it up in the *Week*: "The Constitution is janky. It's antiquated. It's poorly designed. And it's falling apart before our very eyes."

But fear not, suggest other voices. The Founders created a solution: federalism. Commentators and thinkers across the political spectrum suggest that if only we were to double down on federalism—the sharing of power between the federal, state, and local levels—we might be able to push American politics out of the ditch. To some, decentralization appears to be the solution to the most pressing problems in American politics. These thinkers and activists contend that devolving greater authority to lower levels of government will bring with it a host of benefits. It will unleash policy experimentation in state governments, bring constituents closer to their representatives, reduce the temperature of cultural conflict, and result in more efficient, consensual, and representative governance. As Yuval Levin (2016) writes, "the 2016 election has been a surreal nightmare," but "[a] fresh agenda of decentralization and federalism could help address some key downsides of our social, economic and cultural fragmentation, drawing us back to the mediating institutions of civil society, which offer an alternative to both radical individualism and stultifying central control." David Brooks (2007) suggests that "going back to Madison and Jefferson and the decentralized federalism of the founders" is the way to "restore America's constitutional soul."[1]

These appeals tap into a mythological story. The tale says that the framers of the U.S. Constitution supported federalism for ideological rather than pragmatic reasons; they believed in the rules in and of themselves, not because they would get states on board with ratification of the Constitution or for the outcomes they would produce. Moreover, the story goes, the framers' support for a weak national government and strong states was unanimous. Political actors are fond of marshaling this legendary backstory. In 2020 the Texas attorney general proclaimed that "the sooner [the Affordable Care Act] is invalidated, the sooner each state can decide what type of health care system will best provide for those with preexisting conditions, which is the way the Founders

---

1. David Brooks, "Back to Basics," *New York Times*, June 1, 2007, nytimes.com/2007/06/01/opinion/01brooks.html.

TABLE 2.1. How Modern National Parties Challenge Theories of Federalism

	Potential Benefits of the States in Federal System	Challenge from National Parties	Further Developed in Chapters
The Decentralists	Harmony in a diverse republic	Increased inequality between states	3, 4, 5
	Protecting against tyranny	Decentralized democratic institutions vulnerable to exploitation by national parties; decentralized accountability	7, 8, 9
The Brandeisians	Policy experimentation and learning	Policy learning is partisan	5, 6
The New Federalists	Incentives for governmental efficiency	Expanding political inequality by race, wealth, and concentration of organization	5, 6, 7, 8

intended."[2] Here, as usual, the appeal to decentralization has little to do with the substance of the issue or policy. Instead we're meant to conjure up images of Madison, Hamilton, and Jefferson discussing health insurance risk pooling.

But most arguments for federalism are a bit more sophisticated than the Texas attorney general's statement. In this chapter, I examine three sets of thinkers, from three distinct points in American history, who built the intellectual scaffolding that supports American conceptions of federalism to this day. The first, the *Decentralists*, created theories of customization and decentralization, as well as ideas about federalism's protection of liberty, often in support of the Constitution. The second, the *Brandeisians*, put forward a vision of progressive federalism in which states serve as "laboratories of democracy." The third, the *New Federalists*, formalized theories of federalism as an efficient political marketplace, where businesses, workers, and citizens can "vote with their feet." In table 2.1, I summarize the theories of these three groups of thinkers and preview the challenges presented by national parties that I develop in this chapter.

The theories from each of these groups of thinkers have shaped history. They have made their way into popular discourse, into the rhetoric of politicians,

2. "AG Paxton Files Brief Asking SCOTUS to Declare Obamacare Unlawful," Office of the Attorney General of Texas, 2020, https://www.texasattorneygeneral.gov/news/releases/ag-paxton-files-brief-asking-scotus-declare-obamacare-unlawful.

and into the constitutions of other countries. Countervailing theories on the downsides of federalism, however, have been received with less fanfare. To be sure, federalism is a recurring theme in research on the historical development of the porous American welfare state and low levels of redistribution (Pierson 1995; Mettler 1998; Lieberman and Lapinski 2001; Alesina and Glaeser 2004; Weir 2005) and, especially, on civil rights (Miller 2008; King 2017; Robertson 2017; Goodyear-Grant et al. 2019). Comparative politics research has particularly emphasized how American federalism creates veto points that allow concentrated groups to block reforms supported by majorities (Huber and Stephens 2001; Beramendi 2007). And, furthermore, seminal research from Schattschneider (1960) more broadly shows that the ability to alter the "scope" of political conflict, for instance, by moving an agenda item from the state to the national level, can powerfully affect political outcomes.

But compared to the expansive Decentralist, Brandeisian, and New Federalist communities, this kind of critical research on American federalism is neither as long-standing nor as consolidated. However, the political and economic crises of the twenty-first century demand that we take seriously historical institutionalists' insights and reevaluate mainstream theories of American federalism. More fundamentally, shining a light on the interaction of nationalized parties and federal institutions challenges the classic theories of the Decentralists, Brandeisians, and New Federalists. Some scholars have been attentive to the transformation of federalism under nationalized parties. Legal scholar Jessica Bulman-Pozen (2014, 1080), for example, makes great strides in describing the rise of "partisan federalism," in which the Democratic and Republican parties leverage federal institutions to "articulate, stage, and amplify [partisan] competition." But since states, she argues, "participate in national political contests without forfeiting the particularity and pluralism we associate with the local," there is little cause for alarm. My argument, by contrast, is that today's nationalized parties present a more fundamental challenge for the operations of federal institutions, potentially nullifying many of the most important potential benefits of federalism that American intellectuals have touted for centuries.

The Decentralists

Modern Decentralists point to James Madison, a primary author of the *Federalist Papers*, as a key proponent of institutional decentralization. A child of a planter class dynasty in Virginia, Madison seems to fit the demographic profile of a prominent supporter of federalism and states' rights.[3] Madison was not a Decentralist early on, however. In *Federalist No. 10*, Madison suggests that smaller institutional units are more vulnerable to takeover by powerful factions, whereas larger ones are protected by cross-cutting factional interests that are less likely to result in one group dominating. He proposed the Virginia Plan at the Constitutional Convention, which would have provided greater authority to the national government, and less power to states, than the federal system that ended up in the Constitution. But by the 1790s, Madison resisted moves to grant the national government greater authority over the states. There remains a debate among historians about Madison's view of federalism (e.g., Yarbrough 2017).

There is little question, however, that Madison did not anticipate political parties—particularly not the nationally coordinated parties we have today. The modern parties are not the highly regionalized factions the Founders worried about but national teams of politicians, activists, media networks, and primary voters. Despite today's nationally polarized politics, the Decentralists' theories remain dominant. Two of their arguments about federalism stand out in particular: that it is necessary to hold together a large, diverse country, and that it helps protect against tyranny.

Maintaining National Consensus in a Large, Diverse Country

The Decentralists introduced the notion that federalism would preserve national harmony. By allowing states to tailor law toward the particular cultures and desires of their citizens, while also maintaining a national government to hold the edifice together, the United States would avoid the internal conflicts that could threaten its stability. This is how a large and diverse country would persist and flourish. There is an obvious appeal to this line of argument. As conservative commentator Jonah Goldberg (2016) asks, "What would be so terrible about letting diverse communities decide how they want to live and spend their tax dollars?"

---

3. Madison in *Federalist No. 39* describes what we now call federalism, a balance between political equality between individuals and a political equality between states: "The difference between a federal and national government, as it relates to the OPERATION OF THE GOVERNMENT, is supposed to consist in this, that in the former the powers operate on the political bodies composing the Confederacy, in their political capacities; in the latter, on the individual citizens composing the nation, in their individual capacities."

Jonathan Rauch (2007) applies this argument to the culture wars of the 2000s. Rauch contends that on social issues like gay marriage, the best route is "*moral pluralism*: leaving states free to go their separate ways when a national moral consensus is lacking" (emphasis in original). Political issues left to the states "become more tractable over time, as the country works its way toward a consensus." By contrast, bringing an issue to the national level "moves it out of the realm of normal politics, which cuts deals and develops consensus, and into the realm of protest politics, which rejects compromise and fosters radicalism." David Gelernter (2006) writes that "an era where deep and fundamental moral questions divide the nation is in need of a revival of federalism."

And it is true that federalism may have been a force against polarized politics in earlier eras of American history. As Paul Pierson and Eric Schickler (2020, 46) summarize, "Even when the national parties were relatively polarized on a given set of issues . . . state and local parties provided a partially independent, geographically rooted power base to represent competing interests that cross-cut that division." New groups vying to get their issues onto the political agenda would enter into state and local party systems, and there was nothing much the national party could do to prevent it. For instance, beginning in the 1930s, pro–civil rights activists entered into the Democratic Party in northern states despite national Democrats' interests in keeping their coalition (with its important southern segregationist wing) together by keeping civil rights off of the agenda. This made the Democratic Party a truly broad tent, a coalition of the most staunchly anti–civil rights *and* most enthusiastically pro–civil rights candidates.

But today, state and local parties are too integrated into their national party networks to serve as forces against polarization. This is true of formal state and local party organizations, such as the Texas Democratic Party, which are now mostly vehicles for national party actors and nationally oriented issue activists (Paddock 2005; Schlozman and Rosenfeld 2019). This is also true of more informal partisan activists and party-aligned activist groups, such as anti-abortion or environmental activists. Chapter 5 shows how nationally focused issue and ideological activists have helped connect state-level politicians to the national parties, polarizing state legislatures.

Furthermore, a novel theory from Sandy Gordon and Dimitri Landa (2019) sheds light on ways federalism can exacerbate national political conflict. First, states can free ride on each other's public goods provision, which reduces pressure to expand public goods in both the free-riding states and at the national level. Second, there is an asymmetry in state policymaking, as it can only increase regulatory or redistributive standards from the national baseline but not reduce them. Rather than reducing the heat in national conflict over the welfare state or social policy, these features of federalism can increase polarization.[4]

Donald Kettl takes up a similar argument in his book *The Divided States of America: Why Federalism Doesn't Work* (2020). As the title suggests, the book argues that contemporary federalism is a force for national division, not unity. Economic inequality between Americans has been a topic of concern, but Kettl points to the growth of inequality *between* states over the past generation—which has "created more polarization and more friction, and . . . made the United States a collection of states divided" (15). These insights will once again be important in chapter 3, when I describe policy changes in the states in the context of shifting national policy baselines.

Protecting against Tyranny

If you are familiar with the *Federalist Papers*, you will know that it is loaded with references to tyranny. Checks and balances from three coequal branches in the federal government would be the first wall against "the accumulation of all powers, legislative, executive, and judiciary, in the same hands" (*Federalist 47*). But in addition, the Decentralists argued that federalism would provide "double security" against an autocratic takeover, as Madison explained in the *Federalist 51*. "Perhaps the most frequently mentioned function of the federal system is the one it shares to a large extent with the separation of powers, namely, the protection of the citizen against governmental oppression—the 'tyranny' that the Framers were so concerned about," wrote legal scholar Andrzej Rapaczynski (1985, 380).

It makes sense that an extra, constitutionally protected level of government might make it harder for a dictator to take complete power. "In times of crisis," argue legal scholars David Landau, Hannah Wiseman, and Samuel Wiseman (2019, 1190), "state and local governments' control of the personnel engaged in the vast majority of policing, judging, and other governance, as well as key functions such as the running of elections, would meaningfully impede a consolidation of power at the federal level." State and local police derive their

---

4. Despite the way it can exacerbate national conflict, including conflict between the national and state governments, federalism remains a remarkably stable institutional equilibrium (Hafer and Landa 2007).

constitutional authority from the states; their civilian commanders in chief are mayors and, ultimately, governors, not the U.S. president. And as I mentioned earlier, states administer elections for all levels of government.

But what if the opposite is true? What if the power that federalism grants state governments actually leaves the American political system vulnerable to authoritarianism and democratic backsliding? Take a key area of state and local authority: policing. American policing is concentrated at the state and local levels, and rather than protecting against tyranny, it is, for Americans in race-class subjugated communities, imposing it (Soss and Weaver 2017). On the one hand, the decentralization of police departments may make them hard to capture by a single autocrat. But on the other hand is the uncomfortable reality that state and local police forces act as cartels, steamrolling over their mayoral and gubernatorial commanders in chief at the state and local levels. Compared to police forces in other countries, American police act with unprecedented violence, brutalizing African Americans and peaceful protesters with impunity—and state and local civilian authorities appear too institutionally weak to hold them accountable.

Furthermore, as I argue in chapters 7 and 8, state governments' role in administering elections leaves American democracy vulnerable to antidemocratic coalitions who want to tilt electoral rules in their favor. It is easier for an antidemocratic coalition to gain a foothold in a few states than at the national level, and from there they can make it more difficult to vote in elections at any level. In many states, the health of democracy has declined in significant ways in recent years.

Still, we might be concerned about the risks of centralizing election administration in the federal government. Centralizing election authority would make American democracy more vulnerable if an authoritarian coalition were to take power at the national level. Such a coalition might more easily co-opt the centralized electoral institution than those of fifty states, some of which would be under the control of an opposing party. (Donald Trump's efforts to delegitimize and block state certifications of 2020 election results certainly highlight how democracy might have been imperiled had the Constitution vested authority over elections to the president or Senate.) Jessica Bulman-Pozen (2012, 461) goes so far as to suggest that "federalism safeguards the separation of powers"—that federalism not only prevents tyranny directly but also protects other institutional checks against unduly concentrated power.

But the alternative is the status quo: the long-standing, already existing co-optation of a substantial proportion of electoral institutions in the states.

These state administrations have already suppressed votes, gerrymandered districts, and dismantled countervailing power from groups like labor unions—clearing a path for an antidemocratic coalition to take power at the national level. Arguments that emphasize the tail risk of centralized election administration must face not only the fact that Canada, Norway, the UK, and other long-standing democracies have not descended into tyranny under centralized election administration but also the way that *decentralized* administration can increase the likelihood of a would-be autocrat ascending to power at the national level. Centralized election administration might be more vulnerable once an autocrat is in power, but it also might make an autocrat less likely to win in the first place. This is an important trade-off, but many proponents of decentralization neglect the way that federalism has created the risks to democracy that they then call on federalism to stop.

The Decentralists similarly argued that federalism would improve the democratic relationship between the people and their political leaders. Elected leaders at lower levels are, of course, typically stationed geographically closer to their constituents. In theory, they should also be more culturally, ideologically, and demographically similar to their constituents than the average politician at higher levels. "Government by remote control" is what Felix Morley (1959, 5) called national governance in the United States. "The essence of federalism," he continued, "is reservation of control over local affairs to the localities themselves, the argument for which becomes stronger if the federation embraces a large area, with strong climatic or cultural differences among the various states therein."

It is simple to see that institutional decentralization is advantageous if you are out of power nationally. Federalism acts as a kind of insurance for when your coalition is in the national minority. However, decentralized institutions also create *decentralized accountability*. It is more difficult to know which politicians and coalitions to hold accountable when offices and levels of government are more numerous. This presents a trade-off similar to the one regarding decentralization and protecting against tyranny. Decentralization makes it less likely that your coalition will be out of power at all levels, but it reduces the capacity of citizens to understand the quality of governance and ability to hold government accountable. As I argue throughout this book, political and technological changes over the past generation, especially those related to the nationalization of the Democratic and Republican parties, have made the second part of the trade-off, decentralized accountability, a stronger force in American politics.

The Decentralists, who argue that federalism prevents tyranny and preserves harmony in a diverse republic, remain the most prominent historical figures in the historical mythos of American federalism. But the next generation, the Brandeisians, would come close to rivaling their status.

The Brandeisians

"It is one of the happy incidents of the federal system that a single courageous State may, if its citizens choose, serve as a laboratory; and try novel social and economic experiments without risk to the rest of the country." Those are the words of Supreme Court Justice Louis Brandeis from his dissenting opinion in the 1932 case *New State Ice Co. v. Liebmann.*

Although he did not invent the idea, Brandeis's "laboratories of democracy" phrase has persisted as a force in American political thought, both scholarly and popular. The concept is straightforward: states can emulate each other's successful policy experiments and reject the failed ones. States are laboratories in pursuit of the "best" policy solutions, akin to scientists experimenting in pursuit of the cure for a deadly disease. Whether the goal is creating effective public policy or a medical treatment, it is better to have more laboratories on the job than fewer. In the Brandeisian view, federalism means there are fifty state laboratories conducting experiments; it would be a shame if these experiments were confined to one single national laboratory.

Like the arguments of the Decentralists, the Brandeisian theory of laboratories of democracy is popular in the world of think-tank advocacy. As Lindsey Burke (2017) of the Heritage Foundation argues, "States are 'laboratories of democracy.' They can try different policies, and do so without exposing everyone to possible failure. States also compete for residents and businesses, creating a much greater incentive to care about efficient and effective policy than Washington has." The laboratories of democracy idea has also received considerable attention among scholars of political science and public policy, especially in studies of policy diffusion (e.g., Meseguer 2003, 2006; Grossback, Nicholson-Crotty, and Peterson 2004; Volden, Ting, and Carpenter 2008; Gilardi, Füglister, and Luyet 2009; Shipan and Volden 2014). Less attention has been paid, however, to how national parties might disrupt Brandeis's idea.

In chapter 5, I argue that polarized national parties are a wrench in the gears of the laboratories of democracy theory. Politicians, especially at lower levels of government, rely on political and expert organizations for information and other policymaking resources. As these organizations separate into

increasingly partisan networks, beliefs about a policy's effectiveness are likely
to polarize—and policy emulation will tend to occur only between states controlled by the same political party.

There is another problem with the laboratories of democracy idea: spillovers from policy experiments. The optimistic view is that the consequences
of a destructive policy experiment will be confined to a single laboratory. In
recent decades, however, experiments have generated negative spillovers (i.e.,
negative externalities) with consequences that stretch far beyond the borders
of the state "laboratory" in which they were created. For example, chapter 4
describes the "race to the bottom" dynamic, in which a state with lax regulation
and low taxes puts downward pressure on taxation and regulation in other
states. Perhaps more profoundly, democratic institutions in the states affect
the ability of individuals and groups to participate in politics at *all* levels.
When Wisconsin and Michigan implement state policies that restrict labor
unions, they diminish labor's ability to compete in not just state but national
politics. And when North Carolina redraws congressional districts or sup-
presses votes, it affects representation at the national level.

Despite these challenges, the laboratories of democracy theory remains
popular among modern scholars. But another community of thinkers took the
ball further downfield in support of American federalism. In both think tanks
and the academy, advocates and scholars drew up more sophisticated and formalized theories of how federalism incentivizes good governance. These are
the New Federalists.

The New Federalists

The New Federalists drew on insights from the Decentralists about liberty and
from the Brandeisians about policy experimentation in the development of
their theories. But unlike their predecessors, they used tools from modern
social science, especially formal economic theory.

The seminal article for the New Federalists was Charles Tiebout's 1956
piece, "A Pure Theory of Local Expenditures," which, in the social sciences,
helped popularize the idea that people "vote with their feet." The central prem-
ise is that people move "to find the community that provides their optimal tax
and public goods" (Banzhaf and Walsh 2008, 861). The more that people engage in this kind of sorting behavior, choosing to live in places based on the
area's public policies, the better governments will be incentivized to satisfy
their residents. In the aggregate, the political "marketplace" becomes more

efficient. Federalism provides the opportunity for "taxation and expenditure policy [to] be efficiently distributed to maximize total utility," in the words of Jenna Bednar (2005, 193), enhancing overall social welfare.

This theory, if true, provides powerful support for decentralized federal systems that allow states and municipalities to customize policy and make it easy to move across city and state borders. Whereas the Decentralists argued that federalism's allowance for local policy customization helps maintain harmony in a large, diverse country, in which communities are likely to vary greatly in their cultural norms, the New Federalists combined this idea with a focus on residential and capital mobility.

Empirical studies have shown that in some cases people do indeed vote with their feet in ways that incentivize good governance. Economists Matthew Kahn (2000) and H. Spencer Banzhaf and Randall P. Walsh (2008) separately found that better air quality attracts residents and toxic air emissions repel them, increasing the incentive for local and state governments to improve air quality if they wish to grow. Others, like Bill Bishop (2009), make a bolder argument that we have lived through a "big sort," in which millions of Americans have moved to areas to live under the public policies they want and around people with similar political attitudes.

But there are significant constraints on people's ability to vote with their feet. Jonathan Mummolo and Clayton Nall (2017) find that although survey respondents report wanting to live around copartisans, they don't actually move for political reasons, or even for reasons that are especially correlated with partisanship. Their choice of where to move to is instead overwhelmingly determined by the usual mundane factors: affordability, proximity to friends and family, crime rates, and school quality. Moreover, voting with your feet is a power that is distributed unequally. Wealthier people are better positioned to move to areas based on criteria other than affordability and proximity to family, incentivizing governments to adhere to their preferences.

A further constraint on ordinary citizens' ability to vote with their feet is the price of housing, which has skyrocketed in recent years in states and cities experiencing job and income growth. Local zoning control in states like California has aggressively blocked new housing construction and greater density. In many cases, families whose lives would improve by moving to cities with vibrant economies are unable to afford the housing costs. In an era of high economic inequality and growing market power of large firms, these kinds of geographic constraints are less of a problem for employers and wealthy individuals.

Still, it remains scholarly consensus that Americans' ability to vote with their feet incentivizes state and local governments to do a good job. In chapter 5, however, I provide new evidence that challenges even this idea. Among other findings, I show that the economic performance of a state policy has a weak influence over whether other states emulate it, especially if the policy comes from the other political party. To the extent that all Americans would prefer to live in a place with lower crime, better schools, and a healthier economy, state governments don't appear to care very much. Voting with your feet is not a strong constraint on what state governments do in the era of national parties.

If Tiebout's piece represents the seminal article of the New Federalist community, the political economist James Buchanan represents its seminal scholar. Buchanan is a controversial intellectual figure, and Nancy MacLean's 2017 book *Democracy in Chains* ignited a heated (and still, to some extent, ongoing) debate about Buchanan's connections to the Koch brothers and role in conservative movements in support of segregation and opposition to democracy. But there is no controversy over Buchanan's view of federalism. Even the titles of Buchanan's written work on federalism give a clear sense of his normative emphasis, as in his 1995 article in *Publius*, "Federalism as an Ideal Political Order and an Objective for Constitutional Reform."

Buchanan made a number of arguments in support of federalism. By enhancing individuals' and businesses' ability to use the exit option, federalism enhances liberty. By granting citizens control over smaller geographic units, federalism increases the incentive for individuals to learn about and participate in politics (Buchanan 1995b). And most importantly, these microfoundations aggregate up to a system of *competitive* federalism, in which states (or municipalities) compete for residents, investment, and votes in a political marketplace (Buchanan 1995a).

A related argument is that federalism increases efficiency by incentivizing the different levels of government to each specialize in a narrower set of responsibilities (e.g., Nivola 2005). Just as in trade theory, where specialization in an area of comparative advantage enhances welfare, state and local governments and the national government can each specialize in the areas in which they perform best—the national government in questions of foreign policy and trade, for instance, and state and local governments in questions of transportation and public safety. As Pietro Nivola (2005) argues, "the paternalists in Washington cannot resist dabbling in the quotidian tasks that need to be performed by state and local officials," reducing governmental performance across the board.

Chapter 4 responds to these theories directly. As I hinted earlier, the ability to credibly threaten to exit a state or "vote with one's feet" is highly unequal. Whereas ordinary voters are geographically constrained, capital is highly mobile. The latent threat of capital flight, exit from firms or wealthy individuals, puts intense downward pressure on redistributive policies regardless of how much ordinary people support them. This latent exit threat provides a unique structural power to the owners of capital. As Charles Lindblom (1982) theorized, this structural power traps democracies in "the market as prison," limiting the choices that democracies can make about their economic policies and institutions.

Furthermore, Buchanan's argument that federalism incentivizes a more knowledgeable and engaged citizenry is not especially plausible. Lower levels of government are where citizens actually know the least (especially in the contemporary era of state and local journalism on life support). And, as I also show in chapter 4, political participation at lower levels of government appears more unequal than at higher levels, with greater race and wealth gaps in participation in the political process.

Federalism in the Twenty-First Century

As you've read in this chapter, theorizing about American federalism goes back to the Founding. Federalism has also garnered strong support from the academy; postwar social scientists from the New Federalism school developed a broad intellectual community focused on illuminating the implications of the decentralized federal institutions of the American system. But today, the place where you *really* find discussions of federalism is in law, and especially in think-tank advocacy.

Over the past generation, conservative think tanks have helped spread the good word about American federalism. The American Enterprise Institute (AEI), the Cato Institute, the Manhattan Institute, and others publish celebratory reports about the importance of federalism in producing a free and just society. In fact, these conservative think tanks hire fellows specifically to work on federalism advocacy and have entire federalism divisions and committees, such as the AEI Federalism Project.

These federalism advocates have portrayed themselves as losing a battle against centralization, especially during the 1960s and 1970s. Federalism scholar Martha Derthick (2004, 49) lamented the midcentury development of "[a] whole new perception of the state government as subordinates of the national government, properly subject to command," which was "laying the basis for the regulation that spread like kudzu through the garden of American federalism in the 1970s." As the Cato Institute's federalism section subheader reads, "Historically, federalism acted as a safeguard of American freedoms. Under the Constitution, the federal government was assigned specific limited powers and most government functions were left to the states. Unfortunately, policymakers and courts have mainly discarded federalism in recent decades."[5]

Such a proclamation is strangely at odds with reality. While the New Deal and civil rights periods brought major national policies and court rulings that reduced the role of state policy relative to national policy, the past forty years have seen the reverse: a profound shift in policymaking from the national to the state level (a trend we will investigate in the next chapter). As Congress polarized, divided national government became more common, and the Supreme Court's orientation became more conservative, policy-demanding groups and activists shifted resources to the state level. The result has been increased policy diversity between different states and a more important role for state-level policy in the lives of Americans. As a consequence of the nationalization of the parties, the state level has become the center of American policymaking. In many ways, the wishes of the Decentralists, the Brandeisians, and the New Federalists have come true.

Yet few would argue that the American political economy is in a much better place than a generation ago. Rather than ushering in democratic responsiveness, social harmony, and economic prosperity, the shift in policymaking from the national to the state level since the 1970s has coincided with the weakening of democratic institutions, the precipitous rise of economic inequality, and growing mass polarization and discontent.

The next chapter investigates the first consequence of party nationalization in American federalism: *state policy resurgence*. I take stock of major state policy changes over the past generation as state governments moved from the periphery back to the center of American policymaking. As I show in the next chapter, states passed increasingly varied policies in all sorts of areas—taxes, environmental regulation, reproductive rights, drug law, labor relations, and more. And these policy changes were increasingly determined by the party in control of state government. If the mythos of American federalism were true, this should have led to dramatic improvements in American society.

5. https://www.cato.org/research/federalism.

The past two decades have indeed seen some critically important state policies to tackle climate change (Stokes 2020), make health care more affordable (Courtemanche et al. 2017), and more. But these policy victories might obscure the broader drawbacks to the policymaking shift to the state level. Liberal groups and activists bumped up against federalism's disadvantages for diffuse groups like low-wage workers. Criminal justice reformers and abolitionists found policing and incarceration to be a policy area in which both Democratic and Republican state governments pursue "tough on crime" policies and command unaccountable police forces. And defenders of democracy watched as Republican state governments innovated new ways to dilute and suppress votes.

3

From Backwaters to Battlegrounds

IN A 2011 PHONE CALL with a radio host impersonating David Koch, Wisconsin governor Scott Walker explained that he was part of a national movement of conservative governors who "got elected to do something big" across their states (Newell 2011). Democratic governors like Jerry Brown of California and Jay Inslee of Washington similarly called for coordinated efforts by blue state governments to oppose initiatives by the Trump administration and Republican Congress. If their rhetoric is to be believed, politicians at the state level see themselves engaged in major struggles over the direction of public policy in the United States.

But this contentious rhetoric is at odds with how political scientists describe the policymaking role of state governments. The governors are pitching themselves as central to American politics and public policy. Political scientists, on the other hand, tend to suggest that state governments are actually relatively marginal players. There is a long tradition of seeing state governments as "the runt in the American governmental litter" (Allen 1949; Sharkansky 1968; Teaford 2002, 2), with policy agendas that are highly constrained by economic realities (Peterson 1981) and low legislative professionalism (Kousser 2005). Recent research largely continues this characterization. While some studies report important changes in state policy in the polarized era (e.g., Kousser 2002; Hertel-Fernandez and Skocpol 2016; Hertel-Fernandez 2016), the most comprehensive recent studies in this area conclude that state policy outcomes have been generally "stable" over the years (Caughey and Warshaw 2016, 900) and that party control of government still plays only a "modest" role in policy differences between states (Caughey, Warshaw, and Xu 2017, 1342).

So, are state-level politicians overstating their centrality to policymaking in the United States? Or is political science due for an update? In this chapter, I argue the latter. The nationalization of the Democratic and Republican parties led to gridlock in Congress—but in the states, it led to a resurgence of major policymaking.

I first present evidence that state governments have moved from the margins to the center of American politics and policymaking since the 1970s. Over the past generation, the federal government polarized and produced fewer major policies that standardize laws across states (Binder 2003; Hacker and Pierson 2010), and the judiciary became an increasingly "state friendly arena" (Waltenburg and Swinford 1999, 2). Faced with federal gridlock, policy-demanding groups, activists, and social movements on both the right and the left turned to the states to pursue their policy priorities (e.g., Baumgartner and Jones 2010). As parts of two national partisan networks, these policy demanders were able to rapidly shift policymaking resources to states where their party took control and make major changes in short order.

The policy consequences of this shift have been profound. I use data on 135 major state policies to investigate two particular policy dynamics in the fifty states: increased *policy variation* (the substantive differences between states) and *policy polarization* (the relationship between party control and policy outcomes). Recent decades have seen a strengthening relationship between an individual's state of residence and her legal right to obtain an abortion, own a firearm, join a labor union, or use drugs, as well as her tax burden, the strictness of her state's environmental regulatory regime, and the generosity of its welfare state.[1] As it was before the New Deal and civil rights eras, the state level is once again central to Americans' relationship to government.

Scholars have underemphasized the importance of increased policy variation and polarization in the states, and this has led to the underestimation of the role of the states in American governance. But just as important, they have neglected a key area where state policy is *not* very diverse and is remarkably *un*polarized: policing and criminal justice.

These exceptions have much to teach us about American democracy. Indeed, my analysis uncovers that—unlike 14 of 16 policy areas as wide-ranging as environmental regulation, LGBT rights, and health policy—Democratic and Republican states both implemented similar "tough on crime" laws that led to mass incarceration and were equally unwilling or unable to rein in the racial authoritarianism of the police forces under their command. This exceptionalism of policing and criminal justice in defying the polarization pattern highlights a broader lack of attention by political scientists to the role of

---

1. Journalists have been pointing to these trends as well (e.g., Fehrman 2016).

policing in modern racial authoritarianism. As Vesla Weaver and Gwen Prowse (2020, 1177) write, "Despite racial authoritarianism's glaring presence in experiential accounts of U.S. democracy, it has been hiding in plain view in the field of political science. In a field responsible for constructing metrics on democratic stability and political behavior, our failure to theorize racial authoritarianism has had consequences for how U.S. democracy is conceived by the public and policy-makers." This failure has also led scholars and political observers to underestimate the role of state governments, which have constitutional authority over nearly all U.S. law enforcement agencies.

The state level has returned as a critically important part of American federalism and as deeply consequential for the lives of Americans. The resurgence of state policy over the past generation can be seen in the increasingly varied and polarized policymaking in areas like abortion and labor policy, as well as in the bipartisan buildup of authoritarian policing and mass incarceration. Ironically, the rise of nationally coordinated and polarized parties has led to a shifting of policymaking down to the state level.

In the rest of this chapter, I first review literature on the role of state governments within American federalism. Next, I develop my argument about how the nationalization and polarization of the Democratic and Republican parties incentivizes groups to shift their political resources to the state level. I then look empirically at the resulting state policy resurgence, estimating policy variation between states and how this variation is driven by party control of state government. Finally, I investigate the areas of exception, where state policy is not polarized by party—education and especially criminal justice policy—and offer potential explanations for these patterns.

The Minimalist View of States

Three decades after Daniel Elazar (1990) predicted resurgent states in an emerging "neodualist" era of federalism, observers point to intensifying battles over public policy at the state level. However, there has been little empirical investigation of systemic policy changes in the states over time. Though scholars are now less likely to call them the "backwaters" of American politics (Winston 2002, 106), scholars have tended to take a *minimalist view* of state policymaking.

John Kincaid (1990, 144), former director of the U.S. Advisory Commission on Intergovernmental Relations and a prominent scholar of federalism, describes a twentieth century in which the role of states shrank and U.S. federalism became "more adaptable to policy preferences defined increasingly by the national government"—where the federal government moved from "senior partner" to "commanding partner" (see also Posner 2007; Zimmerman 2009).[2] By 1975, even the predominant federalism scholar William Riker (1975, 143) suggested that the existence of lower levels of government "makes no particular difference for public policy."

Additional research lends credence to the minimalist view by highlighting the constraints that face lower levels of government in federalism. Fiscal federalism suggests that the threat of exit from businesses and wealthy residents exerts downward pressure on taxation, redistribution, and regulation (Peterson 1981; Oates 1999), which reduces the potential for variation across states.[3] Fiscal federalism implies that state governments have little policy discretion compared to the federal government: they face a greater threat of exit, and with no ability to manipulate a floating currency, they face economic forces beyond their control and greater pressure to balance budgets.[4] State legislators also lack the policymaking resources of members of Congress (Kousser 2005). Lower salaries increase the incentive to spend time earning money outside of their political offices, and fewer staff limit the ability to research and draft legislation. Even if state legislators face equivalent pressures from voters and interest groups as members of Congress, we would expect those in state capitals to be less productive because of these resource constraints.

Despite these constraints, however, roll-call voting in state legislatures has polarized in recent years (Shor and McCarty 2011). Whether the prior cause of polarization stems from voters, interest groups, or politicians themselves, greater polarization implies greater distance between the policy preferences of Democrats and Republicans,[5] and thus increasing polarization of policy outcomes in the states. But most prominent studies of state policy outcomes still tend to favor the minimalist view (e.g., Dynes and Holbein 2020). While

2. A few conservative commentators counter the minimalist view, arguing, for instance, that liberal state governments like that of the "failed state of California" are too active in attempts "to regulate the internet, to tax corporations on profits earned in foreign jurisdictions, and to impose sales tax collection obligations on internet sellers domiciled elsewhere" (Greve 2011, 6).

3. However, some research challenges the prediction of a "race to the bottom" in the states (Volden 2002; Konisky 2007).

4. Researchers highlight the inability to devaluate a currency as a major barrier to fiscal policy in lower-income Eurozone countries (e.g., Krugman 2013).

5. This is true at least to the extent this polarization is ideological, as well as to the extent that non-ideological partisan brinksmanship incentivizes ideologically distinct policy agendas (Lee 2009).

"Democrats and Republicans may disagree consistently and even violently,"
Devin Caughey, Christopher Warshaw, and Yiqing Xu (2017, 1356) conclude
that "the actual policy consequences of these disagreements are far less dramatic." The increasingly partisan and ideologically consistent rhetoric of
Democratic and Republican governors and state legislators is just that—talk,
with little consequence for public policy (for other examples of minimal effects of party control, see Garand 1988; Erikson, Wright, and McIver 1993;
Jacobs and Carmichael 2002; Konisky 2007). This chapter's theory and empirical analysis challenge this line of research.

How National Polarization Affects State Policy

Political scientists have published countless books and articles about the expanding polarization between the national Democratic and Republican parties in recent decades and its consequences for elections, legislative voting,
and national policy. But there hasn't been much attention on how nationally
polarized parties are filtered through the institutions of American federalism.
This is in part because political science research has tended to see the states as
fifty separate polities, where policy changes occur as a result of political inputs
within each of these separate political systems. In this perspective, an increase
in state policy variation and polarization could be the result of partisan sorting
and polarization of state electorates.

But when we widen our perspective to study American federalism as a
broader system with feedbacks between states and across levels of government
(Karch and Rose 2019), we can begin to theorize why the state level might be
returning as the central locus of major policymaking and policy conflict in
recent decades. In addition to a direct effect of polarization (e.g., Shor and
McCarty 2011), I argue that the development of nationally coordinated and
polarized parties *interacts with American federalism* to shift policymaking down
to lower levels of government.[6] Polarization and divided government at the
national level move policy action down to the state level, where one party is
more likely to have unified control of government. Because the party networks

6. The parties were nationally polarized in earlier eras of American politics, such as during
the late nineteenth century when national polarization over slavery resulted in the Civil War.
The war led to greater centralization of governance at the national level until the end of Reconstruction, when expansion of Jim Crow once again widened the variation across states in areas
of civil rights and racial equity.

are *nationally coordinated*, policy-demanding groups can shift political resources to the right states at the right time to implement their agendas.

Gridlock at the Federal Level

Polarization and divided government have caused a slowdown of national policy
creation (Binder 2003), but federalism may serve as a "safety valve" for policy
demanders who are stymied at the federal level. An expansion of national
policy from the New Deal through the early 1970s "centralized" governance
and standardized the welfare state and civil rights law across the states (Melnick
1996; Mettler 1998; Campbell 2014). Although New Deal programs allowed
states to exclude many Black Americans from benefits (Weir 2005; Katznelson
2013), landmark policies like the Social Security Act of 1935 and the Civil
Rights Act of 1964 decreased interstate policy variation by establishing or raising legal and economic baselines.[7]

However, in the years since the 1970s, polarization has increased in Congress and divided federal government has become a more frequent occurrence
(McCarty, Poole, and Rosenthal 2006). This has led to policy gridlock (Binder
1999) and "drift" (Hacker 2004)—and higher costs of national policy change
for policy demanders. Faced with federal gridlock, policy demanders turn to
states to implement their agendas. Frustrated climate activists may turn their
hopes to the states (Rabe 2004), as might organized labor (Meyerson 2014),
LGBT rights activists (Lax and Phillips 2009), or antistatist and business interests (Skocpol and Hertel-Fernandez 2016). Federal gridlock also means that
these policy-demanding groups can be more confident than in earlier periods
that their state policy victories will not soon be reversed by federal legislation
or court rulings.

Venue Shifting to the State Level

One reason the state governments can serve as a safety valve for policy demanders is because of their partisan diversity. As the parties polarize, policy
demanders are incentivized to ally themselves with one side (Bawn et al. 2012).

7. This process of centralization continued in the welfare and regulatory buildup of the 1960s
and 1970s. Landmark federal policies that decreased state variation during this era include the
Social Security Amendments of 1965 and 1972, the Gun Control Act of 1968, the National Environmental Policy Act of 1969, and the Clean Air Act of 1970.

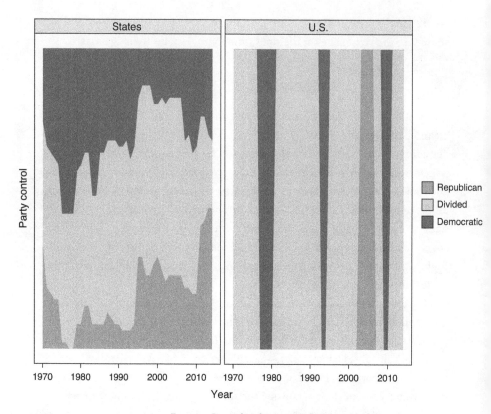

FIGURE 3.1. Partisan Control at the State and National Levels.

Fortunately for them, there will (virtually) always be at least one state government controlled by their aligned party.[8] Moreover, the federal government
has been more likely to be under divided party control than state governments
in recent decades. Between 1970 and 2014, the U.S. House, Senate, and presidency have only been under unified party control about 27 percent of the time
(12 of 45 years), whereas the average state has been under unified control about
50 percent of the time. Regardless of whether this difference in the likelihood
of unified party control is due to federalist institutions or historical happen-
stance, we would expect relatively less gridlock in the states as polarization
increases and, in turn, a relative growth in the role of state governments as
major policymakers.[9]

8. There were no unified Republican states in the year after the Watergate scandal.

9. Constantelos's (2010) study of interest groups based in Michigan and Ontario uncovers
evidence that groups select venues based on party control.

In the rarer moments when important federal policy does pass, polarization and divided government increase incentives for members of Congress to delegate authority to the states (e.g., Mooney 2000; Feeley and Rubin 2009; Chatfield and Rocco 2014). A legislator who would ideally implement his or her preferred policy across all fifty states may accept a decentralized policy as a second-best option if it moves the average outcome (such as the policy regime for the average state or average individual) toward his or her ideal. Moreover, the district-based electoral connection in Congress can improve the relative appeal of the second-best option because "representatives know that when they delegate to state and local agents, policy for *their* constituents will be set by representatives elected by those same constituents" (Chatfield and Rocco 2014, 4). Indeed, the rise of polarization in Congress has coincided with what scholars call a "devolution revolution" (e.g., Soss et al. 2001; Grogan and Rigby 2008; Kelly and Witko 2012). In a similar fashion, the federal judiciary has undergone a "federalism revolution" in which the courts are an increasingly "state friendly arena" (Whittington 2001; Waltenburg and Swinford 1999, 2) precisely during an era of increasingly partisan and narrow decisions (Baum 2015).

But this isn't just the story of the federal government becoming more permissive of decentralization. As chapters 4 and 5 will describe, it is about policy-demanding groups investing in state-level politics. These groups—ideological and issue activists, business lobbies, and wealthy individuals—shifted their attention and political resources toward the states. They and their allies in state governments innovated new ways to use the powers of the state level within American federalism, whether this meant passing major state legislation, marshaling state attorneys general against opponents in the federal government (Merriman 2019), or finding new ways to suppress the vote.

Polarization and divided government at the national level led policy-demanding groups to shift their sights to the state level. The next sections detail four consequences for public policy over the past generation. First, fiscal capacity moved from the national to the state level; as the federal government stalled and the states took up the slack, the states began to occupy a greater share of American taxation and public spending. Second, policy became increasingly varied across states; the average American's policy regime became increasingly tied to their state of residence. Third, party control of state government became the strongest predictor of a state's policy outcomes, with the national Democratic and Republican parties implementing distinct policies. Finally, states expanded their capacity to police and incarcerate their residents, rapidly increasing the U.S. prison population—but, unlike other policy areas, this rise of authoritarian policing and mass incarceration was a bipartisan affair.

Fiscal Activity Moves to the States

One way we can observe state governments transforming from "backwaters" to central players in American federalism is in the balance of fiscal activity between the state and national level. From the 1930s through the 1970s, Congress passed a number of transformational national economic policies. The Social Security Act of 1935 and its expansions in subsequent decades created a system of old age and disability insurance, massively reducing senior citizen poverty. Medicare and Medicaid provided public health insurance for the elderly and low-income families. Laws like the Glass-Steagall Act of 1933 and the Clean Air Act of 1970 funded federal agencies to regulate the financial industry and large polluters. To finance these initiatives, the federal government raised taxes, especially on the wealthy, who famously faced a top marginal income tax rate of 91 percent through the Eisenhower presidency. All of these policies helped narrow the wide economic differences between the states and centralized fiscal activity at the national level.

But by the 1980s, these trends reversed. The federal government not only slowed its production of major economic policies but also dramatically cut taxes and domestic spending. The federal government further devolved economic policy authority to the states in areas like welfare, which converted from the national Aid to Families with Dependent Children (AFDC) to the state-level Temporary Aid for Needy Families (TANF) during the Clinton presidency.

As the national government pulled back, states, particularly more liberal states controlled by Democrats, expanded their fiscal capacity. States like California and Oregon raised taxes on high earners to help finance social programs that the federal government appeared uninterested in providing. Another illustrative example is the provision of public benefits for immigrants. The 1996 welfare reform made legal immigrants ineligible for federal benefits for the first five years of residency. In response, some states moved to cover these new immigrants in their Medicaid, TANF, and State Children's Health Insurance Program (SCHIP) policies using only state funding (Hero and Preuhs 2007), again increasing the relative role of the states.

In figure 3.2, I plot total state government spending, employment, and average state tax rates (covering capital gains, corporations, and income) as a

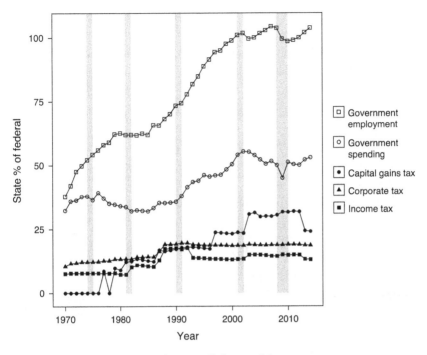

FIGURE 3.2. Fiscal Activity Shifts toward States, 1970–2014.

percentage of its corresponding federal level.[10] Each of these measures of fiscal activity shows an expanding role of state government since the late 1970s. The line marked by empty circles, government spending, increases both because states begin to spend much more on their prison systems through the 1980s and 1990s and because the federal government slows spending (though it's worth noting that this slowdown is concentrated in domestic spending, not military). Similarly, the lines representing taxation (with the shapes shaded black) show the shift toward the state level. In income taxes, for example, the top marginal rate at the federal level of 71.75 percent in 1970 hit a postwar nadir of 28 percent in 1988, whereas some liberal states like California increased top marginal rates to about 14 percent—still much lower than the federal rate but a record for state-level taxation. Shaded years represent recessions, which tend to temporarily increase the role of the federal government compared to the states.

The bulk of public spending, and especially public employment, saw massive shifts from the national to the state level. This trend again partly reflects

10. State percent of federal taxes is in terms of nominal tax rates, not revenue raised.

the national government's slowdown in domestic policymaking, but it is more so the result of the huge buildup of state prison systems in the era of mass incarceration. Per capita spending on prisons and jails, almost all at the state level, more than quadrupled since 1980—closely tracking the expansion of the U.S. prison population.

Fiscal activity has moved downward across the levels of American federalism in recent decades. But fiscal activity is not the only way we can analyze the expanding role of the state level. We can also look directly at major state policy outcomes in many different issue areas, such as abortion, environmental, and labor policy. In the next section, I describe how I use a large data set of state policies to *measure* changes in state policy outcomes over time.

Measuring Policy Outcomes

In this section, I describe my strategy to measure policy outcomes and estimate the changing relationship between party control and policy. I developed a comprehensive data set of state policy outcomes since 1970,[11] but to build it, I stood on the shoulders of giants. I collected data on 35 policies, to which I added data from Jordan and Grossmann 2016, Caughey and Warshaw 2016, and Boehmke and Skinner 2012 to create a data set of 135 policies. (I also extended years of coverage for 16 policies from the other data sets.) Caughey and Warshaw (2016, 902–3 and Supplemental Material) provide a detailed description of many of the policies, which can be binary (e.g., Right to Work laws), ordinal (e.g., mandatory parental notification or consent for a minor's abortion), or continuous (e.g., marginal tax rate on high incomes). Table 3.1 lists the policies.

The data I collected cover policies of considerable importance. They include election laws and state capital gains taxes, as well as various regulations related to public sector unions (Anzia and Moe 2016), abortion rights and coverage (Guttmacher Institute), campaign finance (Barber 2016b), and immigrant workers (National Council of State Legislatures). I also collected data on state laws that preempt localities from raising the minimum wage or requiring companies to provide paid sick leave for employees (see Riverstone-Newell 2017).

---

11. I start in 1970 because of the difficulty in comparing the modern period with the Jim Crow regime, which entailed mass disenfranchisement of Black Americans and a de jure racial caste system.

TABLE 3.1. Ideological Content of Issue Areas

Issue Area	Concept
Abortion	Legal right to and cost of emergency contraception and abortion
Campaign Finance	Restrictions on individual, corporate, PAC contributions; public funding of elections
Civil Rights & Liberties	Penalties for discrimination based on race, gender; religious privileges
Criminal Justice	Punitiveness
Drugs	State legality of federally illicit drugs (especially marijuana)
Education	Spending; public vs. private control
Environment	Restriction on emissions, chemicals; protection of species
Guns	Legal rights to purchase, own, or carry a firearm
Health & Welfare	Generosity (eligibility, benefit levels)
Housing & Transportation	Command and control
Immigration	Legal right to public services for undocumented; regulation of hiring undocumented
Labor	Right to unionize; wage laws
LGBT	Protections or penalties for homosexuality
Taxes	Marginal rate; progressivity
Voting	Cost, access to voting

Of particular importance are my data on criminal justice policies. Although some research focuses specifically on criminal justice (e.g., Yates and Fording 2005), research that summarizes policy across issue areas has neglected incarceration. For instance, aside from a few drug-related policies (e.g., medical marijuana laws), the Caughey and Warshaw (2016) data set only contains data on four criminal justice policies: death penalty repeal, the establishment of probation (only for the 1936–39 period), animal cruelty as a felony, and age-span provisions for statutory rape cases (i.e., the decriminalization of sex between consenting teenagers of similar ages). These policies are generally orthogonal to the rise of mass incarceration. I collected data on laws that criminal justice research considers central to the rise of mass incarceration (for a review, see Travis, Western, and Redburn 2014, chap. 3): truth-in-sentencing laws, which require individuals to serve a minimum percentage of their original sentence; three strikes laws, which increase penalties for an individual's third felony; and determinate sentencing laws, which specify mandatory minimum sentences.[12]

12. In some instances, these "tough on crime" policies were passed by ballot initiative, such as California's three strikes proposition in 1994.

To measure party control of government, I used variables that indicate whether a state is under unified Democratic control, unified Republican control, or divided control (Klarner 2013). While control of the executive branch or one or more legislative chambers may have an independent or partial effect on policy outcomes (Smith 1997), I focused on unified control because polarization and divided government interact to produce gridlock (Binder 1999). Key to the analyses is the comparison of the party-policy relationship across time. Because policy change is rare compared to other political dynamics, estimating a completely dynamic party effect (i.e., by year) is difficult. Precision and clarity are greatly improved by estimating an average party effect for different eras that span multiple years (e.g., Caughey, Warshaw, and Xu 2017, table 3). I primarily compared the association between party control and policy change during two eras: the 1970–99 period and the 2000–2014 period.[13] In practice, this entails interacting the party control variable with a dummy variable for the 2000–2014 period to estimate the marginal effect of party control on policy change during the different eras. Temporal breaks in time-series models can also be estimated empirically. Chow tests reject the null of no structural break in the party-policy relationship between 1999 and 2000 with $p < 0.01$ for every policy measure used in this study, which suggests that there is, indeed, a significant change in the relationship between party control and policy outcomes between the 1970–1999 and 2000–2014 periods.

Unidimensional Measures

Political scientists often summarize public opinion, legislative votes, and, more recently, policy outcomes on a unidimensional left-right orientation. Recent unidimensional policy measures provide a summary of the ideological content of policy on a dimension typically described as "policy liberalism" or "the role of government" (Erikson, Wright, and McIver 1993; Caughey and Warshaw 2016). Each state gets a policy "score" or "ideal point" for each year, representing the left-right orientation of its policies. In this section, I briefly summarize my findings on *unidimensional* measures, as a prelude to more detailed presentation of my study of *issue-specific* policy dynamics.

13. Setting this threshold between 1999 and 2000 strikes a balance between periods that are long enough (precision) and highlights the potentially precipitous increase in policy polarization in the most recent years of hyperpolarization (Mann and Ornstein 2013).

As a first cut at the data, I estimated policy variation and polarization with four unidimensional left-right measures of policy outcomes. The first is the State Policy Liberalism (SPL) measure from Caughey and Warshaw (2016), a set of state-year policy ideal points generated from a dynamic Bayesian IRT model. Second, I estimated the same ideal point model with my expanded policy data set to produce an Expanded SPL measure. The third and fourth measures are Substantive Scales, simple additive indices (averages) that are the sum of a state's liberal policies minus its conservative policies in a given year. These measures serve as expert-coded alternatives to the Bayesian IRT latent dimension estimates and are analogous to the "Policy" measure of Erikson, MacKuen, and Stimson (2002, chap. 9). One of the additive indices weights policies equally, while the other is the average of issue area–specific indices. (Subsequent sections address how the ideological direction of policies is determined.) All measures are normalized to a range between 0 and 1.

This exploratory analysis suggests that policy *variation* has increased across states over time. The spread of policy ideal points has widened greatly since the 1970s. The range and standard deviation estimates are remarkably similar across the measures. The range of ideal points is at least a third larger in the 2010s than in the 1970s and 1980s, and the standard deviation is at least two-thirds larger.[14]

These measures also suggest that this growing variation is related to party control of state government—policy *polarization* has increased. Using dynamic panel regressions, figure A.1 plots the marginal effect of unified party control of government on change in ideal points for the 1970–99 period and the 2000–2014 period. All of the estimates show at least a twofold increase in the magnitude of the relationship between party control and policy ideal points (see also Caughey, Warshaw, and Xu 2017). The expanding variation and polarization evident in the unidimensional analysis motivates the investigation of *issue-specific* policy dynamics. Unidimensional ideal points serve as strong summary measures, but generally, they may create obstacles to inference by obscuring multidimensional variation or conflating extremism and

---

14. The Substantive Scales, which do not use data from earlier years to smooth ideal points over time like the Bayesian IRT measures, show slightly larger increases in range and standard deviation over time (starting from slightly lower in the 1970s and ending slightly higher in the 2010s).

consistency (Broockman 2016), and they rely on relatively strong assumptions about the comparability of policies across issue domains.[15]

More importantly, it is difficult to draw conclusions about the substantive content of policy—its effect on members of the polity—from unidimensional ideal point estimates. Policy scholars may be interested in more specific temporal dynamics in residents' relationship to government. Are state abortion laws more or less restrictive? In which direction have state tax rates, restrictions on campaign contributions, and the generosity of welfare benefits moved in recent decades?

Policy Indices by Issue Area

Issue area measures provide a clearer picture of historical changes in policy substance. Although many studies have employed summary measures of policy outcomes in a single issue area (e.g., Norrander and Wilcox 1999; Hero and Preuhs 2007), mine is the first to compare across many issue area indices. I group the policies into sixteen discrete issue areas: abortion, campaign finance, civil rights and liberties, criminal justice, drug policy, education, environment, gun control, health and welfare, housing and transportation, immigration, labor (private sector), labor (public sector), LGBT rights, taxes, and voting.

In each area, I calculate a simple substantive measure of average policy outcomes: the number of liberal policies minus the number of conservative policies (see also Erikson, MacKuen, and Stimson 2002, chap. 9). Because policies can be binary (e.g., medical marijuana laws), ordinal (e.g., voter ID laws, which can be strict or non-strict), or continuous (e.g., minimum wage level), I normalize each policy to range from 0 to 1. A binary policy, which a state either has or does not have, takes on the value of 0 or 1, whereas an ordinal

15. Additionally, although they may be advantageous in the study of roll-call votes (e.g., Clinton, Jackman, and Rivers 2004), there are two reasons to prefer straightforward additive indices over latent dimension estimates (e.g., factor analysis or Bayesian IRT) for the measurement of *policy outcomes*. Historical, normative, and policy scholarship provides clear priors about the ideological content of policy. Empirically deriving model parameters (the ideological content of policy) from the data rests on the joint assumption that (a) liberal states are liberal because they pass liberal policies, and (b) liberal policies are liberal because liberal states pass them. When this assumption is violated historically (e.g., during the 1960s and 1970s some conservative southern states were early adopters of liberal abortion laws), the model may produce parameters that do not conform to substantive understandings about the ideological content of policy.

or continuous policy, such as a tax or minimum wage, is transformed to the [0, 1] scale. A state's score in an issue area index is therefore the sum of the liberal policies minus the sum of the conservative policies.

This kind of measure relies on three assumptions: first, the ideological "direction" of policy (whether it is liberal, conservative, or neither); second, that policies are of equal substantive importance; and third, that the direction and importance remain constant over time. These assumptions are unlikely to be satisfied in practice, especially equality of substantive importance.[16] However, I argue that these simple index measures strike a balance between agnosticism, precision, transparency, risk of bias, and substantive interpretability.

Determining the *ideological direction* of more than 130 policies is a difficult task. The primary left-right ideological dimension, or "what goes with what," has changed over time, but for the most part political observers characterize policies on the *left* to be those that (1) expand the use of state power for economic regulation and redistribution (Rawls 1971; Foner 1984; Weir 2005; Wang 2005; Brinkley 2011) or increase or protect the rights of historically marginalized groups in society (Black Americans and other non-white racial groups, women, LGBT individuals, immigrants, and religious minorities) (DuBois 1935; Foner 1988; Kessler-Harris 2001; Shelby 2005; Kollman and Waites 2009); and (2) restrict the use of state power for the punishment of deviant social behavior (Simon 2007). Policies on the *right* do the opposite (Himmelstein 1992; Brinkley 1994; Harvey 2007). Although there is considerable nuance throughout political and intellectual history, in short, left policies promote social libertarianism and economic interventionism, while right policies promote traditional (incumbent) social values and oppose state intervention in markets.

Yet even with this large body of historical and normative scholarship, there is still no objective, unifying test of whether a certain moral principle, political action, or legal statute is on the left or right. Many scholars argue that the first dimension of politics represents the "size of government" (Poole and Rosenthal 1997), but this is not always the case. For instance, policies that expand rights and protections for Black Americans, which are understood to be liberal, can involve expansions of state power (e.g., anti-lynching laws) or restrictions on state power (e.g., laws that reduce prison sentences). The same is true of

16. One might argue, for example, that income taxes are more substantively and normatively consequential than capital gains taxes and should thus be weighted more heavily in calculating the issue area indices.

abortion laws, where Medicaid coverage of abortion and bans on "partial birth abortion" both involve greater state intervention but are quite ideologically distinct. It is thus no surprise that there is an ongoing debate about whether the clustering of policies along partisan and ideological lines is due to "natural" ideological or psychological principles (e.g., Haidt 2012) or whether they are the products of idiosyncratic historical coalition partnerships between interests in society that over time became path-dependent (e.g., Karol 2009; Bawn et al. 2012).

I argue that an *issue-specific* left-right conceptualization can improve inference for studies of policy dynamics. Rather than assuming that issues "go together" in unidimensional space, table 3.1 shows conceptual dimensions that determine the ideological direction of policies within each issue area.[17] The left-right dimension for abortion policy, for example, represents the legality and costs (broadly defined) of obtaining an abortion. Other issue areas represent multiple related concepts. Tax policy, for example, is comprised of two concepts: absolute rates and progressivity (the distribution of marginal rates across income levels), and health and welfare policy is comprised of both benefit levels and the strictness of eligibility. I base a policy's *direction*—left, right, or, in a small number of cases, neither—on its expected effect on the issue-specific dimension. This issue-specific conceptualization also helps avoid the problem of sorting and shifts over time regarding which issues "go together" on a single left-right dimension. While the cluster of issues on the left and right has shifted over the nineteenth and twentieth centuries (e.g., Schickler 2013), issue-specific assessments (e.g., whether a policy restricts or broadens access to abortion) have largely remained constant.[18]

Interstate Policy Variation

In this section I estimate change in state policy since 1970. Figure 3.3 plots each issue area policy index. The gray lines represent the policy outcomes for each individual state over time.

---

17. Within an issue area, a policy can be on the "left" or "right," but these terms are simply shorthand for the concepts described in table 3.1.

18. Of the 135 policies shown in table 3.1, I exclude the 15 in the Other category because they (a) have unclear issue-specific ideological content (e.g., animal cruelty felony), (b) are socioeconomically inconsequential (e.g., beer keg registration), and/or (c) are insufficiently varied or numerous to create an issue area (e.g., state lotteries).

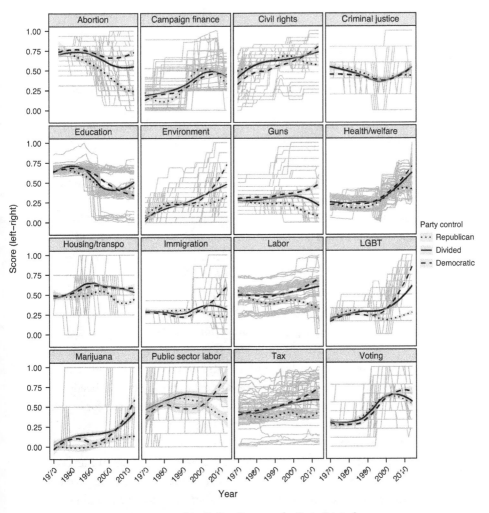

FIGURE 3.3. State Policy Outcomes by Party Control.

States' policy outcomes within each issue area diverge greatly over time; this represents increased *overall variation* in state policy outcomes in each area. Compared to the 1970s, the policy regime under which an individual lives is increasingly determined by her state of residence. For instance:

- Abortion: In 1973, states only differed in Medicaid coverage for abortion and other minor regulations. By 2014, the most restrictive states mandated waiting periods, parental notification, counseling, licensed physicians, a twenty-week gestation limit, and restricted insurance coverage for abortion.

- Environment: In 1970, the greenest states had state EPAs and endangered species laws. By 2014, they had strict regulations of greenhouse gas emissions for cars and utilities, solar tax credits, and a plethora of recycling programs.
- Gun Control: In 1970, the least strict states allowed open carry and the strictest states required dealer licenses and purchaser background checks. By 2014, the least strict states had added Stand Your Ground laws, while the strictest states banned assault weapons and mandated registration and waiting periods for purchases.
- Health and Welfare: In 1970, states varied in AFDC benefits and Medicaid adoption. By 2014, Massachusetts offered generous TANF and SCHIP benefits and had expanded Medicaid, while Alabama did not expand Medicaid, required drug tests for public benefits, and required a monthly income below $268 for a family of three to qualify for TANF.[19]
- Immigration: In 1970, states mostly varied in laws establishing English as official state language, and all legal immigrants were eligible for public welfare and health programs. By 2014, only some states provided public benefits to new legal immigrants.[20] Some states provided in-state tuition for undocumented college students, allowed drivers licenses for undocumented immigrants, and banned the use of e-verify for employment, while other states required all employers to use it.
- Taxes: In 1970, some states had no income or capital gains taxes, while the highest tax state, Vermont, had a 5.54 percent top capital gains rate and 14.88 percent top income rate. By 2014, many states continued to collect no income or investment taxes, but California had a 14.1 percent top capital gains rate and a 14.1 percent top income rate.

Some areas, such as environmental policy, become more liberal over time on average. All of the major policies in this area increase environmental regulation or public spending in pursuit of environmental quality, and the most conservative states on the environment simply do not pass the major

19. This ($268 per month) is about 16 percent of the Federal Poverty Level for a family of three.

20. The 1996 welfare reform made legal immigrants ineligible for federal benefits for the first five years of residency; some states then moved to cover these new immigrants in their Medicaid, TANF, and SCHIP programs using only state funding (Hero and Preuhs 2007).

environmental laws that the "green" states do. Of course, as we gain greater understanding of the reality of climate change—that maintaining the status quo will lead to utter catastrophe—the liberal policy shifts appear less and less substantial relative to the scale of the problem.

State economic policies in the health and welfare issue area also move in a liberal direction over time as states implement programs like SCHIP and expanded Medicaid. In his book *Red State Blues* (2019, chap. 3), Matt Grossmann points to these liberal economic policy shifts in the states as evidence that the conservative policy push has been mostly unsuccessful. Grossmann makes an important point that conservative victories often only block expansions of the welfare state and progressive policies, not fully reverse them.[21] But this is another moment where attention to *federalism*, rather than *state politics*, matters for our inferences. In the economic policy areas that have seen a leftward shift in the states, one must keep in mind that although the average *state* government has expanded its taxation and social welfare provision, U.S. taxation and the welfare state taken *as a whole* have not expanded the same way.[22] For example, while states like California raised income taxes on high earners to a level never before done by a state government, this increase was a fraction of the size of federal tax *cuts* over the same time period. The shift of policymaking to the states is associated with a friendlier overall tax and welfare state environment for the wealthy.

Abortion policy, in contrast to the economic and regulatory policy areas, tracks more conservatively since *Roe v. Wade* (1973). A few states become more liberal on abortion over time as they pass laws to provide Medicaid coverage for abortion and over-the-counter emergency contraception. This liberal trend, however, is swamped by the spread of abortion restrictions in states, such as mandatory parental notice for minors and bans on "partial birth abortion." Though not included in this analysis, prior research finds similar dynamics for Targeted Regulation of Abortion Provider (TRAP) laws, which "single out abortion providers and impose on them requirements and regulations that are excessive and more stringent than those imposed on other medical practitioners" (Medoff and Dennis 2011, 955).

---

21. Research in comparative political economy has long emphasized the difficulty of rolling back the welfare state, as beneficiaries become entrenched and block welfare state retrenchment (Pierson 1994), though more "submerged" forms of retrenchment have affected the American welfare state in particular (Hacker 2004).

22. The Affordable Care Act and, to a lesser extent, SCHIP were welfare state expansions, but the United States also experienced retrenchment in the 1996 welfare reform, as well as more "submerged" forms of retrenchment in welfare state policies around retirement, employee health benefits, and other areas (Hacker 2004).

A third set of issue areas, such as immigration and labor, sees similar growth in *variation* but does not become more liberal or conservative on average since the 1970s. Each issue area shows growing *policy variation* across states, but they also show partisan *policy polarization*: policy outcomes in Republican states are more distant from those in Democratic states. In particular, figure 3.3 shows the correlation between party control and policy outcomes in each area (with the dashed lines representing unified Democratic states, the dotted lines representing unified Republican states, and the solid line representing divided states). There are two issue areas that do not fit this pattern, where increased overall variation appears nonpartisan: criminal justice and education.

The averages of Republican, Democratic, and divided states in figure 3.3, however, are simple correlations, so the growing policy divergence by party control could be simple sorting—states with conservative policies becoming Republican and states with liberal policies becoming Democratic. To test the changing relationship between party control and policy *change*, in contrast, I estimate dynamic panel regressions and compare the marginal effect of party control on policy outcomes for the 1970–99 period and the 2000–2014 period. Figure 3.4 plots these results.

Partisan Policy Polarization

Figure 3.4, which tests the relationship between party control and policy *change*, corroborates the correlations shown in figure 3.3.[23] Again, in 14 of the 16 issue areas, the party effect polarizes after 1999: there is a greater difference in the effect of unified Democratic control relative to that of unified Republican control in the 2000–2014 period than in the 1970–99 period. The amount of polarization depends on the partisanship of policy—that is, whether, for instance, Democratic states increase taxes relative to Republican states. But the overall amount of policy activity in a given area matters. For example, states become less active on civil rights and liberties as time progresses but more active in areas like drug policy, LGBT rights, and voting rights.

Figure 3.4 shows that party control is no better at predicting policy change in criminal justice or education in recent years. Both before and after 2000, party control does not predict change in criminal justice policies. States controlled by Democrats pass punitive and liberal criminal justice policies at

---

23. I follow the dynamic panel models of Caughey, Warshaw, and Xu (2017), who add lagged dependent variables for year $t1$ and $t2$ to traditional two-way fixed-effects models to improve fit.

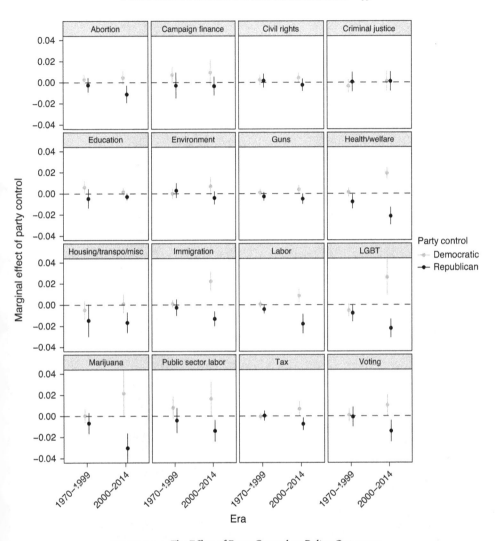

FIGURE 3.4. The Effect of Party Control on Policy Outcomes.

similar rates to divided and Republican states. In both eras, states controlled by Democrats are slightly more likely to pass liberal education policies (e.g., increase spending in K–12 or higher education) and less likely to pass school choice, voucher, and charter laws. However, party control becomes slightly *less* predictive of education policy changes after 2000. In both of these issue areas, the static or decreasing predictiveness of party control stands in contrast to the other 14 issue areas in which party control increasingly explains policy change.

(a)

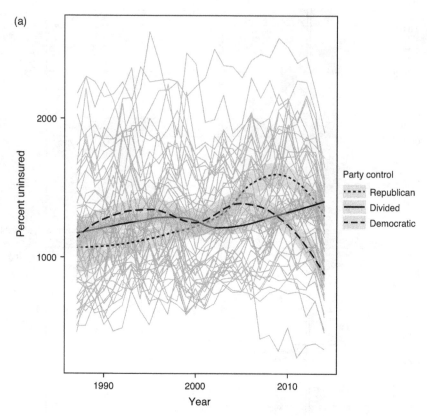

FIGURE 3.5. Party Control and Health Insurance Coverage.
Note: Party control increasingly predicts health insurance coverage over time. Plot (a) shows
the average percent uninsured by state party control over time (using loess). Plot (b) shows
the marginal effect of unified Republican control on the uninsured rate for the 1987–99
period and the 2000–2014 period across three time-series model specifications.

But does this policy polarization matter for the lives of these states' residents? Does it matter for socioeconomic outcomes that there is polarization
in 14 issue areas, such as tax and health policy, but *non-polarization* in criminal
justice and education?

How Policy Polarization Affects the Lives of Americans

The polarization of policy carries major socioeconomic consequences for residents. In the polarized areas of health and environmental policy, party control of
state government increasingly predicts rates of health coverage and carbon intensity of a state's energy supply, respectively. In the non-polarized areas of criminal

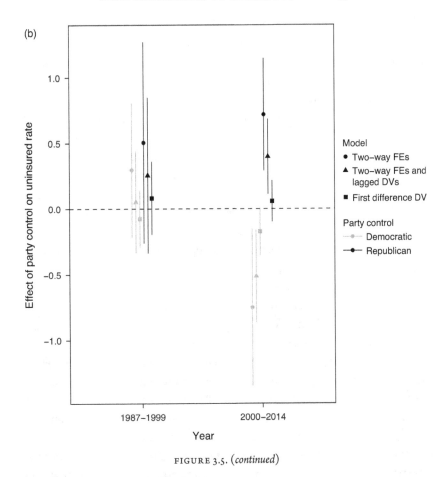

FIGURE 3.5. (*continued*)

justice and education, however, party control *does not* increasingly predict rates of incarceration (overall or among Black residents) or graduation rates, respectively. In this section, I focus in depth on health and criminal justice policy.

The health policy agendas of the national Democratic and Republican parties have been distinct since at least the 1930s. Health policy in the states has been similarly polarized for decades, as Democratic states have tended to have more generous Medicaid eligibility and benefits. As the role of states in health policy expanded with the development of state prescription drug benefits for seniors, as well as federal grants for the State Children's Health Program (1998) and Medicaid expansion under the Affordable Care Act (2014), state health policies increasingly varied—and this variation was increasingly related to party control of government (Trachtman 2020).

Socioeconomic *outcomes* related to health policy polarized accordingly. Figure 3.5 shows the relationship between party control and the *uninsured rate*.

Plot (a) displays state uninsured rates (the gray lines) and the average Republican (dotted), Democratic (dashed), and divided (solid) state from 1987 through 2014. Plot (b) shows the marginal effect of party control for the 1987–99 and 2000–2014 periods from different time-series regression models.

In both the correlation and the regressions, party control of government is increasingly associated with health insurance coverage in more recent years. Whereas prior to 2000, party control does *not* predict change in the uninsured rate, after 2000 unified Republican control is associated with a 0.75-percentage-point increase in the uninsured rate and unified Democratic control is associated with a 0.75-percentage-point decrease in the uninsured rate. These differences in coverage are of considerable social consequence. Health policy scholars, for instance, "estimate the number of deaths attributable to the lack of Medicaid expansion in opt-out states at between 7,115 and 17,104" (Dickman et al. 2014).

Other research highlights how state policy changes and polarization have affected the lives of Americans in other ways. Wisconsin's restrictions on public sector unions' collective bargaining in 2011 increased the gender wage gap among teachers, with women's wages falling relative to men's (Biasi and Sarsons 2020). The expansion of state earned income tax credit (EITC) policies for low-income families increased children's future employment and earnings prospects (Bastian and Michelmore 2018). States that increased their minimum wage reduced criminal recidivism (Agan and Makowsky, forthcoming). State climate policies, such as public benefit funds and renewable portfolio standards, reduced carbon emissions (Prasad and Munch 2012; Wakiyama and Zusman 2021). Although it is hard to estimate precisely, it appears that state assault weapon bans reduce the number of school shootings (Gius 2018).

In contrast, education and criminal justice policies are—uniquely—non-polarized. In education, Democratic state governments pass school choice and charter school laws and spend at similar rates to Republican state governments.[24] In criminal justice even more so, Democratic and Republican states both instituted "tough on crime" laws that led to mass incarceration. The lack of polarization in these areas relative to others has largely reflected the positions of the national Democratic and Republican parties, and a substantial literature describes the bipartisan history of policymaking in these areas (e.g.,

24. However, I do find a modest increase in polarization in K–12 spending per pupil (but not higher education spending), with Democratic governments spending more than Republican governments after 2000.

DeBray 2006; Hursh 2007; Weaver 2007; Alexander 2012; Wolbrecht and Hartney 2014).

Criminal Justice Policy Is Similar in Red and Blue States

Mass incarceration—the internationally unprecedented number and proportion of Americans, disproportionately Black, under correctional control—has drawn increasing scholarly attention with respect to its origins (Weaver 2007; Lacey 2008; Wacquant 2009; Alexander 2012) and consequences (Western 2006; Manza and Uggen 2008; Weaver and Lerman 2010). The same is true of the most public-facing side of the criminal justice system: policing (Forman 2004; Cohen 2010; Fortner 2015; Harris 2016; Stuart 2016; Soss and Weaver 2017). And more importantly, they have generated historically widespread protests based in the Black Lives Matter movement.

The rise of racially authoritarian policing and mass incarceration is the result of changes in law and bureaucracy *in the fifty states*. Of the powers reserved to the states in the Tenth Amendment of the U.S. Constitution, *police powers* are the most prominent and likely the most socially consequential. State and local agencies account for the overwhelming majority of law enforcement, and the federal prison system houses less than 6 percent of the U.S. incarcerated population. There is new but limited research focusing on the interaction of mass incarceration and federalism (Miller 2008; Lacey and Soskice 2015; Miller 2016).

But, curiously, many observers point their righteous indignation not at the state or local level but at national authorities. "I Was Arrested, Jailed and Assaulted by a Guard; My 'Crime'? Being a Journalist in Trump's America," read a July 9, 2020, headline from the UK newspaper the *Independent*. British journalist Andrew Buncombe was arrested for the "failure to disperse" during the Black Lives Matter protests on July 1, 2020, surrounding the then recent police killing of George Floyd.[25] This perspective on the Trump presidency makes some sense. Trump has had a confrontational history with the press, frequently attacking journalists and journalism more broadly, and the independent

---

25. Andrew Buncombe, "I Was Arrested, Jailed and Assaulted by a Guard; My 'Crime'? Being a Journalist in Trump's America," *Independent*, July 9, 2020, https://www.independent.co.uk/news/world/americas/journalist-arrest-seattle-chaz-protest-police-prison-black-lives-matter-a9606846.html.

Freedom of Press Foundation counted 149 assaults of journalists by police and more than 45 arrests between May 25 and June 4, 2020.[26]

Yet the Seattle Police Department (SPD) that arrested Buncombe is not under the authority of the federal government. It is part of the City of Seattle, a well-known liberal city with a Democratic local government, which derives its legal status from Washington State, a well-known liberal state with a Democratic state government.[27] While the broader trends toward a more authoritarian form of governance under President Trump have been rightly noted by scholars, the authoritarianism here is of a different sort. Buncombe's arrest was the result of a police department that felt comfortable arresting and detaining a journalist for the crime of recording events, a police department whose authority derives from the city and state, not the federal government. In fact, prosecutions of peaceful protestors by state and local authorities in both red and blue states skyrocketed during the 2020 Black Lives Matter movement.[28]

Democratic and Republican states alike have enabled police to take excessive and violent action against journalists, protesters, and ordinary (especially Black) Americans. From state and local prosecutors who refuse to bring charges to legislatures that pass laws shielding police from consequences, many state and local actors from both major political parties have converged to enable the expansion of police violence and prison populations. Despite the social importance and comparative punitiveness of American criminal justice policy, its politics has been mostly bipartisan as the parties compete to be perceived as "tough on crime." Vesla Weaver (2007, 261) discusses how after 1968 "even liberal Democrats did not talk about civil rights without deploring crime." Michelle Alexander (2012, 55–56) places responsibility on not only the Republican Party but also on Democrats for adopting "tough on crime" policies, especially during the 1990s. At the local and county levels, Justin de Benedictis-Kessner and Christopher Warshaw (2016, 2020) find

---

26. Trevor Timm, "We Crunched the Numbers: Police—Not Protestors—Are Overwhelmingly Responsible for Attacking Journalists," *Intercept,* June 4, 2020, https://theintercept.com/2020/06/04/journalists-attacked-police-george-floyd-protests/.

27. First-class city, RCW 35.01.010.

28. Adam Gabbatt, "Felony Charges against BLM Protesters Are 'Suppression Tactic,' Experts Say," *Guardian,* August 16, 2020, https://www.theguardian.com/world/2020/aug/16/felony-charges-blm-protesters-suppression-tactic.

TABLE 3.2. Criminal Justice Policies by Party Control

	Policies Passed (Repealed) by Party Control					
	Democratic		Divided		Republican	
	1970–1999	2000–2014	1970–1999	2000–2014	1970–1999	2000–2014
Three Strikes	8	1	11	1	5	0
Determinate Sentencing	6 (1)	1	11 (1)	0	2	0 (2)
Truth in Sentencing	5	0	4 (2)1	0	1	0
Death Penalty Repeal	2	5	1	1	0	0

Note: Democratic and divided state governments passed more punitive criminal justice policies than did Republican governments, though removal of the death penalty mostly occurred in Democratic states. Numbers in parentheses represent repeals.

that Democratic and Republican mayors spend similar amounts on policing in their cities and that the partisanship of county legislatures has no effect on police spending.

As shown in table 3.2, punitive criminal justice policy has not polarized in the states. An exception is the repeal of the death penalty; five Democratic states repealed the death penalty between 2000 and 2014.[29]

Jeff Yates and Richard Fording (2005) find a significant association between Republican control of government and incarceration rates for white and especially for Black people between 1978 and 1995, and I similarly find a statistically significant effect of unified Republican government for the 1978–99 period.[30] The substantive effect, however, is modest and inconsistent across models: the two-way fixed-effect model (the least strict test) shows an increased incarceration rate of about 30 people per 100,000 residents, but the other models show no effect (see Plot (b) in figure 3.6). An increase in a state incarceration rate of

29. Though the states' execution of 1,445 individuals since 1976 is of great social consequence, it is less related to mass incarceration than the other policies because in all likelihood these individuals would have been given a life sentence had the death penalty not been in effect. Moreover, the death penalty is unique because Texas is responsible for more than a third (542) of the executions in the United States since the death penalty was ruled constitutional in 1976.

30. Data on incarcerated populations are from the Bureau of Justice Statistics (ICPSR 36281). Yearly state population estimates by race are from linear interpolation of decennial Census numbers (Weden et al. 2015).

(a)

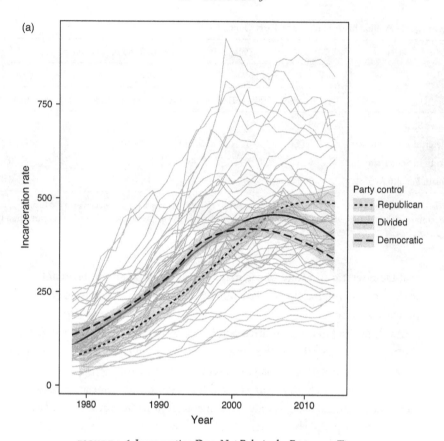

FIGURE 3.6. Incarceration Does Not Polarize by Party over Time.
Note: Incarceration *does not* polarize by party over time. Plot (a) shows the average
incarceration rate per 100,000 residents by state party control over time (using loess).
Plot (b) shows the marginal effect of unified Republican control on the incarceration rate for
the 1978–99 period and the 2000–2012 period across three time-series model specifications.
Models control for the crime rate at year $t-1$ (see Yates and Fording 2005).

30 individuals per 100,000 residents is substantively minuscule in a society in
which one in 36 adults are under correctional jurisdiction.[31]

More importantly, there is no evidence of a polarization of incarceration rates
by party across time. This *decreased* effect of Republican control in the post-2000
period is a stark contrast to the rapid polarization in other policy areas.

31. This is the 2014 estimate from the Bureau of Justice Statistics, and it includes people on
parole or probation.

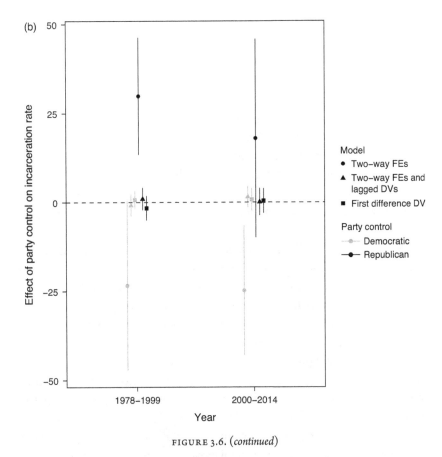

FIGURE 3.6. (*continued*)

I also estimated the relationship between party control and the incarceration rate for Black Americans. Even more than for the overall incarceration rate, the Black incarceration rate becomes *less polarized* after 2000. For most models prior to 2000, Republican control is associated with an increase in the Black incarceration rate of about 100 per 100,000 residents, but the party differences decrease after 2000.

Overall and Black incarceration rates do not appear to polarize in the states, but recent years have seen growing partisan conflict over the use of *private* prisons (Price and Riccucci 2005).[32] The use of private prisons may be more polarized than overall incarceration because it may generate conflict not only

---

32. Price and Riccucci (2005) test the cross-sectional relationship between partisan and ideological variables and private incarceration for the year 1990. To the author's understanding, this is the first test of this relationship across time.

over crime and punishment concerns but also over profit incentives for punitiveness, reports of inhumane conditions, and the fundamental role of the state and the social contract (Shapiro 2011). I estimated the relationship between party control and the percent of inmates who are housed in privately owned prisons, but only beginning in 1999 due to a lack of available data. Analogous bivariate and panel regression analyses suggest a modest relationship between party control and private prisons. After 2010, Democratic states have significantly lower proportions of inmates in private facilities. However, the panel regressions show at most a small effect of party control (less than 1 percent), which is only statistically significant in the model employing the first differenced dependent variable (not the two-way fixed-effects or lagged models).

When it comes to policing and criminal justice policy, it doesn't appear to matter much whether your state or local government is red or blue. The 2020 protests following the police murders of George Floyd, Breonna Taylor, Jacob Blake, and many other Black Americans often focused on pressuring Democratic state and local officials—who in most cases control the police departments who committed these prominent murders—to implement serious policing reform. But progress has been hard to come by.

In the blue state of Minnesota, activists and a unanimous city council proposed a major restructuring of the Minneapolis Police Department, the law enforcement agency whose officer killed George Floyd. The proposal would amend Minneapolis's city charter, a process that requires a citywide ballot measure. However, in a rare procedural move, the state-appointed Minneapolis Charter Commission blocked the item from the ballot.[33]

When it comes to the goal of changing policing and criminal justice policy, we have seen greater social movement pressure and favorable trends in public attitudes—and increasingly progressive rhetoric from state and local Democrats. So why has policy change been slow to come? The answer may be the same mechanism of electoral competition described by scholars like Peter Enns (2016) and Vesla Weaver (2007), that Democratic candidates (at all levels) worry about alienating white voters. Indeed, Democratic leaders vocally argued that calls from some candidates to "defund the police" did electoral

---

33. Liz Navratil and Miguel Otárola, "Minneapolis Charter Commission Blocks Controversial Policing Proposal from November Ballot," *Star Tribune*, August 6, 2020, https://www.startribune .com/charter-commission-blocks-plan-to-remake-police-from-ballot/572016392/. This measure ended up appearing on the 2021 ballot.

harm to the party in the 2020 election. But given the scope of social movement pressure and liberalizing racial attitudes among Democratic voters, there may be another side to the story. Specifically, part of the answer may lie in the organizational power of police. American police departments have come to resemble not street-level bureaucrats in the classic public administration formulation but *cartels* that do not bow to civilian political authority.

When city councils, mayors, and even the federal government threaten to institute reforms, police rebel. They withdraw their labor: calling in sick, taking longer to respond to calls, and generally pulling out of communities.[34] Despite the fact that Covid-19 is considerably deadlier for police officers than violence, a nontrivial number of police officers have resigned or threatened resignation in opposition to local Covid-19 vaccine mandates.[35]

During the George Floyd protests, the NYPD arrested the daughter of Bill de Blasio, the mayor of New York City. The Sergeants Benevolent Association (SBA) then tweeted out details of the arrest, asking, "How can the NYPD protect the city of NY from rioting anarchist[s] when the Mayor[']s object throwing daughter is one of them?" The SBA tweet disclosed Chiara de Blasio's address and other personal details.[36] In some cases, this sort of coercive and threatening activity by police extends even further. After charging a protester with a Class A felony, carrying a maximum sentence of life in prison for the crime of buying red paint, police in Salt Lake City, Utah, began investigating State Senator Derek Kitchen for the alleged crime of sending the protester ten dollars.[37]

In Portsmouth, Virginia, after protesters brought down a Confederate monument, police charged several prominent local figures with felonies, including

34. Alec MacGillis, "What Can Mayors Do When the Police Stop Doing Their Jobs?" *Pro-Publica*, September 3, 2020, https://www.propublica.org/article/what-can-mayors-do-when -the-police-stop-doing-their-jobs/amp?s=07.

35. Becky Sullivan, "Police Officers and Unions Put Up a Fight against Vaccine Mandates for Public Workers," NPR, October 19, 2021, https://www.npr.org/2021/10/19/1047140849/police -officers-unions-vaccine-mandates-covid-19.

36. Eliza Relman, "Alexandria Ocasio-Cortez Accuses New York Police Union of Threatening Mayor Bill de Blasio's Daughter after Her Arrest at Saturday's Protests," *Business Insider*, June 1, 2020, https://www.businessinsider.com/aoc-attacks-nypd-for-threatening-bill-de -blasios-daughter-after-arrest-2020-6.

37. Pat Reavy, "Utah Sen. Derek Kitchen Accused of Helping Pay for Paint Used by Protesters," *Deseret News*, August 19, 2020, https://www.deseret.com/utah/2020/8/19/21376211 /senator-derek-kitchen-accused-helping-pay-red-paint-used-protesters-district-attorney -vandalism.

members of the NAACP, a public defender, a school board member, and the president pro tempore of the Virginia Senate, Louise Lucas, a Black woman.[38] Police in Portsmouth were undeterred by the fact that Senator Lucas had not touched the monument and that Virginia state police had earlier investigated the incident, charging no one.[39] Police also pushed for the removal of the Portsmouth Commonwealth's attorney (i.e., the city's prosecutor), Stephanie Morales, who is Black, from the case by naming her as a potential witness. The vice mayor, Lisa Lucas-Burke, who is also Black, was further charged with a crime for calling on the chief of police to step down.[40]

These are not isolated incidents. They demonstrate a deep and far-reaching problem of authoritarianism and unaccountability in American policing and criminal justice—issues that have sparked condemnation from international organizations such as the United Nations Human Rights Council. As Amnesty International notes, "All 50 states and Washington, D.C. fail to comply with international law and standards on the use of lethal force by law enforcement officers."[41] "The 'land of the free' has become a country of prisons," proclaims the international organization Human Rights Watch. What I hope to highlight is the fact that this authoritarianism is both *bipartisan* and concentrated at the *state level*.

Changes in health and criminal justice policy in the states have been highly consequential for the lives of Americans. The politics of these two policy areas, however, are quite distinct. Health policy in the states has polarized considerably over the past generation based on the party in control of government. This has had major consequences for the health of states' residents, especially with respect to state governments' decisions around whether to expand Medicaid under the Affordable Care Act. Some Republican states' decisions to reject

---

38. Ana Ley, "Portsmouth Council Members May Have Broken Law by Asking for Charges in Confederate Monument Case," *Virginian-Pilot*, September 10, 2020, https://www.pilotonline.com /government/local/vp-nw-greene-moody-psimas-emails-20200910-w3ulihsrtrdcbljvg464tritbi -story.html?outputType=amp.

39. Ana Ley and Gary A. Harki, "A Powerful Black Leader. White Opposition. Criminal Charges. An Old Pattern Continues in Portsmouth," *Virginian-Pilot*, August 22, 2020, https:// www.pilotonline.com/government/local/vp-nw-portsmouth-lucas-history-20200822 -theoupptlfh4pomdqhhc3loxnu-story.html.

40. Ley, "Portsmouth Council Members May Have Broken Law."

41. Amnesty International, "USA: The World Is Watching," https://www.amnestyusa.org /wp-content/uploads/2020/07/WorldisWatchingFullReport080220.pdf.

free federal money to expand Medicaid have resulted in untold health and economic strain for low-income families—and tens of thousands of preventable deaths.

On the other hand, while criminal justice policy in the states has also become increasingly important to the lives of Americans, it has been *non*-polarized: both blue and red states have ramped up racially authoritarian policing and massively expanded their prison populations. Overall, health policy and criminal justice are substantively important and illustrative cases in which major socioeconomic outcomes are polarized to the extent that relevant *policies* are polarized. They are also areas in which state governments have taken on a greater role over the past generation within American federalism.

But 2020 showed signs that criminal justice policy in the states will increasingly resemble health policy in the 2020s. The Black Lives Matter protests following the killing of George Floyd pressured state and local officials to make their actions match their words on issues of racial justice. And though we shouldn't overstate their significance, some state governments—mostly those controlled by Democrats—responded with policy reforms. The Democratic governor and legislature of Virginia passed a law banning no-knock warrants. Colorado and New York banned police chokeholds. Minnesota and other states established new police review boards. These policing reforms are small compared to the scale of the problem of institutional racism in American criminal justice, just as states' expansion of Medicaid is an incomplete solution for American health care. But they have the potential to make meaningful progress.

State Resurgence

There are strong historical and theoretical reasons to expect state governments to be marginal players in American policymaking. Compared to the federal government, states face greater threat of exit from business and wealthy residents. Their legislatures are poorer in terms of the time, money, and information required to change policy. Major interstate differences in policy, such as the legality of racial segregation or gender discrimination in employment, have been washed away by landmark federal policies. Yet this minimalist characterization of states has grown antiquated. Over the past half century, and especially the last two decades, state governments have grown much more important and powerful than in the generation prior. As Bulman-Pozen (2018) describes, "The state side of... policymaking has become increasingly important as polarization has sidelined Congress."

While the federal government grew more gridlocked, states implemented major policies that shape the lives of their residents. Federal laws from the 1930s through the 1970s decreased interstate variation in all of the policy issue areas described in this chapter. Since 1970, in contrast, interstate variation increased as some states implemented restrictions on guns, abortion, labor unions, welfare, and voter eligibility, while others loosened restrictions. Moreover, some of the most significant recent federal policies have served to increase interstate variation rather than decrease it. In addition to welfare devolution in 1996 (Soss et al. 2001), the Supreme Court ruling in *National Federation of Independent Businesses (NFIB) v. Sebelius* (2012) gave states great discretion in the implementation of the Affordable Care Act, and the choice of whether to expand Medicaid and create a state-run health insurance marketplace (Beland, Rocco, and Waddan 2016). There are notable exceptions where Congress and the federal courts have decreased variation in state law, however. In a famous example of "coercive federalism," the National Minimum Legal Drinking Age Act of 1984 threatened to withhold federal highway grants from states that did not increase their drinking age to twenty-one. The area of LBGT rights is also prominent. *Lawrence v. Texas* (2003) invalidated state sodomy bans. Though not included in this chapter's analysis because it occurred after 2014, the *Obergefell v. Hodges* (2015) case legalized same-sex marriage by invalidating state marriage bans.

The upward trend in interstate policy variation is not inevitable, however. In 2017, the federal government came under unified Republican control, and that unified federal government could have acted aggressively against state policies it opposed. However, aside from a momentous tax cut skewed toward the very wealthy, the unified Republican government of 2017 and 2018 failed to pass major national policies. Still, it remains to be seen whether a federal government under the control of one party shifts policymaking away from the states and back toward the national level.

The resurgence of the state level within American federalism prompts new questions about the quality of democracy at the state level. As legal scholar David Schleicher (2018) writes, "any justification for federalism in a democracy—whether it is the greater fit between preferences and policies, sorting, laboratories of democracy, or protection of local identities—will rely heavily on state elections working to create representative, accountable, and locally-differentiated politics" (see also Schleicher 2016). In the coming chapters, I address such questions. Who is setting policy agendas in state governments? How healthy is American democracy at the state level? The next two chapters suggest that, rather than a sea change in public opinion, the major policy changes of the era of state resurgence are the result of increasingly coordinated national networks of activists and organizations that make up the modern Democratic and Republican parties.

PART II

The Nationalization of State Politics

4

Who Governs the State-Level Resurgence?

IN 2015, Governor Scott Walker signed a bill into law that bans abortions after twenty weeks of pregnancy in the state of Wisconsin. Wisconsin for decades had been a moderate state on abortion policy: more restrictive than socially liberal California but more permissive than socially conservative Kansas. However, with the passage of the 2015 law, Wisconsin tied a dozen states for the strictest gestation limit. Because state policies are traditionally understood to be highly responsive to public opinion (Erikson, Wright, and McIver 1993, 2006; Maestas 2000; Lax and Phillips 2009; Caughey and Warshaw 2018), one might assume that the Wisconsin law reflected the preferences of the mass public. It did not. Wisconsin remains near the median in terms of public opinion on abortion, and in the years leading up to 2015, support for abortion rights had actually *increased* slightly in the state.

Cases like abortion policy in Wisconsin—the passage of a substantively significant policy bearing little association to public attitudes—may not be uncommon. As we learned in the last chapter, nearly a half century after the long buildup of federal policymaking capacity, a surprising twist occurred in American federalism: recent state governments have passed a number of significant policies while the federal government has suffered from gridlock. A large number of state laws passed since 2000 are the most socially and economically consequential policy changes in a generation. They include Kansas's abortion restrictions, California's environmental regulations and increased tax rates on high incomes, coastal states' legalization of recreational marijuana, and the restriction of union bargaining rights in the Midwest. Even the most significant federal social policy in a generation, the Affordable Care Act

(ACA), gives states the authority to refuse large parts of it after the Supreme Court's ruling in *National Federation of Independent Businesses v. Sebelius*.

After decades in which the national government took precedence, the state level has returned as a central battleground over which the direction of American politics is fought. Major policy changes at the state level have increased variation in policy outcomes across states. But who is winning this state policy resurgence? Are the states responding to the will of their constituents while the federal government stalls? The answer can inform us about what kinds of political actors are advantaged at the state level.

In the mythos of American federalism, the answer is clear: the states should be especially responsive to the interests and attitudes of ordinary Americans. In the *Federalist 28* (180–81), Alexander Hamilton proclaimed that in the proposed system of American federalism, "the people without exaggeration, may be said to be entirely the masters of their own fate." Indeed, today, polling data suggest that Americans hate Congress, but they seem to love their state and local governments. State and local governments are, in the American mind, closer and more responsive to constituents than the distant national government in Washington.

This chapter asks whether this is, in fact, true. While the conventional wisdom around American federalism persists, I outline a number of underemphasized theories that predict that lower levels of government are especially advantageous for well-resourced, *organized*, and *concentrated* interests. By concentrated, I mean narrower and smaller in size (whether interest group activists on the issue of gun control or an even narrower organized interest like telecommunications firms), in contrast to larger, more diffuse groups (such as voters, low-income workers, or communities threatened by climate change). In politics, and especially in state-level politics, smaller in size does not mean smaller in clout.[1] Activists, campaign donors, and their affiliated political organizations, as well as business and wealthy individuals, have more mobile political resources—like money—than do ordinary voters. They have informational

---

1. Mancur Olson's pathbreaking book, *The Logic of Collective Action* (1965), showed that more diffuse groups faced problems in organizing to achieve their goals simply due to their group's large size. As group size increases, so does the "free rider problem"—the incentive for people to avoid contributing toward producing public goods for the group. This argument helps explain why smaller groups, like a coalition of health insurance companies, are more politically organized, active, and powerful than the much larger group of uninsured and underinsured Americans. I argue that the free rider problem and similar challenges facing diffuse groups are especially severe at the state level.

advantages over voters in low-salience state politics. And compared to ordinary people, business and the wealthy can exercise structural influence by credibly threatening to exit states, taking their investment and tax payments with them.

I then investigate empirically whether changes in state policy and state legislative behavior have been responsive to the interests of ordinary voters or to these narrower interests. I first ask to what extent state governments have been responsive to the attitudes of the mass public. Among the transformational policy changes in the states described in chapter 3, I find that only LGBT rights and marijuana policies—salient, simple policy areas that saw a large shift in public opinion over the past generation—show clear evidence of responsiveness to public opinion. For the rest of the issue areas, state *policies* have changed profoundly, but state *opinion* has been mostly static. And you can't explain change with a constant.

If not the broader public, who is driving these policy changes in the states? While ordinary voters have become more focused on national politics over the past generation, intense activists, donors, and organizations have invested in state-level politics. Crucially, these activists and donors have the benefit of being organized and coordinated in ways that enhance their political influence in the states. Whereas this chapter investigates the limits of constituents' control over state policy, the following chapter (chapter 5) focuses on a class of political actors who have helped nationalize state politics and set partisan policy agendas in the states: interest group activists. Now, however, before turning to an analysis of state policy responsiveness to public opinion, I turn to theories of political advantage within federalism and how they produce unequal participation in state politics across race, socioeconomic class, and organizational capacity.

How Lower Levels of Government Advantage the Powerful

You've probably heard political ads criticize the "fat cats in Washington" as out of touch with American communities. In this telling, representatives in Congress are out of ordinary Americans' reach. American voters appear to agree. While polls typically find that less than 30 percent of Americans trust the federal government, in 2018 Gallup found that 63 percent of Americans trusted their state government. This is the exact same percentage who trusted their state government back in 1973, before the state policy resurgence (McCarthy 2018).

Participation in state and local politics, however, is rarer and more biased toward wealthier and whiter constituents than is participation in national politics. For decades, scholars have described how voter turnout is highest in presidential elections, followed by non-presidential congressional elections in Novembers of even years, but dramatically lower in "off-cycle" elections that only feature state and local races (e.g., Patterson and Caldeira 1983). Sarah Anzia (2011) shows that because few people are paying attention in these off-cycle state and local elections, interest groups have greater influence over politics and policy. As Grant McConnell wrote in 1966, some voters may look up when state officials govern poorly (or even illegally), but "these moments pass; state affairs recover their wonted obscurity and it is assumed that the wrongdoers have been exposed and punished" (see also Rocco 2020).

Studies on participation in local politics also show a starkly skewed politics. In their book *Hometown Inequality*, Brian Schaffner, Jesse Rhodes, and Raymond La Raja (2020) find that voters and activists in local politics are much more conservative and more likely to be white than their communities overall (see also Yoder 2020a on the effects of homeownership on participation in local politics). Local officials are much more responsive to the public opinion of white residents than residents of color, even in areas where whites are the demographic minority. These findings corroborate evidence from earlier studies on inequality in local voter turnout and responsiveness (e.g., Hajnal and Trounstine 2005; Hajnal 2009; Hajnal and Trounstine 2014).[2] As Sherrilyn Ifill argues, "If we celebrate [state and local government], if we romanticize it, without the pragmatism about the role of race in politics . . . we're essentially leaving African-American and other minority communities disempowered."[3]

Candidates for lower offices are also not necessarily more representative of their home communities than "distant" federal officials in Washington. Considerable attention has been given to the fact that candidates for Congress are extremely wealthy (Carnes 2013) and the challenges that all but the most affluent Americans have in running for federal office (Carnes 2020). Jesse Yoder (2020b), however, intrepidly looks into the housing records of California officials, finding that state and local candidates also live in much more expensive

2. In addition, Sances (2016) uncovers a concerning finding that elected property tax assessors are systematically biased in favor of their wealthy constituents compared to appointed assessors (similar to the politics of California's Prop. 13, as described in Martin 2008).

3. *PBS News Hour*, July 31, 2018, https://www.pbs.org/newshour/show/the-arguments-for -and-against-more-powerful-local-government.

TABLE 4.1. State-Level Donors Have Higher Incomes

Recipient	Average Donor Income	Median Donor Income
Presidential Candidate	61.8	70,000–$79,999
U.S. Senate Candidate	65.6	70,000–$79,999
U.S. House Candidate	66.7	70,000–$79,999
Party Organization	64.7	70,000–$79,999
State-Level Candidate	67.1	**80,000–$99,999**

Note: Donor income is scaled from 0 to 100, based on a 12-category scale ranging from 0–$9,999 to $150,000 and above. Data are from the CCES.

homes than do their constituents—even their constituents with nearly identical career and educational backgrounds. He concludes that "wealth disparities appear even at the earliest stages of the candidate pipeline to higher office" (6). For those concerned about government run by the economically privileged, devolving authority to lower levels is unlikely to be of much help.

Before moving on to theories of how lower levels of government might advantage more concentrated and wealthy interests, here I provide a bit more evidence that participation in state politics is less representative than in national politics using the example of campaign contributions (which I will return to in the next chapter). Campaign donors are, of course, a wealthy subset of the American public, and they are also racially unrepresentative (Grumbach and Sahn 2020).[4] But donors to *state*-level candidates are even more unrepresentative. Table 4.1 shows that state-level donors have higher incomes than donors who give money to presidential and congressional candidates, and even higher incomes than donors who give to party committees like the DNC and RNC.

Consistent with these participation gaps in state politics, an important study from Elizabeth Rigby and Gerald Wright (2013) finds that state-level parties tend to take positions on policies that are responsive to the attitudes of their wealthy constituents, but not their low-income ones.

There is also a racial participation gap in state politics. Table 4.2 shows that state-level donors are more likely to be white than are donors who contribute to federal candidates.

4. Women are also underrepresented among campaign donors (Thomsen and Swers 2017). For an intersectional analysis of race and gender in campaign finance, see Grumbach, Sahn, and Staszak 2020.

TABLE 4.2. State-Level Donors Are More Likely to Be White

Race	Presidential Candidate	U.S. Senate Candidate	U.S. House Candidate	Party Organization	State-Level Candidate
% White	81.94	89.1	89.54	87.12	90.04
% Black	10.79	5.39	4.74	6.75	4.4
% Latino	5.92	4.24	4.61	5.18	4.18
% Asian	1.35	1.27	1.11	0.96	1.39

Note: Data are from the CCES.

Not only is there a large participation gap, but participation from average Americans is less influential than participation from wealthier and more organized political actors. In the next section I argue that politics at lower levels is especially advantageous for these organized, concentrated, and well-resourced groups.

A One-Sided Threat of Exit

In the summer of 2020, the rideshare companies Uber and Lyft threatened to leave the largest state in the country and take their business elsewhere. The year before, the California state government had passed Assembly Bill 5 (AB5), a law that classified rideshare drivers as employees rather than "independent contractors." This change would mean that the drivers, for the first time, would be covered by the minimum wage, health-care mandates, and other labor laws—threatening the status quo that Uber and Lyft had enjoyed for years.

The companies went to their political battle stations. They sent teams of lobbyists to the state capitol and began financing an "astroturf" movement against the law (Walker 2014). They contributed money to campaigns. But more crucially, the companies began to exploit the institutions of federalism through the *threat of exit.*

The threat of exit is a major part of the structural power of business (Culpepper 2010). Political economist Charles Lindblom (1982) made this case in his seminal article, "The Market as Prison." The strategy is relatively simple: firms and their financiers threaten to pull their investments and business activity from a jurisdiction unless they receive policy concessions. Often this threat is implicit. CEOs, shareholders, and wealthy taxpayers don't have to even utter a word for politicians to be afraid of what might happen if they became angry enough to leave. But they often do. "If our efforts [at stopping

AB5] are not successful, it would force us to suspend operations in California," threatened Lyft CEO John Zimmer.

Democratic equality, where everyone has a reasonably equal voice to use to influence politics (e.g., "one person, one vote"), is an important standard. The trouble with the threat of exit is that, unlike the vote, not everyone has it equally. When a major firm exits a jurisdiction, it takes its capital and economic activity with it, with potentially profound consequences for state and local tax and consumer bases (for more on structural power, see Culpepper 2015). Moreover, as I describe in the next subsection, ordinary people are much more constrained in their ability to just pack up their lives and move than are firms and investors. Thus, when Lyft and Uber threaten to exit California, they are using a political tool that ordinary people don't have.

The legislative story of AB5 was nothing special. It had received supermajority support from the elected representatives in the state's lower and upper legislative chambers and was then signed by Governor Gavin Newsom. The California public had exercised influence over the law by electing these representatives, but Lyft and Uber had the additional tool of a capital strike (see, e.g., Young, Banerjee, and Schwartz 2018).

To be sure, business interests have a complicated relationship with federalism. Businesses certainly enjoy exploiting their structural power and the threat of exit. "But on the other hand," writes Hertel-Fernandez (2019, 248), "large businesses that cross state lines have a competing interest in passing tax and regulatory legislation through Congress instead of each and every state, as managers would much rather deal with one single set of rules about doing business than fifty different ones."

Yet increased *coordination* of a conservative and business coalition helped firms navigate this trade-off. ALEC, Americans for Prosperity, and other organizations helped create consistent, business-friendly tax and regulatory regimes across many states, while simultaneously keeping policy authority at the state level to maintain the threat of exit as a political weapon (Hertel-Fernandez 2019).

Venue Shopping with Mobile Political Resources

Critically, today political groups and activists can shift millions of dollars' worth of political resources across states in the form of lobbying, campaign contributions, model legislation, and information. A group with the ability to target and influence the agenda of many state governments controlled by their aligned party can make major policy gains while the U.S. Congress stalls.

Ordinary voters and social movements don't have this kind of political mobility. Diffuse voters are immobile, confined to voting within their states for a governor and within their legislative district for state legislative candidates. But more coordinated groups can "venue shop" in search of fertile pastures to implement their agendas (Baumgartner and Jones 2010). Indeed, such an environment is likely to provide political advantages to well-resourced, mobile policy demanders over diffuse voters. A classic literature argued that concentrated and elite interests are advantaged at lower levels of government (e.g., Schattschneider 1960; Riker 1964; McConnell 1966, 139–55), which diffuse and mass interests can counter by "extending conflict" to higher levels (Schattschneider 1960, 63).

Recent studies harken back to the classic literature. They argue that well-resourced organizational networks have increased their investments in state politics with a focus not on their home states but on cross-state agenda setting and advocacy. Organizational and technological innovations have allowed these groups to lobby and provide "model bills" to state legislators (Hertel-Fernandez 2014; Hertel-Fernandez, Skocpol, and Lynch 2016).

Some of the strategies that super-wealthy individuals use to take advantage of federalism are described in *Billionaires and Stealth Politics* (2018) by Benjamin Page, Jason Seawright, and Matthew Lacombe. The authors introduce a theory of "boundary control," a process in which billionaires spend money to usher in unified Republican control in states and then assist these new state governments in developing and implementing policies, especially radically conservative economic policies that are unpopular with voters.

Technology also matters here. As Hertel-Fernandez (2019) describes, groups like ALEC *innovated* new forms of exerting political influence such as using model bills, and the Koch brothers innovated new ways of organizing federated networks of groups like Americans for Prosperity to coordinate wealthy donors, activists, and conservative politicians in the states. Although not as deep pocketed as the Koch network or U.S. Chamber of Commerce, groups like MoveOn.org, in particular, innovated new ways to use the internet to coordinate mostly upper-middle-class liberal activists and donors around state legislative elections on issues like the environment and reproductive rights. Add to this technological moment an environment of extreme economic inequality, and you will have a situation in which well-resourced groups do well.

Broader, more diffuse interests have a harder time in this institutional context. Groups whose main political resource is their mass membership—their ability to mobilize members to vote or engage in social movement activity—have a difficult time moving these resources across states or levels of government. But organization matters. Labor unions, for example, are important representatives of workers in state politics (Bucci and Jansa 2021). They practice what Leslie Finger and Michael Hartney (2019) call "financial solidarity," sharing revenue from member dues in safe union states with unions that face policy attacks in other states. Although unions have suffered significant policy losses in the states since 2010, absent this kind of organization across institutional venues, the setbacks would have been even more severe.

Political venues in the American political system are more numerous and available than ever. Unlike earlier eras of state-centric American federalism, the contemporary state resurgence involves more overlapping policy authority across the national, state, and local levels. As Lisa Miller (2007) argues, "Over the past 50 years, most issues have not simply shifted from one level to another; rather, remnants of activity remain on the levels at which they originated even as issues have migrated across levels" (307). This bleeding of policy authority across levels makes the mobility of political resources all the more important.

Advantages in Informational and Attention

Policy-demanding groups and activists sought big policy changes in the states, and they increased their political investments accordingly. But they faced a potentially power-countervailing force: the *electoral connection*. Voters should be monitoring their governors and state legislatures, ready to reelect them if they do the right thing or throw the bastards out if they don't.

Indeed, classic theories of democratic responsiveness predict that political candidates will be responsive to the policy attitudes of the general electorate's median voter in order to maximize their chances of reelection. A number of influential studies find considerable "dyadic" responsiveness between legislative behavior and constituent opinion at the federal level (Miller and Stokes 1963; Bartels 1991; Canes-Wrone, Brady, and Cogan 2002), as well as "collective" responsiveness at the systemwide level (Page and Shapiro 1983; Stimson 1991; Erikson, MacKuen, and Stimson 2002).[5] A number of major studies of politics at the state level also support the democratic responsiveness theory,

---

5. Comparative analyses of democracies find similar policy congruence and responsiveness (e.g., Brooks and Manza 2008; Soroka and Wlezien 2010).

both at the single-issue level (Clingermayer and Wood 1995; Lax and Phillips 2009) and on one or two left-right dimensions (Erikson, Wright, and McIver 1993; Caughey and Warshaw 2018). As Erikson, Wright, and McIver (1993, 81) argue, "even small differences in state ideological preferences appear to have major policy consequences"—a relationship between opinion and policy so strong that it is nothing short of "awesome" (80).

And beyond these empirical political science studies, recall the discussion in chapter 2 about the long-standing mythos that federalism enhances democratic responsiveness by allowing for policy customization and bringing constituents "closer" to their representatives in the states.

Yet despite both the mythos and the set of empirical studies showing a strong correlation between public opinion and state policy, for the most part, the electoral connection didn't play much of a role in the state policy resurgence we learned about in the last chapter. There were some important exceptions, where voters and social movements put up a strong fight to hold politicians accountable for "out-of-step" policy, such as in opposition to Wisconsin governor Scott Walker's efforts to curb the power of labor unions and to the "Kansas experiment" of high-end tax cuts by Governor Sam Brownback. But even in these examples, Walker survived a recall election against him and was reelected to a second gubernatorial term in 2014; Brownback, in his second term, was appointed U.S. Ambassador-at-Large for International Religious Freedom by the Trump White House.

This is because it is *especially* difficult for voters to hold politicians accountable at the state level. Some studies suggest that the electoral connection is weaker at the state level than the national level because voters pay little attention to state politics (Anzia 2011; Hopkins 2018). In general, voters may select politicians not on the basis of policy positions but on the basis of identity—especially party identification derived via socialization into a party "team" (Green, Palmquist, and Schickler 2002). Indeed, party ID appears to be strengthening as it increasingly overlaps with racial, religious, and other salient social identity cleavages (Schickler 2016; Mason 2018). Voters see politics as a national battleground between these partisan "teams" and are unlikely to split their tickets by voting for one party at the state level and one at the national level. It is thus no surprise that state legislative elections are dominated by national forces, with parties' success in the states closely tied to their success in national offices (Rogers 2016). As Daniel Hopkins (2018, 13) argues in *The Increasingly United States*, "Americans today are primarily engaged with national and above all presidential politics," taking cues on how to feel about state and local politics from the national level. "Once we account for political partisanship," he continues, "knowing [an American's] place of residence adds little to our understanding of a variety of political attitudes."

For voters to hold politicians accountable for their policy choices, public policy must be "traceable" for voters (Arnold 1992)—the connection between policies and social outcomes must be clear. In their book *The New Economic Populism*, for example, William Franko and Christopher Witko (2018) argue that when citizens are aware of and informed about economic inequality, they can pressure their state legislators and, in some states, implement ballot initiatives to raise the minimum wage or taxes on millionaires.

However, the precipitous decline of state politics journalism has made policy even less traceable for voters. Pew reported a staggering 35 percent decline in the number of full-time newspaper reporters covering state politics, policy, and administration just between the years 2003 and 2014 (Enda, Masta, and Boyles 2014).[6] As the state-level staff for major papers like the *Pittsburgh Post-Gazette* and the *Charlotte Observer* declined, the ratio of state politics reporters to Americans swelled to about 400,000 to one (Wilson 2014). As the number of state politics reporters declined, so did coverage of the reams of legislation coming out of state legislatures. As thirty-year New Hampshire state legislative reporter Norma Love described (quoted in Wilson 2014), "There may be 1,000 bills or 1,200 bills filed, so you have to target the ones you could cover." This decline in newspaper coverage of state politics has not been offset by increased TV coverage or online state politics reporting. Local TV news, which increases voter knowledge of home-state politicians (Moskowitz 2021), has been on the decline. In fact, even the local TV news that survived the industry decline has become increasingly focused on national politics (and more ideologically conservative)—the result of media conglomerates like Sinclair Broadcast Group buying up local stations (Martin and McCrain 2019).

A substantial body of empirical research finds evidence consistent with a fractured relationship between constituents' and state politicians' policy positions. In a pathbreaking study, David Broockman and Christopher Skovron (2018) surveyed state legislators and found that their beliefs about their constituents' policy views were extremely skewed—state legislators systematically overestimate the conservatism of their districts on policy questions. Both Democratic and Republican (and liberal and conservative) legislators thought

6. Pew updated the report and found a 23 percent decline in full-time state politics reporters between 2008 and 2017.

their constituents were more conservative than they actually were. In fact, the study found that half of conservative-leaning legislators thought they represented a district with more conservative policy views than the most conservative district in the entire country. Steven Rogers (2017) shows that punishment for "out-of-step" legislative votes rarely leads to electoral punishment for state legislators. In sum, Kathleen Bawn and colleagues (2012) make a compelling argument that policy-demanding groups and activists (and their aligned politicians) exploit voters' "electoral blind spot"—but there are some good reasons to believe that the electoral blind spot is especially wide at the state level.

Did Ordinary Voters Drive the State Policy Resurgence?

In chapter 3, we saw that the states have become increasingly important policymakers. But who is driving these major changes in state policy? In this section, I ask whether it was the mass public. Specifically, I investigate the relationship between public opinion and state policy outcomes.

If voters are behind the major state policy changes of recent years, we're likely to find two empirical patterns. First, we should find *cross-sectional* responsiveness, which asks whether political units with more conservative opinions are more likely to have conservative policy outcomes (e.g., Erikson, Wright, and McIver 1993; Gray et al. 2004).[7] Cross-sectional responsiveness requires variation in opinion across states. If only a certain subset of states has a given policy, one would expect that aggregate opinion in those states with that policy should be more supportive than opinion in states without the policy. Compared to states with more liberal constituents, states with more conservative residents should have more conservative policies.

Second, *dynamic* responsiveness asks whether temporal changes in opinion within states are associated with policy changes (Lowery, Gray, and Hager 1989; Stimson, MacKuen, and Erikson 1995; Caughey and Warshaw 2018). As we saw in chapter 3, policy has polarized; the question here is whether opinion has polarized in ways that predict these policy changes. One reason we might see both diverging state attitudes and diverging state policy—evidence of dynamic responsiveness—is geographic sorting. As I mentioned in chapter 2, Bishop (2009) argues that Americans have increasingly opted to live in communities that tend to share their political views (see also Sussell and Thomson

7. A related question is whether binary policy outcomes are congruent with opinion majorities (e.g., Lax and Phillips 2012).

2015). To estimate dynamic responsiveness, I once again turn to a difference-in-differences setup, which estimates the within-state relationship between opinion and policy.

As seen in chapter 3, party control of government has large effects on policy outcomes in the states. But this pattern may itself be driven by public opinion. I investigate whether party control explains policy outcomes above and beyond that which is predicted by public opinion. Policy attitudes in states may leave little variation in policy outcomes unexplained, because politicians who are "out of step" on policy issues are voted out of office (Downs 1957; Erikson, Wright, and McIver 1993; Canes-Wrone, Brady, and Cogan 2002) and incumbent politicians self-sanction in order to avoid anticipated electoral punishment (Stimson 1995). If party control has a substantial influence over policy outcomes *net of public opinion*, it will be important to investigate other potential causes for why the parties in government propose and pass distinct policy agendas in the states.

Significant state policy changes have increased variation in policy outcomes across states in recent years. In this situation, cross-sectional responsiveness requires that opinion in states that implement these significant policies is relatively more supportive than opinion in states that do not. Similarly, dynamic responsiveness necessitates opinion divergence in the corresponding policy area to accompany the divergence in policy outcomes. A correlation between opinion and policy outcomes over time is possible if at least one of these two changes occurs: (1) state policy opinion becomes more liberal (or conservative) in states where the liberal (or conservative) policy is passed; (2) state policy opinion becomes more conservative (or liberal) in states where the liberal (or conservative) policy does *not* pass.

Challenges to Studying Responsiveness

The relationship between opinion and policy is key to democratic theory, but successful estimation and inference in this area is no simple task. A first major challenge relates to the difference between *responsiveness*—the correlation between opinion and policy—and *congruence*—whether majorities of residents are getting the policy they want (e.g., Matsusaka 2010; Lax and Phillips 2012). Typically, it is much more difficult to estimate congruence because there are few situations where researchers are able to put state opinion and state policy on the same substantively meaningful scale. Gabor Simonovits, Andrew Guess, and Jonathan Nagler (2019) call this the problem of estimating "responsiveness without representation," where even when we observe dynamic or cross-sectional responsiveness, policy can be incongruent with opinion. Across all fifty states, it could be the case that policy in some issue areas is intercept-shifted such that it is "off center," with the average resident of the average state wanting a very different policy than the status quo (Hacker and Pierson 2005; see Bartels 2015 for a cross-national analysis). Indeed, this is what Simonovits, Guess, and Nagler (2019) find with respect to state minimum wage laws: while states with higher public support for minimum wages have more generous minimum wage policies (responsiveness), the average resident of *every state* wants a more generous minimum wage than their state currently has (incongruence). Unfortunately, there are a limited number of survey questions that can be put on the same scale as policy, and focusing on congruence would greatly reduce the range of issue areas that I could analyze. For this reason, I follow the bulk of the literature in measuring responsiveness rather than congruence.

Other challenges arise from choices in measurement. Although a large literature contends that there is a strong link between the liberalism of a state's population and the state's policy outcomes, measuring the public's opinions on a single liberal-conservative dimension may create obstacles to aggregation and inference (Broockman 2016). Larry Bartels (2015, 3), for instance, goes so far as to describe single-dimensional analysis, such as the relationship between "public mood" and policy of Stimson 1995, as "provid[ing] no way to assess the degree of congruence between what citizens wanted and what they got."[8] A stronger test of democratic responsiveness is whether the public's policy preferences are translated into policy change in the corresponding issue area.

The drawback here is that policy issue preferences may be measured more noisily than is found in a single left-right dimension of ideology. Still, researchers have made strides in estimating the policy- and issue-area specific relationship between opinion and policy. Jeffrey Lax and Justin Phillips (2012) offer a particularly thorough multidimensional analysis of policy congruence to constituent majorities at the state level, but congruence only at one snapshot in time. Daniel Lewis, Frederick Wood, and Matthew Jacobsmeier (2014) study the relationship between judicial behavior and gay rights opinion over time.

8. Despite the difficulty in substantively interpreting responsiveness on a single dimension, as a robustness check I test the association between the "policy mood" measure of state opinion by Enns and Koch (2013) and significant policy outcomes, finding substantively similar results.

This chapter investigates the relationship between temporal trends in opinion and state policy outcomes in many different issue areas.

Finally, some challenges are largely insurmountable. Polling introduces measurement error, though aggregate opinion may cancel out random error and have more stability and "rationality" (Page and Shapiro 2010). Correlations are unsatisfying for questions of causal inference, and there are times where exogenous variation cannot plausibly be exploited. However, as I have described, some theories include correlations as necessary conditions, and estimates of the correlation between opinion and policy can shed light on the largely unstudied origins and representational consequences of recent significant policy changes in the states.

Public Opinion Data and Methods

I use repeated policy-related questions from the American National Election Study (ANES), Gallup, and the General Social Survey (GSS) to estimate temporal dynamics in the policy opinions of residents of the fifty states. The sample of policy areas is determined by the intersection of my sense of the policy's substantive social and economic significance and the availability of repeated measures of public support. I list the policy questions for which I estimate state-level support, along with the survey-years from which the questions are taken, in table A.1.[9]

As I did with policy outcomes in chapter 3, I measure public opinion by issue area. (Table A.1 shows the issue area that corresponds to each survey question.) Most studies of responsiveness have measured opinion and policy at the level of the single policy (Clingermayer and Wood 1995; Lax and Phillips 2009) or on a single left-right ideological dimension (Erikson, Wright, and McIver 1993). Scholars have argued that dimension aggregation reduces measurement error in opinion estimates (Ansolabehere, Rodden, and Snyder 2008). However, in light of new evidence that dimension reduction may conflate consistency with extremism and lead to spurious relationships between opinion and outcome variables (Broockman 2016), new research tends to disaggregate attitudes into "social" and "economic" dimension measures of opinion and policy (Caughey and Warshaw 2018; Caughey, Dunham, and Warshaw 2018). I argue that these dimensions are still a bit too broad to capture important variation in public attitudes on policy: within the large buckets of social

---

9. For the feeling thermometer questions, the top 51 levels are coded as 1.

and economic issues, many individuals are likely to hold unconstrained policy attitudes that reflect real attitudes.[10]

In order to increase the precision of state subsamples, I employ varieties of the popular multilevel regression with poststratification (MRP) method. MRP involves the estimation of a multilevel model with individual-level effects nested within states and regions and then the use of Census weights for poststratification. The method has been extensively validated in recent years in samples of approximately 1,500 respondents nationwide.[11]

The multilevel models first estimate the effect of individual demographic factors on opinion using random intercepts. The individual model is nested within a model with fixed effects for state-level characteristics. I use state Democratic vote share in the last presidential election and state income as predictors along the lines of Gelman 2009. I also include a state's percent of evangelical residents (see Lax and Phillips 2009). States are nested within regions. Finally, estimates are population reweighted at the state level using Census Current Population Study (CPS) data downloaded from the Census's *Data Ferret* program. MRP uses partial pooling of the data based on demographics and region. Because Census weights vary as geographic concentrations of demographic groups change over time, the model is able to pick up variation in state-level opinion even in cases where respondents in state survey subsamples answer questions identically across time.

For each state-year, I average the MRP estimates in each issue area. These issue-area averages are the primary opinion measures used in subsequent analyses. I merge my opinion estimates with the measures of issue-specific policy outcomes used in chapter 3. For use in regression models, I recode policy outcomes and/or opinion such that policy liberalism is matched by poll question liberalism, with higher values indicating more liberal and lower values more conservative.[12] A positive coefficient for opinion thus *always signifies*

---

10. For instance, among social issues, an individual may hold liberal views on LGBT rights and conservative views on abortion. Similarly, among economic issues, an individual may oppose labor unions but support raising taxes to support the poor. While such unconstrained survey responses may at times reflect "errors," they often signify policy attitudes with consequences for vote choice (Ahler and Broockman 2017).

11. The cluster sampling design of the ANES (meant for representative national, not state, samples) makes estimates using ANES questions less reliable than the CCES, but state estimates are a vast improvement over raw ANES subsamples (Stollwerk 2012).

12. For example, because the labor unions question asks for respondent support for labor unions and Right to Work laws are oppositional to organized labor, I recode the MRP estimate as opposition to labor (i.e., 1—support for labor).

greater responsiveness within policy areas. In contrast, a positive coefficient for party control means that the party is more likely to make policy more liberal (i.e., the same interpretation as the models of policy in chapter 3), such that the coefficient for Democratic control will probably be positive and that for Republican control probably negative. In the cross-sectional responsiveness models, I estimate the contemporaneous relationship between opinion and policy in 1988 and in 2012. In dynamic responsiveness models, I estimate the relationship between opinion in year $t - 1$ and policy in year t (see Caughey and Warshaw 2018).

Public Opinion Results

In this section, I present three types of analyses of the opinion-policy relationship. First, I describe *national* responsiveness to public opinion by plotting the average state opinion and average state policy in each issue area across time. This helps gauge systemwide dynamics in opinion and state policy over the past generation. Second, I compare *cross-sectional* responsiveness—whether states with more liberal opinion have relatively more liberal policies—in 1988 and 2012. This analysis addresses whether the relative positions of state policy correspond to their relative positions in opinion, and whether this correspondence has grown stronger or weaker over time. Third, I estimate *dynamic responsiveness* to opinion, which asks whether state policy responds to opinion change over time. To address the possibility that party control of government mediates the opinion-policy relationship, I execute *mediation analysis,* a generous test that adds together the direct effect of opinion on policy with its indirect effect on policy through party control of state government.

Describing Opinion and Policy across Time

I plot average state opinion and average state policy outcomes over time in figure 4.1. We are interested in the temporal correlation between opinion and policy—whether opinion change is associated with policy change across time. Average state opinion is shown in the solid line, and average state policy is shown in the dashed line. In many issue areas, while there may be temporary fluctuations, opinion is largely static since the 1980s in such areas as abortion, environment, health and welfare, labor, and taxes.

Policy change cannot be well explained by static opinion, and yet, as we saw in chapter 3, some of these issue areas experienced sea changes in policy but little change in mass attitudes. Abortion policy is a clear example. Since *Roe v.*

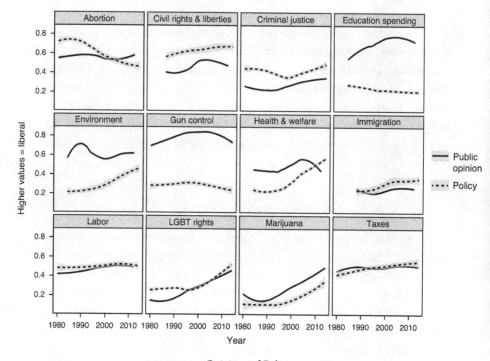

FIGURE 4.1. Opinion and Policy across Time.

Wade (1973), many states innovated and implemented increasingly restrictive abortion policies—but figure 4.1 suggests that, on average, opinion has remained stable during this time period.

Conversely, some major changes in average state opinion are associated not with correspondent policy change but with policy stasis. Average state opinion becomes much more generous on education spending since the 1980s. It is commonly known that increased education spending is a perennially popular item in the mass public, but it becomes even more popular in recent decades. However, as more Americans desire increased education spending, education spending *decreased* in the average state.

Then there are some issue areas in which changes in average state opinion track the average state's policy outcomes relatively closely. Public opinion on LGBT rights and marijuana policies moves markedly leftward between the 1980s and 2012—and so does state policy in these areas. Descriptively, these issue areas show evidence of healthy democratic responsiveness. In the next sections, I more systematically estimate cross-sectional and dynamic responsiveness.

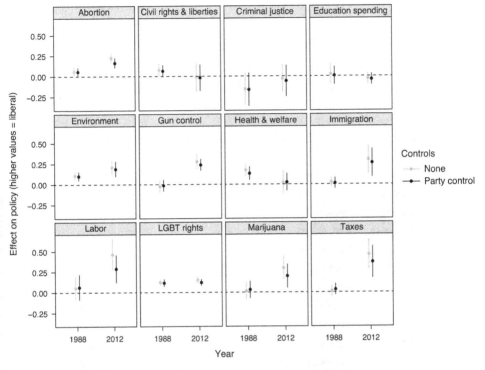

FIGURE 4.2. Cross-Sectional Responsiveness to Public Opinion.

Cross-Sectional Responsiveness

The next step is to estimate the *cross-sectional* relationship between opinion and policy. Figure 4.2 plots the results of cross-sectional regressions of the opinion-policy relationship by issue area. Positive coefficients suggest that public support for a policy (relative to other states) makes a state significantly more likely to implement the policy.[13]

Cross-sectional responsiveness is modest in 1988. Only in abortion, environment, health and welfare, and LGBT rights do we observe evidence that states with more liberal opinion are significantly more likely to have more liberal policies in the issue area. The rest of the issue areas show policy outcomes that are unassociated with state opinion.

13. The size of confidence intervals varies across issue areas due to the different number of survey and policy items used in the aggregate measures (see, e.g., Ansolabehere, Rodden, and Snyder 2008).

The cross-sectional opinion-policy correlation tends to be stronger in 2012. In abortion, environment, gun control, immigration, labor, marijuana, and taxes, the coefficients are significantly greater than zero—and significantly greater in 2012 than in 1988. As argued earlier, cross-sectional responsiveness is a necessary but insufficient condition for democratic responsiveness overall.

Some issue areas see no change in cross-sectional responsiveness during this time period. The correlation between opinion and policy in LGBT rights is evident in both time periods. In contrast, cross-sectional responsiveness remains minimal in both 1988 and 2012 for criminal justice and education spending. However, in health and welfare policy, and to a lesser extent civil rights, cross-sectional responsiveness *weakens* between 1988 and 2012.

Taken as a whole, these findings on cross-sectional responsiveness are a potentially hopeful sign. Even if state opinion is static across time, such an increase in cross-sectional responsiveness between 1988 and 2012 may mean that policy has *come into alignment* with public opinion. This might occur, for example, if a state's median opinion on abortion was more conservative than its policy status quo in 1988 and abortion policy moved rightward to meet this opinion. Furthermore, as we observed in chapter 3, the range of policy outcomes in the states has expanded greatly in recent decades because *state governments are doing more important and variable policymaking*. Statistically, increasing the variation of a Y variable improves the correlation between X and Y—so this greater cross-sectional responsiveness is in part thanks to the greater variation in state policy outcomes across time.

But there are limits to assessing responsiveness cross-sectionally. An important tradition of literature argues that voters adopt policy positions from elites (e.g., Lenz 2013; Achen and Bartels 2016; Broockman and Butler 2017).[14] Such studies have criticized cross-sectional studies of responsiveness (e.g., Erikson, Wright, and McIver 1993) for being susceptible to reverse causality. A potentially more effective test of the opinion-policy relationship is to estimate *dynamic responsiveness*, the relationship between opinion change and policy change within each state.

---

14. Survey questions are also somewhat endogenous to a society's political agenda. It is precisely when elites propose or discuss policy agenda items that surveys ask the public about them.

Dynamic Responsiveness

In this section, I estimate dynamic responsiveness in the states. The models use state and year fixed effects to estimate the within-state relationship between opinion and policy. In contrast to estimates of cross-sectional responsiveness, this analysis of dynamic responsiveness suggests that opinion change within states is not a significant predictor of policy change. Within a given state, increases in policy support are negligibly associated with an increased likelihood of passing the policy.

But because opinion is typically believed to be causally prior to party control, party could be a *mediator* for public opinion. State public opinion on policy questions could lead voters to elect politicians from the party that will implement their preferred agenda. I test this idea with causal mediation models.

These mediation models are a generous test for policy responsiveness, because they combine the direct effect of opinion on policy with the mediated effect of opinion on policy through party control. The estimation process can be described in three steps. First, the models estimate the direct association between opinion and policy. Second, they estimate the effect of a one standard deviation increase in opinion on the mediator, *party control*, in order to estimate the effect of this change in the mediator on policy outcomes. Finally, the direct effect of opinion on policy and the mediated effect of opinion through party control are combined. I plot the results in figure 4.3.

In each issue area shown in figure 4.3, the left estimate represents the mediated effect of party control. This is determined by the correlation between opinion and party control. Because public support for conservative policies (and opposition to liberal policies) is usually positively correlated with unified Republican control and negatively correlated with Democratic control, these estimates should be positive. While they are indeed positive (the only exception is immigration), the estimates are minuscule because *dynamics in policy opinion are not strongly correlated with party control.*

The middle estimates represent the "direct" effect of opinion on policy. Most importantly, the rightmost estimates are the total effect of opinion on policy: the sum of the direct effect of opinion and the effect of opinion as mediated by party control of government. This makes mediation analysis quite a generous test of dynamic responsiveness.

Yet even under the favorable conditions of mediation analysis, public opinion remains an inconsistent predictor of policy in the states. Again, only LGBT

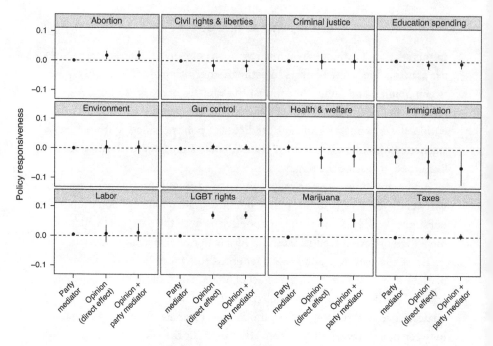

FIGURE 4.3. Responsiveness to Public Opinion by Issue Area.

rights and marijuana policy show strong responsiveness to dynamics in state opinion.

Taken as a whole, the results in this chapter tell a two-sided story of state policy responsiveness over the past generation. On the one hand, the cross-sectional results suggest that, to a greater extent than in the past, states with more conservative opinion are adopting right-wing policies, while states with more liberal opinion are adopting more liberal policies. On the other hand, the descriptive and dynamic responsiveness results show that this has not been the result of increased public liberalism or conservatism *within* states.

Why LGBT Rights and Marijuana?

LGBT rights and marijuana policy are the two issue areas that show consistent evidence of opinion change leading to policy change—a key health metric of democratic responsiveness to mass attitudes. The strong responsiveness we observe in these areas stands in stark contrast to the weak or even negative relationship between opinion and policy in other areas. What explains this variation across different issue areas? Political scientists increasingly summarize many policies and issue areas on one or two left-right dimensions, but the results of this study suggest that responsiveness operates differently depending on the issue. In this section, I argue that there are three explanations for the distinct politics in LGBT rights and marijuana policy over the past generation.

First, public opinion has shifted greatly on LGBT and marijuana policy over the past generation. Such a sea change in opinion might produce a clearer signal to politicians of public attitudes than issue areas with more static opinion. Popular culture surrounding LGBT individuals and relationships, as well as the use of marijuana, has transformed since the 1970s. As late as the 1990s, television sitcoms portrayed marijuana use as a dangerous pathology; by the mid-2000s, the U.S. version of *The Office* featured an episode in which uptight Dwight is mocked by the other characters for his strict anti-marijuana attitudes. To an even greater extent, thanks to social movement pressure, the 1990s and 2000s saw the rise of positive portrayals of LGBT individuals in shows such as *Will and Grace* and *Ellen*.[15]

Second, LGBT rights and marijuana policy are social issues that feature greater partisan polarization in the mass public than do economic policies. Despite substantial *policy* polarization between red and blue states on issues like the minimum wage, many economic policies designed to support lower- and middle-income Americans remain popular and less polarized across red and blue Americans, as well as red and blue states. Hopkins (2017) suggests that this partisan geography strengthens the incentives for national parties to pursue these distinct social policy agendas.

Third, LGBT rights and marijuana policy are relatively simple to understand. Many scholars have suggested that policy complexity shapes politics (Makse and Volden 2011), especially by advantaging information-rich actors and disadvantaging more information-poor voters (e.g., Bartels 2009; Lenz 2013). Compared to taxes and environmental regulation, LGBT rights and marijuana policy are straightforward problems with relatively straightforward policy solutions (e.g., same-sex marriage and medical marijuana). Politicians often claim credit for economic outcomes that may have little to do with their or their party's policy decisions (Arnold 1992), but this is less possible in the areas of LGBT rights and marijuana.

But there is a final reason why the LGBT rights and marijuana policy areas might be more responsive than others: LGBT rights and marijuana policy

15. Note that I am not making a normative comparison between marijuana policy and LGBT rights, or between LGBT individuals and people who use marijuana.

activists used a strategy of influencing public opinion to achieve policy change. In other areas, activists, political organizations, and large businesses and wealthy individuals used other tactics to influence state governments. As Theda Skocpol (2013b, 118) has argued, "shallow, inert aggregate individual opinions" are unlikely to matter much in policy battles—"only *organizationally mobilized* public opinion matters" (emphasis added).

In the next chapter, I describe how national activists and activist groups became more coordinated and invested in state politics in recent years. While state opinion has been mostly static, these activists have increased their participation in state politics—and transformed state governments in the process.

5

National Activists in State Politics

IF NOT ORDINARY VOTERS, who might be driving state policy resurgence? As I argued in the last chapter, state politics might be advantageous for people and groups with more time, money, information, coordination, and mobility. In this chapter, I turn my sights away from ordinary voters and toward groups of people that tend to have these kinds of political resources: *activists*— specifically, *interest group activists* who are coordinated by political organizations. This chapter describes how activists on the left and the right invested in state politics in recent decades in ways that polarized state legislatures and set ambitious policy agendas for parties in government. In particular, I look at activists with enough wealth to spend money in politics and with enough coordination to make that money influence what politicians do in office.

These activists are different from ordinary Americans. They participate more in politics. They vote more, but they also are more likely to contact their legislators, attend governmental hearings, and donate money to political candidates. This participation is facilitated and coordinated by activist *organizations*—lowering the cost of participating and increasing its influence over politicians. Some activists are so wealthy that they can finance entire organizational networks, as the Koch brothers have done in pursuit of their radically conservative ideological goals (Hertel-Fernandez 2019). Social movement activists, on the other hand, may only have their body and their voice, which they might use in political protests (Schlozman 2015). I focus here on a middling group: activists who are coordinated by issue and ideological organizations and who contribute money to campaigns. I call these individuals *interest group activists* (hereafter IGAs).

In response to the growing difficulty of passing federal legislation through polarized and usually divided national government, these IGAs and their affiliated organizations have invested greater political resources in state politics. Across the ideological spectrum, groups like MoveOn.org, National Right to

Life, and the NRA innovated in the use of the internet to rapidly coordinate activists around state legislative and gubernatorial elections and battles over state policy. These groups and their affiliated IGAs helped take what was previously unexciting state politics and connect it to national battles over the direction of public policy—polarizing state legislatures and ushering in a resurgence of major state policy.

In this chapter, I focus on a particularly important form of political participation for groups and IGAs: contributing money to campaigns. Recent studies suggest that campaign contributions from different kinds of donors—interest groups, party committees, or individual donors—affect the behavior of legislators in office (La Raja and Schaffner 2015; Barber 2016b). Specifically, these studies suggest that the balance of fundraising from individuals relative to organizations has contributed to legislative polarization in the fifty states. Individual contributions appear to polarize, while interest group contributions appear to moderate, state legislatures. Curiously, however, as polarization has grown precipitously, there has been little shift in the aggregate share of fundraising from individuals compared to interest groups. What's missing in the money in state politics literature, and what can really help us understand polarization and the resurgence of states, are IGAs.

Research may have neglected IGAs because they can't be studied solely as atomized individuals, nor as formal organizations; they have elements of both. I argue that variation in the *types of individual donors* who contribute to candidates offers a more complete explanation for legislative polarization in the states. Specifically, it matters to what extent that candidates' individual donors are affiliated with and coordinated by interest groups. While previous work focuses on whether individual donors are different from PAC donors (Barber, Canes-Wrone, and Thrower 2015; Barber 2016a, 2016b), individual donors are often affiliated with political organizations like political action committees (PACs). Indeed, interest groups such as Americans for Tax Reform, the NRA, and MoveOn.org *are comprised of individuals*.

Conceptualizing individual donors who are affiliated with interest groups as IGAs may help explain the nationalization and polarization of state politics in recent years. In this chapter, I operationalize IGA donors as individuals who contribute both to issue or ideological groups and to legislative candidates. I first provide evidence that IGA donors are distinct from otherwise similar co-partisan donors. Survey data suggest that IGA donors report more extreme ideological and policy attitudes than otherwise similar individual donors. Moreover, the benefits of organization, such as coordination and informational resources, may lower the cost of political influence for IGA donors. Consistent with this theory, I find that IGA donors are significantly more likely to report contacting legislators.

I then use campaign finance data to investigate the relationship between IGA donors and legislative behavior in the states. Over time, the average donor to a state legislative candidate has become much more likely to be an IGA donor. I find that the proportion of legislators' contributors who are IGA donors has large and significant effects on their legislative behavior—as large as the effect of public opinion or contributions from formal party committees and interest groups. Since 2000, increases in the proportion of donors who come from ideological group extended networks are associated with legislative polarization. I use a novel data set of state legislative primary dates to estimate the effect of IGA contributions during the primary and general election periods. Consistent with theories that emphasize the role of parties, groups, and activists in the nomination process (Bawn et al. 2012; Hassell 2016), I find that the effect of IGA contributions is mostly concentrated in primary elections.

While IGA donors may be polarizing agents, actors affiliated with party establishments are expected to be moderating influences, because they care more about winning general elections than ideological purity (La Raja and Schaffner 2015; Hassell 2018). However, I find that *party insiders*—individual donors affiliated with state party committees such as the Montana State Republican Party and the Democratic Legislative Campaign Committee (Hassell 2016)—have no consistent relationship with legislative behavior.

Donors and politicians act strategically in ways that make it difficult to study causal relationships in campaign finance research. It could be the case that politicians cause changes to donor behavior rather than the other way around (what social scientists call endogeneity). But while we should be cautious about interpreting these effects as causal, this investigation of individual affiliates of interest groups provides a partial explanation for partisan polarization of legislative behavior and policy agendas in the states and for the nationalization of state politics.

Individuals and Organizations in Campaign Finance

Political observers are often surprised to learn that conventional wisdom in political science maintains that money—at least in the form of campaign contributions—exerts little influence in politics.[1] Indeed, many studies have

---

1. Legal scholars, journalists, and pundits have echoed these arguments (Schuck 2014; Porter 2012; Smith 2016).

found minimal effects of campaign contributions from PACs (Wawro 2001; Ansolabehere, de Figueiredo, and Snyder 2003). Individual donors, who may contribute for ideological reasons, are dismissed as facing collective action problems that limit their influence (Ansolabehere, de Figueiredo, and Snyder 2003). Puzzlingly, however, a separate set of studies suggests that politicians are more responsive to the preferences of wealthy individuals and interest groups than those of ordinary citizens (Gilens 2012; Gilens and Page 2014; Bartels 2009; Page, Bartels, and Seawright 2013).

But research in three new areas has uncovered evidence about how money in politics influences politicians. Instead of buying the roll-call votes of opponents, one literature finds that interest groups, especially business groups, seek to buy access to policymakers in order to influence policy outcomes (Fouirnaies and Hall 2015, 2016; Grimmer and Powell 2016). The access theory is a strong alternative to theories of vote-buying (Ansolabehere, de Figueiredo and Snyder 2003).[2] In addition to complicating unidimensional analyses of business in politics,[3] the access theory widens our understanding of tools that individual campaign donors may use to influence legislative behavior (Kalla and Broockman 2016).

In addition to the research on contributions and access, a second literature finds that spending limits on different forms of contributions (e.g., corporate PACs, party committees, or individuals) affect the behavior of state legislators (Flavin 2015; La Raja and Schaffner 2015; Barber 2016b). Important recent studies, for instance, find that the Supreme Court's ruling in *Citizens United v. FEC* to eliminate limits and disclosure requirements on certain kinds of campaign spending caused state legislatures to become more Republican (Abdul-Razzak, Prato, and Wolton 2020), become more conservative (Harvey and

---

2. Vote-buying is unlikely on salient issues, though the rise of "dark" money after *Citizens United v. FEC* may allow for more overt issue conversion. Business organizations often combine campaign contributions with lobbying to shape the less salient details of policy and use negative agenda control to exploit policy "drift" (Hacker 2004; Hall and Deardorff 2006; Hacker and Pierson 2010).

3. Fossil fuel companies, for instance, may donate to Democrats in oil- and coal-producing states to buy access and ultimately limit environmental regulation, but the Democrats' liberal positions on unrelated issues like gay rights or abortion make such Democrats—and, by extension, their corporate donors—appear moderate on a single dimension. In addition, scholars of structural and instrumental business power have long chronicled the ability of business to shift and redefine the "center" in ways that will not appear in measures of relative ideology on a single dimension (Lindblom 1982; Hacker and Pierson 2002, 2010).

Mattia, forthcoming), and pass more pro-corporate policy (Gilens, Patterson, and Haines 2021). This research, like the study at hand, suggests that shifts in the sources of campaign contributions can shape the behavior of parties in government over time.

A third set of studies has focused on organizational networks funded by mega-wealthy individuals and corporations. Alexander Hertel-Fernandez's book *State Capture* (2019) is a trailblazing example of this line of research. Hertel-Fernandez traces the "conservative troika" of conservative organizations that invested massive political resources in state politics in recent decades: ALEC, the State Policy Network (SPN), and Americans for Prosperity (AFP). Each of these groups specialized in particular ways of spending money in politics—whether on lobbying and model bills, subsidizing activist activity, or contributing money to campaigns—gaining them major policy victories on issues like tax cuts and environmental deregulation. Recently, these groups have pressured state governments to take extreme policy measures during the Covid-19 pandemic. In May 2020, for example, ALEC circulated a letter urging state governments to reject federal money. "The idea of the federal government 'bailing out' the states would be harmful to taxpayers, federalism, and ultimately the states themselves," the letter argues.[4] Like rejecting federal funds to expand Medicaid, however, it is unclear how rejecting this money serves any state interest except a radical ideological opposition to government itself.

Yet despite this important progress in understanding money in politics, we're still missing something about how activists have *organized* to influence state politics. Prior studies draw a sharp line between atomized individual campaign donors on the one hand and official party committees and interest group organizations on the other (La Raja and Schaffner 2015; Barber 2016a, 2016b; Grimmer and Powell 2016). Michael Barber (2016b, 297–98) argues that individual donors are motivated by ideology, whereas interest group donors are motivated by a desire for access to important legislators. Correspondingly, he finds that individual contribution limits are associated with moderation and PAC limits with polarization.

However, there has been little change in the proportion of fundraising from individuals versus PACs in recent years. As shown in panel (b) of figure 5.1, the average state legislative candidate's share of funds from PACs increased from 36.7 percent in 2000 to 38.1 percent in 2012 (approximately 3 percent of one

4. "State Leaders Say 'No Thanks' to Federal Bailout," July 28, 2020, https://www.alec.org /article/state-leaders-say-no-thanks-to-federal-bailout/.

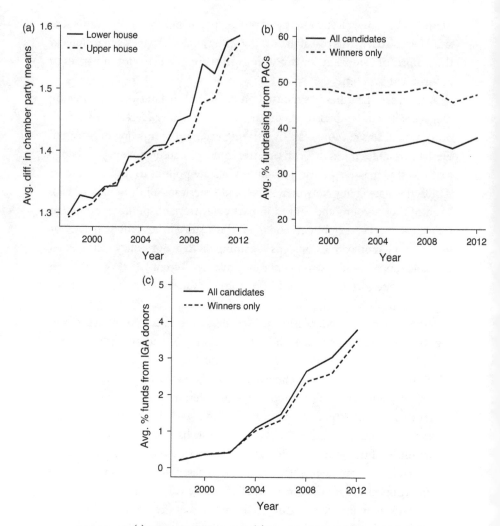

FIGURE 5.1. (a) Legislative Polarization (b) Percent of Contributions from PACs
(c) Percent of Contributions from IGAs.
Note: Legislative polarization (difference in party chamber means) has increased (a),
but the aggregate share of contributions from PACs has remained static (b). In contrast,
the share of contributions from IGA donors has increased (c).

standard deviation in candidates' share of funds from PACs). Among only
winning candidates, the share decreased from 48.6 to 48.5 percent during this
period. While Barber (2016b) offers persuasive evidence that the balance of
PAC and individual funding affects legislative behavior, these small aggregate
changes suggest that it may not be a principal cause of the precipitous rise of

legislative polarization in the states during this period, which is shown in panel (a) with NP-scores (Shor and McCarty 2011). The proportions of funds from party committees and party insiders also remain remarkably constant during this time period.[5]

In contrast, panel (c) shows a rapid increase in candidates' share of fundraising from IGA donors. In 2000, the average candidate received less than 0.25 percent of her funds from IGA donors. By 2012, IGA donors comprised nearly 4 percent of the average candidate's funds—an increase of over tenfold. Although IGA donors remain a relatively small proportion of candidates' overall fundraising, this shift from virtual nonexistence to a clear presence in state legislative campaigns may influence candidate incentives if IGA donors are systematically different from other individual donors—and if increased IGA contributions is a proxy for other forms of group activist participation, such as volunteering on campaigns and lobbying legislators.

Individual Donors as Group Activists

The distinction between individuals and organizations in politics might be considerably fuzzier than political science tends to suggest—and understanding this fuzziness could be important to understanding the politics behind the big changes in state governments over the past generation. From the perspective of the individual, people who are organized can coordinate to amplify their political voices. From the perspective of the organization, groups can marshal activists, suggesting they have much greater political resources at their disposal than what sits in their official 501(c) and PAC bank accounts. A group's most important resource, which has been largely neglected by political scientists, is its donor network—the individuals who provide the funds that enable the formal, legally defined organization to exist and persist (Walker 1991). Groups are more than simply their formal PAC and 501(c) organizations; they are better understood in addition as *extended networks* of donors,

---

5. The McCain-Feingold (Bipartisan Campaign Reform) Act of 2002 restricted party committees' use of "soft money" in campaigns, which La Raja and Schaffner (2015, 111–12) argue decreased the relative influence of formal parties in state politics. It is possible that the Act incentivized greater activity from outside groups such as those that organize IGAs. As a robustness check, I execute the main analyses for the years 2004–12, when the Act was in effect, and find a similar estimate.

activists, and members.[6] Indeed, extended networks are not unfamiliar to political science; a long tradition of research has defined political parties as coalitions of policy-demanding groups in society (Key 1947; Schattschneider 1960; Truman 1951; Karol 2009; Masket 2009; Bawn et al. 2012; Hacker and Pierson 2014; Achen and Bartels 2016).

Groups seek access to politicians in order to shape policy outcomes (Fouirnaies and Hall 2015, 2016; Barber 2016a; Grimmer and Powell 2016), but people closely affiliated with these groups can also contribute money directly to candidates. Groups may have a larger effect on legislative behavior indirectly through the contributions of affiliated individuals than they do from the contributions that come directly from the group's legally incorporated PAC and 501(c) organizations. These affiliated individuals are in both a politician's donor network and an interest group network; that is, the candidate's and the group's networks overlap.

It is well known that donors are different from non-donors (e.g., Barber 2016b). However, there are two reasons to expect differences between donors who give to both legislators and groups and those who give only to legislators (shown schematically in figure 5.2). First, an individual's donation to an interest group signals interest in the group's goals, which, in the case of activist groups, centers around ideological and policy outcomes (Bawn et al. 2012). Second, organized groups can overcome obstacles to collective action more effectively than unaffiliated, atomized individuals. Interest groups can hire staff, provide information, and marshal resources that help to coordinate individuals within their network and prevent free riding (Olson 1965). In this way, organizations can amplify the political voice of their members beyond those of atomized, unaffiliated individuals.

Recent research suggests that campaign contributors have greater access to politicians than individuals who do not contribute. In a groundbreaking field experiment, Joshua Kalla and David Broockman (2016) found that legislators and their staff are more likely to grant donors a meeting than nondonors. Such access may provide individual donors with the opportunity to influence legislative behavior. What often goes unreported in discussions of the Kalla and Broockman (2016) study, however, is that the donors seeking access to state legislators were affiliated with a national progressive interest group, CREDO Action, which maintains a superPAC. With resources and

---

6. The organization of workers in firms also affects the individual workers' campaign finance behavior and, quite likely, their influence in politics (Stuckatz, forthcoming).

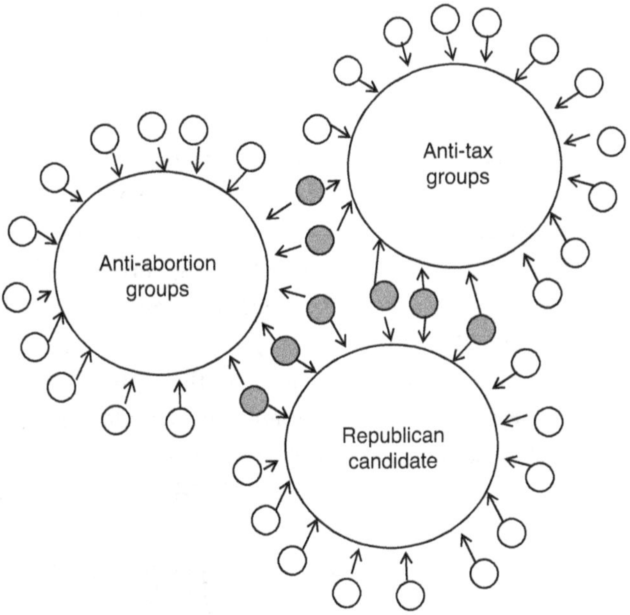

FIGURE 5.2. Group and Candidate Donor Networks.
Note: Large circles represent interest group PACs or a legislative
candidate. Small circles represent individual donors. Shaded donors are
those who contribute to both a legislator's campaign and at least one
interest group PAC.

coordination provided by the organization, the signals that such a group of
donors sends to politicians are likely to be more coherent and effective at influencing behavior than those of unaffiliated, atomized individual donors.

The methods that groups use to coordinate members in order to achieve
political goals are varied. A tradition of research on parties suggests that the
"extended networks" of party coalitions—comprised of "policy-demanding"
activists and organizations—are influential in the nomination process (Schattschneider 1960; Karol 2009; Masket 2009; Bawn et al. 2012; Hassell 2016).
These activists and organizations have informational and other resource advantages over ordinary voters in primary elections (e.g., Anzia 2011). Given the
overwhelming uncompetitiveness of state legislative general elections
(Klarner 2015), supporting their preferred candidates in the nomination process is a viable way to ensure that activists' policy goals are pursued by parties
in government.

Lobbying candidates and incumbent officeholders is another potentially fruitful method of influence for groups of activists. Groups use a variety of strategies to facilitate lobbying from their activist members. Some organizations sponsor trips to legislatures and town hall meetings. Others contact members to generate large amounts of phone calls to legislative offices before key legislative votes. The National Rifle Association (NRA), for example, provides an extensive array of guidelines, information, and resources for individuals to contact lawmakers and lobby for gun rights effectively. The group's website even allows members "to identify and contact [their] lawmakers directly from [the] site."

These coordinating mechanisms may lower the costs of lobbying candidates and legislators for organizationally affiliated individuals relative to unaffiliated individuals. In addition, group affiliation may increase the influence of individuals' political signals to candidates and legislators. By wearing an NRA hat and drawing upon a common activist language, for instance, an individual firearm activist may be perceived as a greater potential electoral threat to candidates.

Ideological Activists and Party Insiders

In this chapter, I investigate the effect on legislative behavior of donations from IGA donors, individuals who contribute to legislators *and* to single-issue and ideological interest group PACs, as well as the effect of donations from *party insiders*, individuals who contribute to both legislators *and* to state legislative party committees. Understanding the structure and goals of the organizations with which these individual donors are affiliated helps shape our expectations about their potential role in polarization.

Ideological or single-issue groups are expected to support candidates who are ideologically pure, consistent, and active on their pet issues (Wilcox 1989; Bawn et al. 2012). Outside of business and labor groups, these ideological groups include the vast majority of what political observers and social scientists consider to be politically active interest groups: conservative Christian groups, environmental organizations, women's rights groups, antiwar groups, libertarian groups, anti-tax groups, Tea Party groups, politically active African American and Latino organizations, and many more.

In addition to interest group activists, of particular interest is the role of formal party committees in the polarization of American politics (Bonica 2013; La Raja and Schaffner 2015; Barber 2016b; Hassell 2018). In contrast to policy-demanding ideological groups, party committees are expected to prioritize electability above other considerations (for an alternative explanation, see Hassell 2018). A popular theory thus posits that contributions from party organizations lead to more moderate politicians (La Raja and Schaffner 2015; Schuck 2014).[7] But this might not be the case in today's era of nationalized parties, where state party organizations are on the sidelines or tools of the national party. In the words of Daniel Schlozman and Sam Rosenfeld (2019, 166), "State parties, central players in the American party system since Martin Van Buren, have become pawns in a mercenary, money-driven, candidate-led, nationalized, and deinstitutionalized game." Indeed, empirical evidence suggests that modern party gatekeepers themselves appear to prefer to recruit ideologically consistent candidates over moderates, especially in the Republican Party (Broockman et al. 2021).

There are additional reasons to expect party organizations and insiders to be less of a moderating force on Republicans. Compared to their Democratic counterparts, Republican groups active in state politics, such as the Republican Governors Association (RGA), Republican State Leadership Committee (RSLC), and Republican Attorneys General Association (RAGA), have been more active, extreme, and nationally coordinated. From 2010 through 2018, these Republican groups spent $835 million compared to just $475 million for their Democratic counterparts, playing an important role in ushering in the wave of very conservative Republican legislators and governors in the 2010 election cycle. The Democratic Governors Association (DGA), Democratic Legislative Campaign Committee (DLCC), and Democratic Attorneys General Association (DAGA) are cross-pressured ideologically by their relationships with large businesses and wealthy donors (though as Paul Pierson and I show elsewhere [2016], large firms and the super-wealthy donate much more to the Republican groups).

Like formal party committees, *party insiders*, individuals who contribute to legislators *and* to state party committees, may have partisan incentives. Hans Hassell (2016), for instance, provides evidence that party organizations can direct party insiders to support their preferred candidates. However, evidence from Rhodes, Schaffner, and La Raja (2018) suggests that party insiders

---

7. For a countervailing theory, see Malbin 2017, 545–47. Malbin suggests that the *Citizens United* ruling allowed party leaders to use 501(c) organizations to spend unlimited amounts on campaigns. This spending appears to have been concentrated in general elections, not primary elections in support of moderate candidates.

(closely related to what the authors call "party-oriented donors") may contribute in less strategic patterns than other donors. Not only are individuals who mostly give to party committees less likely to be wealthy and politically engaged; they also "either demonstrate no clear strategy in their giving behavior or choose to simply focus on giving to what is arguably the most 'obvious' target of donations—their preferred political party" (Rhodes, Schaffner, and La Raja 2018, 513). Hassell (forthcoming) further finds that party insiders intervene in primaries even in safe districts for their parties and often do so in opposition to other party insiders—evidence that suggests party insiders prioritize policy and ideology over the pragmatic pursuit of partisan majorities. Overall, the role of party insiders in state politics is still an open question.

How Campaign Donors Influence Politics

IGA Donors Are Especially Influential

There are strong theories for why party committees and PACs are likely to support moderate candidates in contrast to individual donors (e.g., La Raja and Schaffner 2015; Barber 2016b). However, there has been little empirical focus on variation in attitudes and behavior among individual donors (but see Barber, Canes-Wrone, and Thrower 2015; Barber 2016a). In this section I investigate the political attitudes and self-reported participation of different kinds of individual donors. This task helps further solidify our theoretical expectations about how IGA donors and party insiders may influence legislative behavior. I first examine whether IGA donors systematically differ in ideological and policy attitudes from otherwise similar individual donors. I then ask whether IGA donors are more likely to contact legislators, one way that donors may use to influence legislative behavior.

Do donors affiliated with activist groups have distinct ideological and policy views from those of similar copartisan donors? My analysis of data from the Cooperative Congressional Election Study (CCES) suggests that they do (Ansolabehere and Pettigrew 2014). As seen in figure 5.3, copartisan nondonors, legislative donors, party committee donors, and IGA donors differ significantly in their self-reported ideological placement.[8] These predicted ideologies are derived from the models that include the constituent terms for

---

8. Individuals who report donating to a legislative candidate and a "political group" are coded as IGA donors in the CCES data.

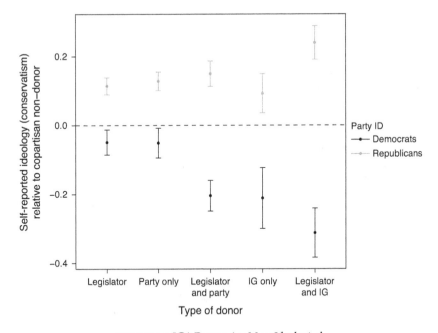

FIGURE 5.3. IGA Donors Are More Ideological.
Note: Interest group activist donors have more extreme ideological self-placement. Estimates
are derived from full interaction models (separated by party ID) with covariates including
race, gender, age, education, and family income.

these interactions as well as demographic controls, all of which are omitted
here for brevity.

In the era of sorted and polarized electorates, party identification is the most
powerful predictor of attitudes, as expected, but the within-party differences
are non-trivial. Republican IGA donors are significantly more conservative
than Republican non-donors and legislative donors; Democratic IGA donors
are significantly more liberal. On the 7-point ideological self-placement scale,
the average Democratic IGA donor is about 0.31 units more extreme (liberal)
than Democratic non-donors and 0.26 units more extreme than Democratic
legislative donors. For both parties, donors who give to party organizations (or
party organization and legislators) are a middling group, with ideological self-
placement in between legislative donors and IGA donors.

Non-donors, legislative donors, party donors, and IGA donors also differ
significantly in their policy views. Again, the IGA donors are the most extreme
(or consistently partisan). Democrats who donate to both legislative candidates and interest groups are more supportive of abortion rights, gay marriage,

and a path to citizenship for undocumented immigrants than are their non-donor and legislative donor counterparts, while IGA Republican donors are more conservative on abortion, cap and trade, gun control, immigration, and the minimum wage. Republican IGA donors are about 8 percentage points less supportive of increasing the minimum wage than Republican legislative donors and nearly 17 percentage points less supportive than Republican non-donors. Republican IGA donors are 6 and 3 percentage points less likely to support legal abortion rights than Republican non-donors and legislative donors, respectively. In every other policy area, Republican IGA donors are consistently more conservative and Democratic IGA donors consistently more liberal than their legislative donor counterparts, but the differences are not significant at the $p < 0.05$ level.

IGA Donors Contact Legislators

Not only do IGA donors hold more consistently extreme attitudes than their copartisan counterparts; they are also more likely to contact their legislators. Figure 5.4 shows the predicted probability of contacting the incumbent legislator (again holding constant respondent race, gender, age, education, and income). Fewer than 50 percent of Republican and Democratic non-donors contact their legislator, and about 65 percent of those who donate to legislators do so. In contrast, more than *three in four IGA donors* report making contact with his or her legislator.[9]

As described, contacting legislators is a plausible mechanism by which interest group activist donors can influence the behavior of legislators across time. Because contacting legislators is a costly action, this finding is consistent with arguments that organizational coordination can serve to reduce the costs (e.g., with informational resources as in the NRA example described earlier) or increase the social benefits of participation.

Challenges to Causal Inference

The previous section established that IGA donors are more ideologically extreme and more likely to contact legislators than other donors—patterns that lead us to expect IGA donors to play a role in the polarization of state legislatures.

9. The survey question asks about contacting the U.S. House incumbent, which I use as a proxy for contacting state legislators.

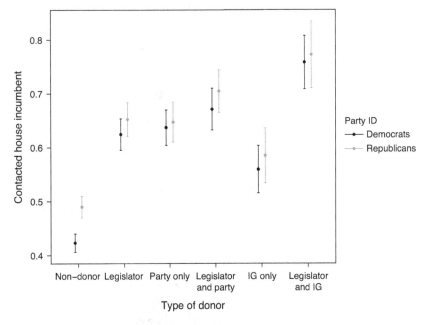

FIGURE 5.4. IGA Donors Contact Their Legislators.
Note: Interest group activist donors are more likely to contact their legislators.

However, the causal relationship between contributions and legislative behavior is likely to be multidirectional. As previously argued, IGA donors may systematically support more extreme candidates and influence the behavior of incumbent legislators through lobbying or threatening to support a primary challenger. Legislators may also become more extreme partly in order to *attract* increasingly numerous group activist donors, and party gatekeepers may recruit candidates for their ability to build networks of activist donors.

Candidate and legislator behavior, however, may be the prior cause of increased IGA contributions. State legislators may have other incentives to become more extreme, such as a desire to advance to higher office in an increasingly nationalized and polarized partisan context. This extremism, in turn, may galvanize IGA donor activity.

Although there will remain some degree of uncertainty over the direction of causality, establishing a correlation between IGA contributions and legislative behavior suggests an important role for IGA donors in polarization. Even if candidates and legislators are the prior cause of increased IGA contributions, candidates may only be able to become extreme because they know they can rely on a funding base with increasing concentrations of IGA donors.

Overall, regardless of whether politicians' behavior leads IGA donors or vice versa, it is likely the case that IGA donors are necessary for the observed equilibrium of legislative behavior of the past two decades.

Data and Methods

Calculating the Composition of Donor Networks

I use the Database on Ideology and Money in Elections (DIME), which provides consistent contributor and recipient identifiers for nearly all campaign contributions at the state and federal levels from the Federal Elections Commission (FEC), Center for Responsive Politics, and National Institute on Money in State Politics (Bonica 2013).[10]

I code a contributor as an ideological activist for a given election cycle if during the cycle the individual donated to an interest group PAC defined by the Center for Responsive Politics as "ideological/single-issue." Analogously, I define *party insiders* as individuals who have donated to a state or national party committee in a given electoral cycle (see Hassell 2016).

Legislative Behavior

The outcome of interest is a measure of legislator ideology derived from roll-call votes from Shor and McCarty 2011, analogous to the DW-NOMINATE scale developed by Poole and Rosenthal (1997). One must be careful when interpreting these kinds of unidimensional left-right scales, because "moderate" and "extreme" are relative to a dynamic policy agenda, in which the substance of a moderate or extreme roll-call vote changes over time. In popular discourse, the term "moderate" is often interchangeable with the word "good" in ways that are disconnected from the substantive content of policy (Roberts 2015). And in some formal modeling studies, "moderate" means congruent with the ideology of a district's constituents. But in this chapter, "extreme" roll-call voting simply means "more consistently liberal or conservative" and, in the polarized era, "more consistently with members of his or her own party." Increasingly polarized roll-call voting in state legislatures is connected to the *policy* polarization that we learned about in chapter 3 (though some of the

---

10. The FEC requires disclosure of individual donors who contribute over $200 in an election cycle.

policy polarization comes from non-legislative institutions such as ballot initiatives and judicial rulings).

Legislative behavior is measured in year $t+1$, where year t is the election year. I thus test the effect of the composition of candidates' donor networks during an election season on their behavior while in office.[11] For ease of interpretation, all variables are rescaled to have a mean of 0 and standard deviation of 1.

I construct traditional time-series cross-sectional (TSCS) regression models to estimate the effect of dynamics in the composition of donor networks on legislative behavior. All models contain state fixed effects in order to restrict the analysis to within-state variation across time, as well as legislative chamber fixed effects (i.e., a dummy variable for upper legislative chamber). I depart from some recent literature on state legislative behavior by estimating separate models for Democrats and Republicans. Evidence from Grossmann and Hopkins 2015 suggests that "the Democratic Party is better understood as a coalition of social groups seeking concrete government action" (119) compared to the Republican Party. As a consequence, Democratic IGAs—group networks of individuals—may be more influential on Democratic legislative behavior than their Republican counterparts. Furthermore, although business and trade groups tend to support relative moderates (e.g., Bonica 2013), their policy goals tend to be conservative (i.e., deregulatory or anti-tax) in issue areas relevant to their firm or industry. This may mean business and trade PAC contributions, the bulk of PAC money in politics, have a greater moderating effect on Democrats.

The relationship between IGA contributions and legislative behavior could be confounded by public opinion if, for instance, legislative districts are becoming more solidly Democratic or Republican. I adjust for public opinion by including a variable for district Democratic presidential vote share from Rogers 2017 in the main analyses.

The main models also include year fixed effects to control for time trends. Because the percent of IGA contributions to candidates has risen precipitously since 2000 (as shown in figure 5.1) and state legislatures have polarized during the same period (Shor and McCarty 2011), models that include year fixed effects are likely to show a much smaller correlation between ideological activist donors and legislative behavior. Year fixed effects protect against potential confounding variables that may influence both the composition of

11. As a robustness check, I also construct models in which I only use Shor-McCarty scores from legislators' first term in office, and find similar results (see also Barber 2016b).

donor networks and legislative behavior over time. However, it may be the case that the universal increase in proportions of ideological activist donors over time is exogenous. For example, technological changes such as the expansion of the internet may have caused an increase in the aggregate proportion of IGA funds in elections, while also leading to changes in media that increased polarization. By contrast, if the internet increased polarization only by facilitating IGA participation, time may not be a confounder. In such a case, estimates from the models without year fixed effects are preferred.

Primary Elections

In order to test the extent to which potential influence over legislative behavior arises from primary election or general election fundraising, I fit additional models that separate contributions into primary and general election periods. To do so, I calculate candidates' funding amounts from different sources in the primary and general election periods using a new data set of state legislative primary dates.

A research assistant collected state legislative primary dates between 2000 and 2012 from state government websites. The primary dates' data set includes special elections that vary by legislative district. To my knowledge, this is the first nationally comprehensive data set of state legislative primary dates.

However, state legislative primaries are mostly uncompetitive, and groups and individuals may contribute during the primary election period in order to support a candidate in the general election. As a robustness check, I undertake a similar analysis of funding during the primary and general election periods for candidates running for open seats. Open seats are a proxy for primary election competitiveness because they lack long-term incumbents who tend to hold large resource advantages (Ansolabehere et al. 2010).

Results

I first plot the bivariate relationship between candidates' concentration of IGA donors and legislative behavior in figure 5.5 using loess regressions. As expected, legislators with larger proportions of interest group activists in their donor networks have more extreme (or consistently partisan) roll-call voting behavior.

Both Republicans and Democrats appear more extreme in office when they rely on greater numbers of IGA donors. At lower concentrations of IGA

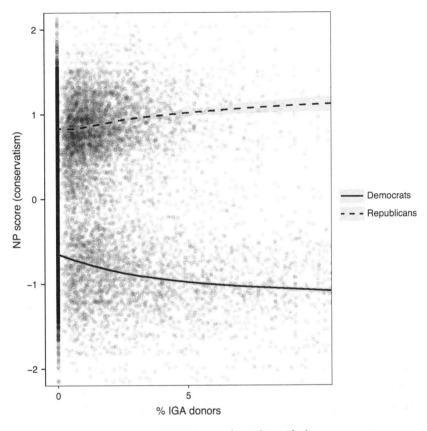

FIGURE 5.5. IGA Donors and Legislative Ideology.

donors (i.e., moving from 0 to 1 percent IGA contributions), the slope is steeper for Democratic legislators. Overall, the slopes of these loess curves are quite symmetric.

However, the relationship between IGA contributions and legislative behavior in figure 5.5 may be confounded by time, geography, and other sources of fundraising that may be correlated with IGA contributions. Figure 5.6 shows the relationship between the concentration of IGA contributions and legislative behavior for Democrats and Republicans, respectively, conditional on these potential confounders.

Figure 5.6 reports that Democratic and Republican candidates with greater concentrations of IGA contributions have more extreme roll-call voting records once in office. A one standard deviation increase in candidate funds from IGA donors is associated with more liberal NP-scores for Democrats (a shift

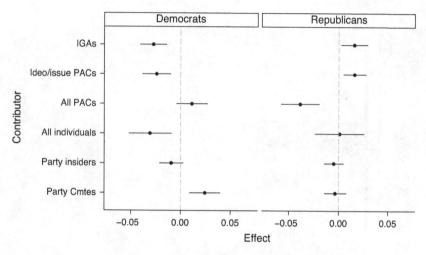

FIGURE 5.6. The Relationship between Contributions and Legislative Ideology.

of between 0.028 and 0.041 units). Similarly, a one standard deviation increase in IGA contributions for Republicans is associated with between a 0.016- and 0.029-unit rightward shift.

The magnitudes of the effects are substantial. For context, in 2012 the average Democratic state legislator was 0.11 units more liberal and the average Republican 0.18 units more conservative than in 2000. The aggregate increase in IGA donors shown in panel (c) of figure 5.1 can explain about 25 percent of the liberal shift for Democrats over this period and about 9 percent of the conservative shift of Republicans. (The similar effect sizes explain a lower proportion of Republicans' rightward shift because the GOP has moved farther right than Democrats have moved left.)

Importantly, this finding for IGA donors remains robust even when controlling for contributions from the activist *organizations* with which IGA donors are affiliated. Ideological/single-issue groups and their extended networks of individual activists appear to have independent effects on legislative behavior. Contributions from these ideological and single-issue PACs such as the NRA and MoveOn.org are associated with legislative extremism for both parties, as expected, and their effects are of similar magnitude to those of IGA donors. If groups are to be conceptualized as formal organizations and individual affiliates, then the effect of these activist groups could be as large as the sum of the effects of the ideological PACs and IGA contributions.

The models also control for candidates' share of funding from PACs and individual donors. I find effects that are consistent with those of Barber (2016b), in which greater overall PAC contributions relative to individual contributions are associated with moderate legislative behavior. For Democrats, the effect of percent individual contributions is significantly different from zero and significantly larger in magnitude than the effect of IGA donors. For Republicans, the effect of percent PAC contributions is significantly different from zero but statistically indistinguishable from the effect of percent IGA contributions.

In contrast to IGA donors, contributions from party insiders have no consistent relationship to extreme roll-call voting in state legislatures. Figure 5.6 shows that party insiders are associated with greater extremism for Democrats and moderation for Republicans, but these associations are not statistically significant.

Aggregate Effects of IGAs on State Parties

The analysis thus far has focused on explaining differences between legislators in the same state based on their sources of fundraising. But if the Democratic and Republican parties increasingly operate as coordinated teams, then it might be more informative to take a more macro perspective. How have changes to the parties' *aggregate* fundraising from IGA donors changed the parties in government? One advantage here is that while the data do not allow me to do a within-legislator difference-in-differences design, I can do a within-*state* difference-in-differences design at the aggregate state party level. Figure 5.7 uses this kind of aggregate difference-in-differences model to estimate relationship between a state party's contributions and legislative ideology.

The results show that as the share of IGA fundraising for Republican candidates in a state grows, the Republicans in the state legislature become more conservative. The effect is larger than those of the legislator level analysis shown earlier and is massive in substantive terms: a one standard deviation increase in the percent of money that comes from IGA donors makes the state's average Republican legislator 0.33 standard deviations more conservative in office. Ideological and single-issue fundraising has a smaller but still substantial rightward effect on Republicans.

We don't see the same effects for Democrats. Whereas the earlier analyses showed symmetrical effects at the level of the individual legislator—that is, within a state, more IGA funding is associated with more liberal Democrats and more conservative Republicans—this analysis at the state legislative level suggests that fundraising from IGA donors has had little effect on Democrats.

An additional advantage of this aggregate analysis is that I can include a variable for state-level public opinion. While the candidate-level analysis earlier required me to use district presidential vote share, here I can use the public

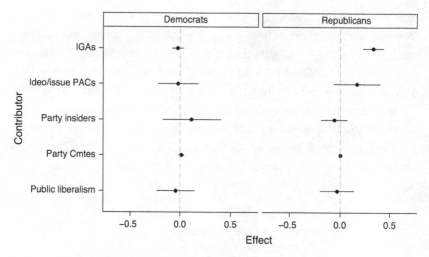

FIGURE 5.7. IGA Contributions and Legislative Polarization at the State Party Level.

liberalism measure of Caughey and Warshaw (2018), which is based on a sophisticated modeling of hundreds of survey questions about all kinds of public policies.[12]

However, the results show that compared to the effects of IGA donors on Republican state parties, the effect of public opinion on state legislative behavior has been tiny. In the last chapter, I looked directly at the relationship between state opinion and policy in particular issue areas. The analysis here instead looks at legislative ideology based on roll-call votes as the outcome but provides another stark piece of evidence consistent with more coordinated, active, and well-resourced groups, not public opinion, driving the transformation of state politics.

Primary and General Election Contributions

Activist groups are understood to influence parties in the nomination process (Bawn et al. 2012; Hassell 2016). In this section, I present results of models that separate sources of campaign contributions in the primary and general election periods.

Figure 5.8 reports the results of models of the composition of donor networks separated into the primary and general election periods. Critically, the

12. Here I use average of the "social liberalism" and "economic liberalism" public opinion measures. Robustness checks use the separate variables.

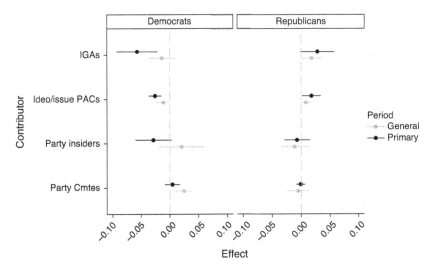

FIGURE 5.8. Donor Networks at the Legislator Level (Primary and General).

large effects for percent ideological activist donors are concentrated in the primary election period. An increase in percent IGA contributions in the primary period of one standard deviation is associated with a 0.015- to 0.0589-unit shift leftward for Democrats and a 0.031-unit shift rightward for Republicans.

Ideological/single-issue PAC contributions in primaries are also associated with more extreme legislative behavior, but the effect is considerably smaller than that of IGA donors. Party insiders again appear to moderate Democrats, with their greatest effect in primary elections. Again, however, party insiders have no significant relationship to Republican legislative behavior.

In general elections, IGA contributions and formal ideological/single-issue PAC contributions still have effects in the expected direction (extremism). The effect magnitudes are consistently smaller than those for primary election periods but are still apparent and, in most cases, statistically significant at the $p < 0.1$ level. Overall, the results corroborate theories that emphasize the role of activist groups in the nomination process.

Organized Money Matters

Organized groups are more than their staff members, their offices, and their formally incorporated nonprofit organizations. They are networks of activists and patrons. This investigation of the role of organizationally affiliated donors offers a more complete picture of the influence of groups on the polarization of state legislatures and the resurgence of state policy. It also provides an additional explanation for the way state policy changed dramatically in recent years without much change in public opinion. A large body of literature suggests that legislators are more responsive to elites and groups than mass attitudes (Bartels 2009; Gilens 2012; Gilens and Page 2014), but campaign contributions—a tool in which wealthy individuals and organized groups hold advantages over ordinary citizens—are often found to have minimal effects.

I find that the percentage of a legislative candidate's donors who are affiliated with interest groups may influence legislative behavior. Both Republican and Democratic state legislators with larger proportions of IGA donors are more extreme than their copartisan counterparts in their states. This relationship is robust to holding constant legislators' overall contributions from PACs and individuals, which previous research has shown to influence legislative behavior (Barber 2016b).

However, individual campaign donors with close ties to formal party organizations do not appear to be a moderating influence. There is evidence that these party insiders are influential in the candidate nomination process (Hassell 2016), but they may not systematically select for more moderate candidates. While the decline of party committee influence may play a role in the polarization of state legislatures (La Raja and Schaffner 2015), the results in this chapter suggest it is unlikely that party insiders mitigate polarization in today's state politics. This finding is consistent with arguments that the composition of party insiders and party organizations has changed. Party operatives, once local elites, are increasingly recruited from the ranks of national ideological and issue activist groups (Schlozman and Rosenfeld 2019).

This chapter investigated the role of activists affiliated with ideological and single-issue groups, but such groups represent a mere fraction of organizationally mobilized money in state politics. In contrast to this study, other emerging research investigates the influence of super-elite groups like ALEC (Hertel-Fernandez 2014, 2019), the Koch network (Skocpol and Hertel-Fernandez 2016), and business groups (Hacker and Pierson 2010), which have few activist affiliates outside of large donors and individuals who are directly employed by the interest groups. Such super-elite groups often attempt to mobilize grassroots or "astroturf" movements in support of their causes (Walker 2014), but the ratio of resources provided by major patrons relative to activist affiliates is much higher than for the ideological and single-issue groups addressed in this study. Ideological and single-issue activist groups are more likely than business and super-elite groups like Americans for Prosperity to prioritize social issues over economic issues. In addition, wealthy individuals and corporations have a broader set of ways to use money in politics than do even the relatively deep-pocketed activist groups' IGAs. Super-elite groups appear more likely to employ or partner with 501(c)4 or 501(c)6 organizations with the ability to raise, spend, and transfer unlimited sums of "dark" money from anonymous contributors toward political activities. Corporations even strategically give to charities in the districts of key legislators in order to increase their political influence (Bertrand et al. 2020). Future research should not neglect the larger context of groups' political resources and expenditures in drawing conclusions.

Three additional areas of further research are ripe for investigation. First, the relationship between organized groups and individual activists needs theoretical and empirical development. Why do donors contribute to activist groups, and how does the affiliation with interest groups shape the political participation of individuals? What variation in coordinating strategies exists among interest groups, and what are the results of such variation? In this data, most IGAs contribute to both interest groups and legislators in their first cycle of giving.[13] However, a more granular analysis of contribution timing should investigate whether interest group contributions to a legislator predict similar contributions from their affiliated IGAs, or vice versa. Such investigation can shed light on the "origin story" of IGA donors.

Second, further research can disentangle the mechanisms of IGA influence. Although this study makes progress in uncovering mechanisms in various ways, such as disaggregating IGA contributions in primary and general elections, these IGA contributions are likely to be correlated with other forms of political participation. Additional research may discover creative ways to exploit quasi-exogenous variation in specific forms of IGA participation, such as lobbying candidates or volunteering in campaigns.

Third, a policy-oriented focus on the influence of activists is warranted. The donors in the field experiment by Kalla and Broockman (2016) were coordinated by an interest group to lobby legislators about a complex piece of legislation on chemical regulation. Organized groups provide individual activists with resources to effectively lobby on specific policy issues. While this study estimates the effect of activist donors on legislative behavior measured on a

---

13. It is important to note that donor identities are matched across time with only moderate precision such that the data may understate the prior contribution behavior of individuals over time.

single left-right dimension, subsequent research should investigate policy-specific effects in areas such as environmental regulation, labor relations, gun control, abortion, and civil rights.

Activists got organized, and they invested in state politics. They voted in state legislative and gubernatorial primaries, they lobbied incumbents, and, as this chapter describes, they donated money. In the process, groups organized around issues like guns, environmental protection, and abortion, and ideological groups like MoveOn.org and Tea Party organizations, set policy agendas for Democratic and Republican state governments. They transformed American federalism by fusing together the national and state levels into a single political battleground.

With nationalized parties—coordinated in part by the activist organizations described in this chapter—what happens to policy learning and diffusion between state governments? The next chapter takes up this question. The nationalization of party networks through activists and organizations, especially in the arena of campaign finance, has profound implications for the role of states as "policy laboratories." The hope of Louis Brandeis's idea of "laboratories of democracy" is that state governments learn from each other about which policies are helpful and which are harmful. But learning requires information. All governments, and especially those at lower levels, seek economic, legal, scientific, and political information from nongovernmental expert and activist groups in order to make policy. Over the past generation, as organizations have polarized and nationalized, so has the information that partisan state governments rely on to make policy. As I explain in the next chapter, the nationalization and polarization of the parties' organizational networks reduce state governments' incentives to learn from the policy experiences of states controlled by the other party—with major consequences for states' ability to act like Brandeis's theorized policy laboratories.

6

Partisan Laboratories
of Democracy

THE LAST CHAPTER investigated the rise of organized national activists in state politics—an important organizational shift that contributed to the nationalization of the Democratic and Republican parties in the states. This chapter turns to a consequence of party nationalization, especially when party nationalization is driven by organizations: the decline of learning between state "policy laboratories." In particular, as the parties and party-aligned organizations polarize into two national networks, we see reduced policy learning and emulation across states controlled by different parties.

So far, we've challenged the conventional wisdom that the state level isn't very important for policy and that state governments are especially responsive to local constituents rather than coordinated national activists. In this chapter, I take on another piece of conventional wisdom about American federalism: that states are "laboratories of democracy." In the generations since Louis Brandeis introduced this theory, federalism has been lauded for incentivizing policy experimentation and learning. State governments engage in policy experimentation and may "act as scientists, watching these experiments and learning from them" to produce more effective governance (Shipan and Volden 2012, 790). This sort of institutional learning, in which governments faced with uncertainty can observe and emulate best practices in other states, has been thoroughly investigated in empirical studies of policy diffusion (e.g., Meseguer 2003, 2006; Grossback, Nicholson-Crotty, and Peterson 2004; Volden, Ting, and Carpenter 2008; Gilardi, Füglister, and Luyet 2009; Shipan and Volden 2014).

But just as the *Federalist Papers* had done before, Brandeis's comments about federalism neglected *political parties* in describing governments' incentives. A plethora of observational studies have separately investigated learning, whether governments emulate successful policies (e.g., Volden 2006), and homophily, whether states emulate the policies of similar states, such as those controlled by the same political party (e.g., Grossback, Nicholson-Crotty, and Peterson 2004). However, there has been little analysis of the *interaction* of homophily and success. Do the parties structure institutional learning in American federalism? Are state governments *unbiased learners*, emulating successful policies regardless of the source, or are they *partisan learners* that emulate copartisan success but ignore successful policies from outpartisan sources? This chapter tackles this question.

A survey experiment of officials by Daniel Butler and colleagues (2017) suggests that officeholders are unbiased learners, interested in learning about policies of outparty governments when presented with evidence of policy success. However, I argue that copartisans, not outpartisans, will be most affected by evidence of success. If policies are understood to be "owned" by party brands (Cox and McCubbins 1993),[1] parties have an incentive to avoid providing evidence of success for outparty-owned policies, as this could improve the outparty's "party valence brand" (Butler and Powell 2014). Furthermore, resource-constrained state governments often obtain information about policy from party-aligned organizations (Ahn et al. 2013; Hertel-Fernandez 2014; Campbell and Pedersen 2014), which may systematically bias institutional learning under federalism. If these partisan and partisan-aligned organizations shape perceptions of success in favor of copartisan policies and against outpartisan policies, we may expect copartisans, not outpartisans, to be those most sensitive to information signals. In turn, policy learning may be biased such that governments of different parties do not converge on the most economically or politically effective policies as classic theories of federalism predict.

This study tests the predictions of models of policy learning. I first test a traditional model of unbiased learning. I then introduce a simple theoretical model of *partisan learning*, based in the incentives of partisan state governments in the context of nationalized parties. In the partisan learning theory, state governments discount information about the expected success or failure of policy based on the partisan control of another government.

The empirical analysis shows moderate support for theories of unbiased learning. Electoral and, to a lesser degree, economic success predict policy

---

1. Petrocik 1996 and subsequent studies have focused on the related concept of party ownership of broad issue areas such as the environment or the economy.

diffusion. However, empirical tests of *partisan learning* suggest that state governments primarily learn from copartisan governments. Interacting the partisanship of the source with the informational signal shows that a policy's economic or electoral benefits are mostly independent of its likelihood of diffusion, unless the potential diffuser polity is controlled by the same political party as the potential recipient polity. Further analysis suggests that shared partisanship plays a role beyond shared ideology: legislative ideological proximity between governments has an independent effect on the likelihood of diffusion but, in contrast to shared party control, does not affect learning.

This chapter has implications for our understanding of federalism and policy polarization. Federalism, in theory, is a "political marketplace" with strong incentives for governments to converge upon the most effective policies—yet chapter 3 shows that Democratic- and Republican-controlled states are pursuing increasingly distinct policy agendas. Party brands, a classic explanation for legislative polarization, provide a mechanism for the non-convergence of state policy. And following on chapter 5's investigation of interest group activists, an important additional mechanism is the increasing partisanship of expert and interest group organizational networks that provide informational resources and other "legislative subsidies" not just to Congress but even more importantly to subnational governments with fewer policymaking resources.

Learning about Policy

Studies of diffusion have been prominent in each of the intellectual communities described in chapter 2: the Decentralists, the Brandeisians, and the New Federalists. The Decentralists and New Federalists tend to emphasize the potential advantages of states' ability to customize policy to their particular constituencies. This tradition experienced an intellectual resurgence in the second half of the twentieth century (e.g., Buchanan and Tullock 1962). Studies find that diffusion is more likely to occur between geographic neighbors (e.g., Case, Rosen, and Hines 1993) and between polities with similar racial demographics (e.g., Jones-Correa 2000), partisanship and ideologies (Grossback, Nicholson-Crotty, and Peterson 2004; Volden 2006), dominant religions and cultures (Grattet, Jenness, and Curry 1998; Simmons and Elkins 2004), and economic conditions (Volden 2006).[2]

2. States with similar geographies and demographics are likely to face similar social problems, which, in turn, require similar policy solutions compared to geographically and

Overall, the customization theory predicts that governments will tend to emulate the policies of *similar* states. The most important dimension of similarity in contemporary American politics is, of course, partisanship. Studies have shown that states controlled by the same party are much more likely to emulate each other's policies (e.g., Grossback, Nicholson-Crotty, and Peterson 2004; Volden 2006).[3]

By contrast, theories in the Brandeis tradition of "laboratories of democracy" emphasize policy experimentation and learning. The numerousness of states facilitates improvements in governance by increasing available information about policy effectiveness. In the words of Stefan Sinn (1992, 191), "If a multitude of policy experiments takes place it is more likely that the 'best' policy package is discovered than if one harmonized policy package produced by a cartel of governments is implemented." Over time, learning—via belief updating in response to new information—causes all actors' beliefs about the effectiveness of policy choices to converge on "true" best practices (Breen 1999).

In this informational context, studies of public choice suggest that intergovernmental competition for residents and investment provides incentives for governments to learn. Seminal studies have characterized state (and local) governments in federalist systems as actors in market competition for residents who "vote with their feet" (e.g., Tiebout 1956; Oates 1972). Theories of fiscal federalism also posit that governments compete for investment. Politicians will be more likely to support policies that are perceived to deliver strong economic performance. Politicians may hope to improve the economy for its own sake, but the *electoral connection* is the primary mechanism: politicians are aware of the association between economic performance and incumbents' election prospects.

If constituents engage in retrospective voting, office-seeking politicians have incentives to learn about and implement *economically successful* policies. Public policy choices have considerable influence over the economy (e.g., Hacker and Pierson 2010), and the state of the economy greatly affects

demographically dissimilar states. States in close geographic proximity tend to be dependent on similar sources of economic activity: coastal states may have large shipping, fishing, and tourism industries, while Appalachian states are home to extractive mining industries. These sectors of economic activity may demand distinct regulatory policies in ways that lead to geographic diffusion. States with similar racial demographics also face incentives to adopt similar policies. Hero and Tolbert (1996), for instance, show that a state's distribution of racial groups largely explains its "political culture" (see also Elazar 1972).

3. For a comparative example, see Gilardi and Füglister 2008.

incumbents' reelection prospects (Fiorina 1978; Erikson 1989; Lewis-Beck and Stegmaier 2000). When deciding whether to adopt a policy, governors and state legislators will be attentive to the economic trends, such as those in growth and unemployment, in states with that policy on the books.

Parties in government are also likely to be attentive to the *electoral success* of policies. Fabrizio Gilardi (2010) finds evidence that governments are more likely to support policies that appear to generate positive electoral outcomes for incumbents in other jurisdictions. I similarly investigate the relationship between electoral success and policy emulation.

Theories of learning and intergovernmental competition persist in scholarly and conventional wisdom. Scholars argue that federalism improves policy experimentation and learning and reduces rent extraction by states (e.g., Dye 1990; Qian and Weingast 1997; Kappeler and Välilä 2008; Volden, Ting, and Carpenter 2008). A generation of conservative politicians and judges has championed these theories under the banner of "New Federalism" (Conlan 1988). With a few caveats about the challenges of externalities or free riding, theories of institutional learning persist as a dominant framework for understanding American federalism (Bardhan 2002; Romano 2002; Devine, Katsoulacos, and Sugden 2005; Shipan and Volden 2012; Calabresi and Bickford 2014; Levin 2017). As Senator James Inhofe summarized, "it's more efficient when it's done from the states" (quoted in Stein 2018).[4]

I refer to this theory, in which electorally interested state governmental actors have incentives to emulate successful policies from any source and ultimately converge on best practices, as the *unbiased learning model*. Empirical findings have tended to be consistent with the unbiased learning model. Studies find that more economically or politically effective policies are more likely to spread to other jurisdictions (Berry and Berry 1990; Volden 2006; Makse and Volden 2011; Glick and Friedland 2014; Shipan and Volden 2014). There is also evidence that governments emulate the policies of jurisdictions with constituents who are satisfied with government services (Lundin, Öberg, and Josefsson 2015).

---

4. Former Utah state senator Michael Waddoups prominently argued that "in general, state governments are better managed, have better fiscal controls, are more innovative, and reflect the will of the people far more than the Federal Government." Citizens for Economy in Government, "Towards More Efficient Massachusetts State Government" (1975), https://archive.org /stream/massachusettsmat4497stat/massachusettsmat4497stat_djvu.txt.

Partisan Learning

Although theories of similarity and learning have both received considerable attention, there has been little investigation into the potential *interaction* of similarity and learning. The most important dimension of similarity in contemporary American politics is partisanship, and parties, in turn, may structure policy learning.

Butler and colleagues (2017) find that politicians are less interested in learning about policies that are incongruent with their ideology or partisanship—but that evidence of success can mitigate this bias. Evidence of success, in other words, affects those predisposed to opposing the policy. Butler and colleagues (2017) make a major contribution by randomizing treatment and focusing on the upstream stages of policymaking. However, the experiment is unable to directly test whether evidence of success affects copartisans and outpartisans differently. The experimental treatment involves a single policy, one that is ideologically liberal, and nearly 90 percent of liberal respondents were interested in learning about the policy regardless of the "success" condition. That the "success" treatment only affected conservative and Republican respondents may reflect a ceiling effect. In addition, the "success" treatment is binary. In practice, there is great variation and granularity in the information that elected officials may receive about the political and economic experiences of other states.

In contrast to Butler and colleagues' study, I argue that we should expect evidence of success to have a greater effect on *copartisans*, those who are more predisposed to *supporting* the policy. This is for two reasons. First, parties have incentives to avoid implementing successful outpartisan policy because this could improve the outparty brand or reputation. Second, parties rely on increasingly polarized networks of outside organizations for policymaking resources, such as information.

Policy Success and Party Brands

A single-minded reelection seeker will want to support policies that she believes will improve the economy and satisfy voters in her district. However, she is cross-pressured by partisan incentives. Politicians have an incentive to work on behalf of their party because the health of their collective party brand affects their individual likelihood of reelection (Cox and McCubbins 1993). Partisan incentives of this sort have been used to explain puzzles in politicians' behavior, such as legislative votes that are "out of step" with district opinion and legislators' delegation of authority to party leaders. Party brands have been regionally distinct in the past, but over the past generation they have become increasingly national (Abramowitz 2010; Abramowitz and Webster 2016; Schickler 2016; Hopkins 2018).

The quality of party brands depends to some degree on policy performance. Parties that implement successful policies in a key issue area may obtain issue ownership (Petrocik 1996). Parties may also improve their valence brand through good governance. Experimental evidence (Butler and Powell 2014) suggests that voters reward or punish incumbent candidates for their party's performance in "nonideological" behaviors, such as maintaining low unemployment or passing a budget on time. A party brand is a function of the real-world success of the policies that it owns.

Not only do parties in government have incentives to implement successful policies to distinguish themselves from the outparty; they have incentives to *avoid* implementing successful outpartisan policies. By implementing a policy, a state government creates additional data points which, in expectation, serve to decrease uncertainty about the policy's level of success. Helping to implement a successful policy may bring legislators and governors individual electoral benefits, but if the policy is owned by the outparty, it comes at the cost of improving the outparty brand.

Recent policy dynamics in the states may reflect these incentives. For example, the Republican legislators and governor of Wisconsin may be tempted to emulate neighboring Minnesota's recent minimum wage increase, whose implementation is correlated with above-average economic growth. However, the minimum wage is owned by the Democratic brand; the Democratic government of Minnesota implemented and executed the policy. If it were to emulate the policy, Wisconsin's Republican government would provide more evidence that this Democratically owned policy is successful, which would in turn improve the national Democratic brand. For the Republican government of Wisconsin, the cost of this improvement to the Democratic brand likely outweighs the benefits of implementing the successful policy in their own state.

Partisan Organizations and Heuristics

Partisan identity also shapes politicians' use of cognitive heuristics and positions in organizational networks. Partisan heuristics and organizational networks are likely to influence perceptions of policy success and, ultimately, behavior in government. First, partisanship is a strongly held social identity that affects cognitive processing (Green, Palmquist, and Schickler 2002), and this social group identity may affect the behavior of elites in addition to the mass public. Political elites may employ the availability and representativeness heuristics as cognitive shortcuts in decision making. Considerations about copartisan states are likely to be more *available* than about outparty states; good news about policy success in copartisan states may be assumed to be more *representative* of a broader trend than news from outpartisan states. Indeed, as Kurt Weyland (2005, 282–86) describes with regard to the spread of pension privatization in Latin America, policymakers' use of these heuristics led to a "cumulation of distortions" that is not well predicted by theories of unbiased (or, as the author calls it, "rational") policy learning.[5] Overall, politicians are likely to suffer from similar cognitive biases as high-information voters, rejecting considerations from outpartisan sources and accepting them from copartisan sources (e.g., Zaller 1992).

The bipartisan National Governors Association (NGA), for instance, has declined in clout compared to the Democratic Governors Association (DGA) and Republican Governors Association (RGA) (Jensen 2016, chap. 3). These governors associations hold conventions to support networking and information provision. Greater participation in partisan compared to bipartisan governors associations is likely to increase the partisan bias in exposure to information, potentially leading governors to place greater weight on the experiences of copartisans via the heuristics described above.

Second, the complexity and noisiness of policy analysis allow considerable room for *organizations* to shape politicians' beliefs about policy success. Organizations often provide the resources necessary to generate a policy idea from the "primeval soup" of potential solutions for an issue in the problem stream (Kingdon 1984). A key policymaking resource is policy analysis, which affects beliefs about the expected effects of policy (Wildavsky 2017). Where policymakers derive these resources depends on the structure of the "policy community" (Kingdon 1984, vii). From the perspective of policy-interested organizations and entrepreneurs, "access to centers of power" affects their ability to influence policy alternatives (Zahariadis 2014, 78). Like scholars who emphasize the role of policy-demanding groups in parties (Bawn et al. 2012), I argue that extended networks of partisan-aligned activist and expert

5. I sidestep the debate about whether the heuristics involved in partisan learning violate "rationality" or indicate "bounded rationality" (for a deeper discussion of heuristics and rationality, see Simon 1985).

organizations can provide these logistical and informational resources. Niko-laos Zahariadis (2014, 78) cites the case of the privatization of British rail, which moved from the problem phase to the policy design phase of the policy process "because it was pushed for by think tanks with very strong connec-tions to the governing party."

In the U.S. case, recent decades have seen the organizational landscape grow increasingly partisan such that policy-interested organizations and en-trepreneurs are increasingly likely to only provide policymaking resources to a single political party. Policy analysis, "model bills," lobbying, and other "leg-islative subsidies" are less likely to cross party lines (Ahn et al. 2013; Hertel-Fernandez 2014; Campbell and Pedersen 2014; Krimmel 2017).[6] Labor unions, for instance, have long been relatively more aligned with the Demo-cratic Party but were present and somewhat influential in the extended group networks of both parties, providing key information to policymakers about the economic interests and circumstances of their rank-and-file members. However, Laura Bucci and Kevin Reuning (2020) find that as labor union density has declined over the past generation, unions are less central to parties' organizational networks.

Even if electorally motivated politicians wish to obtain *unbiased* informa-tion about policy success, their partisan organizational networks may select or spin information in biased ways. Information about weather anomalies in a legislator's district only seems to affect Democratic state legislators' climate policy activity (Bromley-Trujillo, Holman, and Sandoval 2019), for instance.

The American Legislative Exchange Council (ALEC) is a prominent ex-ample of an organization that may influence policy learning in the states. The organization is credited with facilitating the development and diffusion of Stand Your Ground laws across states, along with many other policies. Consid-erable attention has been paid to the practice of legislatures copying the exact legal language from "model bills," but ALEC also attempts to marshal evidence of their policies' success in other states in order to facilitate emulation. Before becoming governor of Wisconsin, Scott Walker had been an ALEC member as a state legislator. As he described, "Probably more important than just the model legislation, [ALEC] had actually put together reports and such that showed the benefits of truth-in-sentencing and showed the successes in other states. And those sorts of statistics were very helpful to us when we pushed it through" (quoted in Hertel-Fernandez 2019, 108). Note that although social

6. See Hall and Deardorff 2006 for a formal model of lobbying as a legislative subsidy.

scientists often contest the veracity of the empirical claims from partisan and other political organizations such as ALEC (e.g., Hertel-Fernandez 2019), these organizations may still have some incentive—though probably a very weak one—to report true information about policy success because they, like politicians, want their aligned party to control the levers of government.

Studies by Gilardi (2010) and Gilardi, Füglister, and Luyet (2009) have made progress in investigating the interaction of partisanship and information signals in policy emulation. Gilardi (2010), for instance, tests whether European governments emulate cuts to unemployment benefits more often when the policy shows signs of economic or electoral success depending on the governments' partisanship.[7] However, it remains unknown whether the historical record in the fifty states is consistent with the theory of partisan learning and whether it generalizes across space, time, and policy type. This chapter fills the gap in our theoretical and empirical understanding of governmental learning.

Model of Partisan Learning

The theory of partisan learning is straightforward. Figure 6.1 compares the predictions of the *unbiased learning model* and the *partisan learning model* as they relate to the expected probability that government i emulates policy q from government j. The two key variables are the partisanship of the potential diffuser, government j, and the information signal about state j's experience with policy q. Government j is either copartisan or outpartisan (with the solid line representing the likelihood of emulating government j's policy when j is copartisan, and the dotted line when j is outpartisan). The information signal represented on the x-axis, evidence of success, takes a value between 0 to 1, with higher values indicating greater likelihood that policy q is successful.

Like a traditional spatial model, the model first assumes that parties in government receive ideological, group-based, or partisan payoffs for implementing policy. Second, parties in government receive payoffs for policy success. Third, parties in government receive more information about policy success of copartisan policies, whereas they observe outpartisan policies with greater uncertainty. An additional mechanism is that emulating a successful policy

---

7. Gilardi (2010) finds that left parties in European Union countries tend to care most about unemployment benefits' effect on the unemployment rate, while right parties tend to weight its electoral effects more heavily.

improves the national brand of the party that "owns" the policy, a disincentive against emulating successful outpartisan policies.

The following list summarizes the hypotheses generated from the model predictions:

- (H_1) Partisan Similarity: Shared party control increases the likelihood of policy emulation.
- (H_2) Unbiased Learning: Signals of success increase the likelihood of policy emulation.
- (H_3) Partisan Learning: Signals of success from copartisan states increase the likelihood of policy emulation more than signals of success from outpartisan states.

H_1 predicts that there is a payoff to emulating a policy from a copartisan government that is independent of policy success. The payoff could be ideological or based in responsiveness to group pressure or the party's electoral base. Ideology and partisanship are highly correlated in the polarized era (e.g., Shor and McCarty 2011), and legislators and executives may risk implementing policy associated with negative economic or electoral outcomes if there are countervailing ideological or group-based payoffs. At the same time, there are potential nonideological partisan payoffs to emulating copartisan policy, such as financial support from party committees or extended networks of partisan groups (e.g., Hassell 2016) or incentives based in partisan competition (e.g., Lee 2009). These payoffs associated with partisanship generate the gap between the y-intercepts in figure 6.1.

In all models the information slope is positive, independent of the characteristics of the information source. Evidence of success strictly increases the likelihood that state government i adopts the policy. This prediction corresponds to H_2.

H_3 distinguishes between the *unbiased learning* and *partisan learning* models. The slopes represent the relationship between evidence of success and the likelihood of emulation. In the unbiased learning model, the slope for evidence of success is equal or larger when government i is outpartisan.[8] By contrast, in the *partisan learning model*, the slope is larger when government i is copartisan than when it is outpartisan. The difference between the copartisan information and outpartisan information slopes is the discount that

---

8. The outpartisan and copartisan slopes differ in panel (a) of figure 5.1, but equal slopes are also consistent with the unbiased learning model.

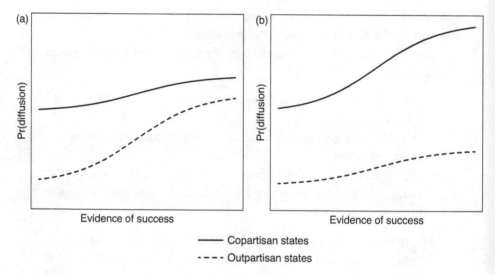

FIGURE 6.1. (a) Unbiased Learning (b) Partisan Learning.

government j gives to information from outpartisan sources. *H3a*, the partisan learning hypothesis, predicts that the information slope is significantly greater when government j is copartisan.

In the regression context, it is simple to translate these hypotheses into an interaction model. *Evidence*$_{jqt}$ represents the information signal from state j's experience with policy q as of time t. Shared partisanship *Copartisan*$_{ijt}$ is a time-variant feature of the state dyad. The outcome is the probability that state government i emulates policy q from state government j at time t. The model takes the general form:

$$Pr(Emulation_{ijqt}) = \alpha + \beta_1 Copartisan_{ijt} + \beta_2 Evidence_{jqt} + \beta_3 Copartisan_{ijt} \times Evidence_{jqt}$$

In short, *H1* predicts that β_1 will be positive; *H2* predicts that β_2 will be positive; and *H3* predicts that β_3 will be positive.

Measures and Estimation

Policy Data

Existing studies of policy diffusion tend to analyze data on a single policy type, such as lottery adoption (Berry and Berry 1990), antismoking laws (Pacheco 2012), or characteristics of SCHIP programs (Volden 2006). Authors often generalize their substantive conclusions beyond the policy area in their data (e.g., Baybeck, Berry, and Siegel 2011, 245).[9]

I once again use the large data set of state policies described in chapter 3.[10] To be sure, policy administration may vary across states even when formal policies do not. Jamila Michener's book *Fragmented Democracy*, for instance, looks beyond formal differences in state Medicaid policy, such as eligibility criteria, showing that differences in implementation and administration have profound effects on the democratic inclusion of people marginalized by race and class. As federalism scholar Philip Rocco (2020) likes to joke, "if you know one state Medicaid program, you know one state Medicaid program." There are many additional examples of state administration and implementation, rather than formal policy, affecting the lives of Americans. A particularly extreme example was the poisoning of municipal water in Flint, Michigan, with lead at the hands of the city's "emergency city manager," who had been appointed by Governor Rick Snyder in 2013. For reasons of practicality, this data set focuses on formal de jure state policy.

Not all forms of policy success are relevant to every policy type. Because reelection incentives are considered paramount for politicians (Downs 1957; Mayhew 1974), signals of electoral success are expected to be important for all types of policies, from abortion laws to tax policy. By contrast, signals of economic success, such as reduced unemployment, are likely to be much more relevant to economic policies such as the minimum wage than for social policies such as gay marriage laws. It is safe to assume that this belief is common among politicians and most voters. This is not to say that social policies do not affect economic activity. A recent North Carolina law that restricted the use of restrooms by transgender people led firms to relocate conventions, sporting events, and other economic activity. The expansive data set of policies used in this study provides the opportunity for separate analyses of economic and social policies, with the expectation that signals of economic success are more closely associated with economic policies.

9. As Baybeck, Berry, and Siegel (2011) claim, "Although our empirical analysis is limited to the case of lottery adoptions, we believe that our strategic theory of diffusion via competition is more widely applicable, since many policy choices made by governments (national, state, and local) influence 'location choices' made by persons or firms, which in turn have positive or negative consequences for the governments."

10. I remove policies that have been passed by ballot referenda or court ruling. To date, Desmarais, Harden, and Boehmke 2015 is the most comprehensive study of policy diffusion in the fifty states, but it investigates characteristics of diffuser and adopter states rather than the interaction of partisanship and success.

Similar to studies of war (Bremer 1992; Cunningham, Skrede Gleditsch, and Salehyan 2009), the unit of observation in studies of policy diffusion is a pair of polities, a *dyad*. Each dyad represents two states, state$_i$, the potential *recipient* state, and state$_j$, the potential *diffuser* state, in year t. This dyadic structure allows variables to represent characteristics of the potential adopter state (state$_i$) and the potential diffuser state (state$_j$), as well as similarities or differences between state$_i$ and state$_j$. But because I test theories of diffusion across more than one hundred different policies, the unit of observation could be more accurately described as the state-policy *triad*. A single observation shows whether or not policy q diffused from state$_j$ to state$_i$ in year t. In year t for policy q, the dyad data contain 2,450 observations (50 times 49).[11] Models of economic policy emulation have an N of 4,001,315 observations; models of social policy emulation contain 3,608,671 observations.

As a first cut at the data, I plot the average likelihood of a policy diffusing from one state to another over time in figure 6.2. Partisan diffusion, in which states emulate policy from states controlled by the same party, occurs more frequently in recent years. For most of the time period, the probability that diffusion occurs between any pair of states is similar regardless of whether they share the same partisanship. But in the mid-2000s, this begins to change as same-party dyads become more likely to emulate each other's policies than cross-party dyads.

This is descriptive evidence that to the extent that states are "laboratories of democracy," they are increasingly members of separate partisan "scientific" communities. However, this descriptive analysis doesn't tell us whether policy success matters for policy emulation within or across parties. In the next section, I detail my plan to systematically assess the role of shared partisanship, policy success, and their interaction in policy diffusion.

Measures

The independent variables are designed to test the predictions of unbiased learning, geographic learning, and partisan learning theories. The first set of independent variables describes the similarity between state$_i$ and state$_j$. The variable *Same Unified Party*$_{ijt}$ is a dummy variable that describes whether the

11. I follow Boehmke (2009) in excluding state-policy triads in which both states already have the policy such that convergence is not possible. In addition, for analyses that include a variable for party control of government, however, Nebraska is excluded due to its nonpartisan legislature. This results in 49 times 48 = 2,352 observations for policy q in year t.

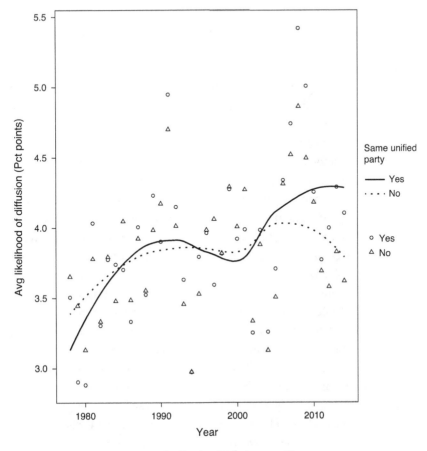

FIGURE 6.2. Partisan Diffusion over Time.

governorship and legislative chambers of the two states in the dyad are both controlled by the same political party in year *t*. Specifically, it takes a value of 1 if state$_i$ and state$_j$ are both controlled by the Democratic Party, 0 if state$_i$ and state$_j$ are both controlled by the Republican Party.[12] I interact information about policy success in state$_j$ with *Same Unified Party*$_{ijt}$ and/or *Proximity*$_{ij}$ in the

___

12. Unified party government is the relevant variable, rather than disaggregated control of the governorship or a legislative chamber. The interaction of divided government and polarization is understood to produce policy gridlock (Binder 2003). Prior research shows minimal effects of these disaggregated variables (e.g., Volden 2006, 300). Finally, for practical reasons, the inclusion of additional three-way interactions for partisan control requires considerably more computational resources and may decrease substantive interpretability.

key hypothesis tests. In the main analyses, all success independent variables are rescaled to have mean 0 and standard deviation of 1 for ease of interpretation.

Economic Success. A set of independent variables tests *economic* learning. I primarily use three measures of economic success: change in *employment*, change in *economic growth*, and state income per capita. These are widely used measures of economic success for practitioners and scholars interested in the relationship between politics and the economy. These measures of economic success show evidence of use in retrospective voting and strongly predict incumbents' likelihood of reelection (e.g., Fiorina 1978; Bartels 2009).[13] Again, these variables are measures of the economic performance of state$_j$. Δ *Unemployment*$_{jqt}$ is the change in the employment rate between state$_j$'s policy implementation of policy$_q$ and time t. The unemployment rate is collected from the Bureau of Labor Statistics (BLS).[14] Note that because unemployment is undesirable, the sign on the coefficient for unemployment should be negative. Δ *GSP*$_{jqt}$ is the change in gross state product (GSP) between j's implementation of policy$_q$ and time t. State GSP data are collected from the Bureau of Economic Analysis (BEA) and adjusted by the BLS's yearly inflation estimate.[15] In contrast to change in unemployment and GSP, I use a measure of per capita income due to the consistent finding in diffusion research that states tend to emulate wealthy "leader" states (e.g., Tolbert, Mossberger, and McNeal 2008; Boushey 2010). State income per capita data are from Jordan and Grossmann 2016.

Electoral Success. Finally, a set of independent variables are designed to test the importance of *electoral* learning. All of these variables are measures of the performance of state$_j$, the potential diffuser state. Following Gilardi 2010, the variable Δ *Incumbent Governor Vote Share*$_{jqt}$ represents the change in vote share for the incumbent governor (or, in the case of open seats, for the incumbent party) between the implementation of policy q and time t. Similarly, Δ *Incumbent Legislator Vote Share*$_{jqt}$ is the average change in vote share for incumbent state legislators and senators (again, for the incumbent party in open seat elections) and is collected from Klarner et al. 2013.

---

13. Employment and growth are virtually universally accepted measures of economic success. In practice, of course, politicians have a variety of visions of what constitutes success. Those with more left-leaning ideology, for instance, are likely to see policies that increase economic inequality as normatively negative, while those with right-leaning ideology may be indifferent to a policy's effect on inequality.

14. https://www.bls.gov/lau/.

15. https://www.bea.gov/data/gdp/gdp-state.

Policy Diffusion. The dependent variable, *policy diffusion$_{ijqt}$*, is coded as 1 if state *i* adopts (or moves closer to) policy *q* of state *j* in a given year, 0 otherwise. For example, diffusion = 1 for the observation representing medical marijuana in year 1999 for the states of Oregon (state$_i$, the potential recipient) and California (state$_j$, the potential diffuser), because in that year Oregon implemented a medical marijuana law that already existed in California. For continuous policies (e.g., tax rates or Medicaid income eligibility) and ordinal policies (e.g., voter ID laws, which can be non-strict or strict), diffusion equals 1 if state$_i$ *moves closer* to the existing state$_j$ policy (see also Volden 2006).[16] The data structure is symmetric such that policy repeals are treated equivalently to policy creation. Just as they are with the implementation of new policies, politicians are concerned with the success or failure that can arise from repealing policy. Policy repeals also have considerable substantive importance. For example, many states repealed the death penalty after the Supreme Court reauthorized its use in 1976.[17]

Dealing with Time. The policy learning theories predict that state *i*'s decision to emulate state *j*'s policy *q* in year *t* is determined by the success of state *j* in the time since it implemented policy *q*. This suggests that state governments do not discount experiences that happened many years earlier. However, studies suggest that politicians behave myopically, or face a myopic electorate (e.g., Bartels 2009). For example, incumbent politicians engage in greater spending in election years. If this is the case, state governments may adopt policies that show recent success. In table A.2, I provide additional analyses in which success variables measure state *j*'s experience between year *t* and *t* − 1.

Estimation Strategy

The principal models for this analysis are logit and multilevel logit regressions. Prior diffusion research has tended to use conventional logit models with standard errors that are clustered by dyad, which allows for non-independence

16. In robustness checks, coding diffusion as a continuous variable for continuous or ordinal policies (based on the percent of the range between existing state policies) does not substantively affect regression results.

17. I draw from Boehmke 2009 in eliminating observations where the probability of emulation is precisely zero, such as when no states have policy *q* on the books. I further implement the correction from Boehmke 2009 of removing observations in which state$_i$ and state$_j$ have the same policy in time *t* − 1 such that there is no potential for emulation.

within dyads. I estimate logit models of this variety, varying whether models include fixed effects for years (to account for temporal heterogeneity in the likelihood of policy diffusion) and specific policies (to account for heterogeneity in the likelihood of the diffusion of different policies, such as Medicaid coverage of abortion or collective bargaining rights for firefighters).[18] With independent variables X for state dyad d, policy q, and year t, γ_j represents policy fixed effects and δ_t year fixed effects:

$$\hat{y}_{dqt} = \alpha + \beta X + \gamma_q + \delta_t + \varepsilon_{dqt}$$

However, the assumption of independence across dyads is unrealistic because the same polity is included in multiple dyads (Gilardi 2010). The New York–New Jersey dyad should not be assumed to be independent from the New York–Connecticut dyad, for instance. I thus estimate a non-nested multilevel model that corresponds to the groupings and interdependencies in the data.[19] Specifically, I model random intercepts at the state$_i$, state$_j$, year$_t$, and policy$_q$ levels (see Gelman and Hill 2007):

$$\hat{y}_{ijqt} \sim N(\beta X + \alpha_i + \alpha_j + \alpha_q + \alpha_t + \varepsilon_{ijqt})$$

The equations for the random intercepts α for state i, state j, policy q, and year t:

$$\alpha_i \sim N(\mu_{\alpha i}, \sigma_i^2)$$
$$\alpha_j \sim N(\mu_{\alpha j}, \sigma_j^2)$$
$$\alpha_q \sim N(\mu_{\alpha q}, \sigma_q^2)$$
$$\alpha_t \sim N(\mu_{\alpha t}, \sigma_t^2)$$

This multilevel model structure uses partial pooling of the data, a balance between cross-sectional and within-unit variation (Gelman and Hill 2007). The time-series cross-sectional (TSCS) specification described above is analogous to that of Shor and colleagues (2007). A model intended purely for prediction rather than theory testing should use a more complex multilevel model structure.

18. Rates of policy change vary greatly across policies. States frequently make changes to policies such as the minimum wage or income tax rate, but change is rare for other policies such as state equal rights amendments (ERAs).

19. The design is crossed, not hierarchical or nested, because each state i co-occurs with each state j and each year t.

TABLE 6.1. Traditional Partisan Models

	Economic Policies		Social Policies	
	1	2	3	4
(Intercept)	−18.573	−18.573	−5.001***	−5.002***
	(33.629)	(33.629)	(0.145)	(0.145)
Same Party Control	0.064***	0.061***	0.050⁺	0.045⁺
	(0.012)	(0.012)	(0.026)	(0.026)
Dist. Leg. Ideology	−0.026***		−0.110***	
	(0.004)		(0.009)	
Dist. House Ideology		−0.021***		−0.083***
		(0.005)		(0.011)
Dist. Senate Ideology		−0.008⁺		−0.036***
		(0.005)		(0.011)
AIC	555582	555582	156336	156342
Deviance	554829	554827	155575	155579
Log-Likelihood	−277721	−277720	−78103	−78105

Note: Multilevel logit coefficients with standard errors in parentheses.

$^{***}p < .001$; $^{+}p < 0.1$

For multilevel models, and, to a greater extent, for traditional models with clustered standard errors, bias can arise when the number of geographic units is too small (Angrist and Pischke 2008; Stegmueller 2013). The bias becomes undetectable when the number of units surpasses approximately 20, especially when the multilevel model includes only random intercepts (Stegmueller 2013), so there is little concern of small sample bias.

Results

The following section presents results for three varieties of models: traditional partisan similarity models, traditional learning models, and models of partisan learning.

Party and Ideology

Table 6.1 shows the results of unbiased partisan models of policy diffusion (Hypothesis 1). The results are straightforward and as expected. The coefficient for *same party control* is positive, relatively large in magnitude, and

TABLE 6.2. Unbiased Learning Models

	Economic Policies			Social Policies		
	1	2	3	4	5	6
(Intercept)	−4.490***	−4.406***	−4.490***	−8.559***	−8.141***	−8.562***
	(0.074)	(0.068)	(0.076)	(0.593)	(0.430)	(0.594)
Δ Incumbent	0.002		0.002	0.011+		0.010
	(0.003)		(0.003)	(0.006)		(0.006)
Δ Incumbent Leg.	0.007*		0.005*	0.024***		0.027***
Vote Share	(0.003)		(0.003)	(0.007)		(0.007)
(State j)						
Δ Unemployment		−0.007*	−0.009*		0.037***	0.036**
(State j)		(0.004)	(0.004)		(0.011)	(0.011)
Δ GSP (State j)		−0.011**	−0.012**		−0.010	−0.017
		(0.003)	(0.004)		(0.011)	(0.013)
Income per		0.079***	0.086***		−0.035	0.046+
Capita		(0.008)	(0.009)		(0.023)	(0.024)
AIC		1088256	1244328	265692	289994	265511
Deviance		1087386	1243420	264825	289101	264628
Log-Likelihood		−544051	−622085	−132779	−144928	−132685

Note: Multilevel logit coefficients with standard errors in parentheses.
*$p < .05$; **$p < .01$; ***$p < .001$; +$p < 0.1$

statistically significant (though only at the $p < 0.1$ level for social policies). The coefficients on *dist. leg. ideology* are large and negative, suggesting that more states with more ideologically proximate legislatures are more likely to emulate each other's policies.

Learning

Table 6.2 tests traditional models of learning (Hypothesis 2). The results provide more modest and inconsistent support than did the partisan analysis presented earlier. Evidence of electoral success, especially for legislators, significantly increases the likelihood of diffusion (see columns 1 and 4). This is true for the 72 economic policies and, to a greater extent, for the 68 social policies in the data.

Evidence of economic success appears much less influential. For economic policies, while decreased *unemployment* increases the likelihood of diffusion for economic policies (as expected), the sign for Δ *GSP* points in the wrong direction. However, states are considerably more likely to adopt economic policies from wealthier states than poorer states. For social policies, Δ *unemployment* has the incorrect sign. On average, the coefficients for the economic success variables are marginally positive.

Overall, the results are mixed for the traditional models of learning.

Partisan Learning

This section describes the results of empirical tests of models of *partisan learning* (Hypothesis 3), in which information about electoral and economic success is hypothesized to have heterogeneous effects depending on the partisanship of the information source. In these models, an indicator for shared partisan control of government is interacted with measures of economic and electoral success. The coefficient for information variables without the party interaction represents the effect of information from *outpartisan* sources on the likelihood of emulation. The effect of information from *copartisan* sources is the sum of this coefficient and the coefficient on the variable interacted with the *same party* variable.

Regardless of informational signals, shared partisan control of government maintains its robust positive association with policy emulation.

Signals of success from *outpartisan* states are inconsistently associated with emulation (the gray point estimates in the figure). Change in incumbent gubernatorial vote share of the potential diffuser state is unrelated to emulation. The other electoral success variable, change in incumbent legislative vote share, however, is positively related, though only modestly.

The economic success variables from outpartisan states yield more inconsistent results. Recall that our theoretical expectations for the effect of economic success are better applied to tests of economic policy emulation than social policy emulation. The sign on the coefficient for the potential diffuser state's change in unemployment rate is as expected for economic policies (negative, indicating decreased unemployment increases the likelihood of emulation). For social policies, the relationship is stronger, but in the wrong direction (positive). This pattern is inverted for change in population: population change has an unexpected negative association with economic policy emulation but a large positive association with social policy emulation. Change in state GSP has a small, unexpectedly negative effect. Finally, as in the earlier learning models, a state's wealth (higher per capita income) is strongly predictive of economic policy emulation. The relationship is negative and significant for social policy emulation, by contrast.

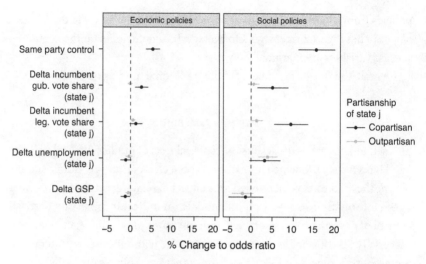

FIGURE 6.3. Partisan Learning.

The relationship between electoral success and emulation is stronger between *copartisan* states (the black point estimates in the figure). As seen in the
coefficients for the interaction variables, the electoral success variables are
strongly and significantly associated with diffusion for both economic and
social policies (though the coefficient for state legislator electoral success is
statistically insignificant).

Unlike electoral success, economic success remains inconsistently related
to emulation for copartisan states. Decreased unemployment is associated
with copartisan emulation of economic policy ($p < 0.1$) and social policy (in-
significantly). However, change in population has an unexpectedly negative
and reasonably strong association with emulation. Change in GSP has no effect. Within-party, state wealth is again a strong predictor of diffusion.

Figure 6.3 plots the marginal effects, expressed in percent change to the
odds ratio, of information signals from copartisan and outpartisan sources.

Ideology Results

Is institutional learning structured by political parties, or is partisanship simply a
proxy for ideology? Because legislative partisanship and ideology are highly correlated, ideology, not parties as organizational networks, could be the reason that
emulation of success tends to occur within-party. Republican-controlled governments, for example, may be willing to emulate successful policies from conservative Democratically controlled governments. Although legislative polarization

TABLE 6.3. Ideology and Learning

	Economic Policies		Social Policies	
	1	2	3	4
(Intercept)	−18.562 (34.514)	−18.576 (33.629)	−5.018*** (0.147)	−4.994*** (0.147)
Δ Incumbent Gub. Vote Share (State j)	0.005 (0.004)		0.006 (0.008)	
Dist. Leg Ideology	−0.033*** (0.004)	−0.030*** (0.005)	−0.114*** (0.009)	−0.101*** (0.012)
Δ Incumbent Leg. Vote Share (State j)	0.005 (0.004)		0.017 (0.009)	
Dist. Leg. Ideology × Δ Gub. Vote Share	0.004 (0.004)		−0.007 (0.007)	
Same Party × Δ Leg. Vote Share	0.003 (0.004)		−0.009 (0.008)	
Δ Unemployment (State j)		−0.015* (0.008)		−0.005 (0.017)
Δ GSP (State j)		−0.036*** (0.010)		−0.071** (0.023)
Income per Capita (State j)		0.018 (0.015)		0.020 (0.036)
Dist. Leg. Ideology × Δ Unemployment		−0.006 (0.004)		0.013 (0.010)
Dist. Leg. Ideology × Δ GSP		−0.005 (0.006)		0.019 (0.015)
Dist. Leg. Ideology × Income per Capita		−0.008 (0.004)		−0.018 (0.010)
AIC	527322	555554	149989	156101
Deviance	526575	554787	149236	155326
Log-Likelihood	−263588	−277700	−74927	−77978

*p < .05; **p < .01; ***p < .001

has increased dramatically in state legislatures in recent years, there still exists a small number of states in which Democratic chamber medians are to the *right* of other states' Republican chamber medians (Shor and McCarty 2011).[20]

In table 6.3, I fit additional models that interact information signals with *legislative ideological similarity* (instead of shared party control), using data

20. The Democratic chamber medians in Arkansas, Alabama, and Indiana are equal or to the right of the Delaware Republican chamber median, for example.

from Shor and McCarty 2011.[21] Separately, legislative ideological proximity predicts emulation, as do signals of electoral and economic success. However, there is little action in the interaction of success and ideological proximity. Whereas the interactions of success and shared party control show large effects in figure 6.3, not a single estimate of the interaction of success and ideological proximity is statistically significant. Success in copartisan states matters more than success in outpartisan states—but success appears to have the same effect regardless of State B's legislative ideology.

This finding lends additional support to the theory of partisan learning. In the polarized era, partisanship and ideological similarity are highly correlated (e.g., McCarty, Poole, and Rosenthal 2006; Lee 2009; Shor and McCarty 2011). But shared partisanship is more than ideology; it is organizational. Partisan organizational networks may shape policy learning.

Conclusion

Theories of states as policy laboratories that are engaged in intergovernmental competition suggest that there are strong incentives to emulate policies associated with efficient, effective, and successful governance. A recent study from Butler and colleagues (2017) provides experimental evidence in support of this view. Federalism, this view suggests, can mitigate the centrifugal forces of mass and elite polarization by incentivizing learning and the emulation of best practices.

This chapter challenges this theoretical tradition. Politicians have incentives to avoid implementing policies that would improve their competitors' party brand. Party and partisan-aligned committees, think tanks, and lobbying organizations provide much of the policy analysis and information that cross the desks of state legislators, governors, and their staffs. This may generate partisan learning networks. If learning primarily occurs within the same political party, it is unlikely to mitigate polarizing pressures facing state governments.

I find that, regardless of the source, economic success is inconsistently related to emulation. Contrary to the predictions of models of intergovernmental experimentation, learning, and competition in federalism, trends in unemployment and economic growth have little to do with policy emulation. This is not especially surprising in light of the divergent policy agendas of Democratic- and Republican-controlled states that I described in chapter 3. Policy divergence in

21. The Shor and McCarty (2011) data begin in 1992.

Minnesota and Wisconsin—states with very similar geographies, demographies, and economies—is unlikely to be explained by traditional Brandeisian models of federalism.

While economic trends have little effect, the results show that states are more likely to emulate the policies of wealthier states. This is consistent with prior studies that focus on "leader states," which have greater resources to engage in experimentation and are thus more likely to be emulated down the road (Walker 1969; Volden 2006). However, I find that the *interaction* of shared party control and wealth matters: states are more likely to emulate the policies of wealthy states when they share party control in both economic and social policies.

Overall, the relative lack of evidence for economic policy learning underscores the basic challenges facing any government hoping to learn from other states' policy experience. Policies interact with each other in complex and multifaceted ways such that the true effect of implementing a policy in a given state might depend on the state's existing policy regime. Still, the potential for such large obstacles to policy learning hasn't dulled support for Brandeis's laboratories of democracy theory.

In contrast to the inconsistent results of signals of economic success, I find that evidence of *electoral* success has a robust relationship to policy emulation—but only when this evidence comes from states controlled by the same party. Remarkably, evidence of electoral success in outpartisan states has virtually no effect on the likelihood of policy emulation. It matters not whether a Democratic governor experienced electoral gains after implementing a popular policy; a Republican state government remains unlikely to pass the policy. It may be the case that governors and state legislators are indifferent to the potential electoral costs of implementing policies that are "out of step" with their constituents. But partisan information networks may also drive this pattern. When governments consider implementing a policy, any prediction of the mass public's reaction comes with great uncertainty. In this context, partisan information networks may lead officeholders to overestimate the popularity of copartisan policies and underestimate the popularity of outpartisan policies.

Additional research should investigate the mechanisms undergirding the partisan learning model. In addition to strong qualitative and theoretical evidence, the finding that success from copartisan governments, but not ideologically proximate governments in general, increases the likelihood of emulation increases our confidence in the partisan organizational network mechanism.

However, this analysis cannot completely rule out an ideological learning mechanism: it could be the case that politicians use party control of government as a heuristic for ideology such that emulation of ideological distant copartisan governments is a cognitive error (e.g., Lau and Redlawsk 2001).

Overall, the predictions of Brandeisian models of unbiased institutional learning under federalism are not borne out in historical data over recent decades. Optimistic interpretations of federalism often emphasize the potential for institutional incentives to cut against partisan and ideological incentives. This optimism is deeply embedded in traditional understandings of American political institutions. But scholars of federalism should be attentive to this interpretation's limited empirical support in observational data.

It's concerning that the state policy data don't show much support for this prominent theory of the benefits of federalism. But the fact that one of federalism's virtues might not be real isn't as concerning as what I show in the next two chapters: that federalism leaves the United States vulnerable to democratic backsliding.

PART III

Democracy in the States

7

Laboratories of Democratic Backsliding

THE TRUMP PRESIDENCY has generated new concerns about authoritarianism and democratic backsliding in the United States (Gessen 2016).[1] This concern comes in many flavors. Prominent think-tank moderates and Never-Trump conservatives express dismay at the erosion of parliamentary norms. Liberal Americans worry about the Trump coalition's apparent comfort with undemocratic and violent rhetoric toward its political opponents. Human rights activists point to increasingly authoritarian immigration policy. Nearly all of this concern has been directed at one level of government: national.

The crisis of democracy has also sparked new concerns among scholars. Recent research has focused on conceptualizing and measuring the health of American democracy (Dionne, Ornstein, and Mann 2017; Lieberman et al. 2019). Scholars of American politics, most of whom had considered American institutions to be so robust that the potential for backsliding was unnecessary to study, increasingly turned to comparative and historical scholars for insight. Prominent cross-national measures of democracy from the Varieties of Democracy Project (V-Dem), Bright Line Watch, and Freedom House now operate somewhat like the Doomsday Clock of the Cold War era.

Yet there has been no such systematic inquiry into *subnational* dynamics in American democracy. This lack of attention is curious in light of American federalism, an institutional system that gives state governments the authority to administer elections and other democratic processes. To the extent that thinkers have systematically addressed the role of federalism in this precarious

---

1. See also, for example, the September 2018 special issue of the *Atlantic* titled "Is Democracy Dying?"

period, it usually involves a reassertion of classic, optimistic theories about its importance in safeguarding institutions. Members of the conservative establishment argue that federalism mitigates the political frustrations of intense and polarized masses, allowing them a safety valve of local policy change while they are out of power at the national level (Levin 2017). Proponents of "progressive federalism" similarly suggest that federalism allows racial minorities to hold power in areas where they comprise majorities (Gerken 2012). Still others remind us that state governments, with their own authority clearly written into the U.S. Constitution, provide a check against a presidential power grab of all levers of authority in the American political system.

In many important ways indeed, governors, state legislators, and state judicial branches have challenged the actions of the Trump administration in areas such as climate and immigration. But faith in state governments betrays a tradition well known to scholars of race and ethnicity: state and local governments directly and indirectly enforced racial hierarchy for most of U.S. history (DuBois 1935; Foner 1988). In a broader sense, the United States was not a democracy until the national government enforced authority against state governments through the Voting Rights Act of 1965 (Mickey 2015; King 2017). More recent challenges to American democracy, such as the rise of mass incarceration and the carceral state (Soss and Weaver 2017), are also concentrated at the state level (Miller 2008). And in an uncanny pattern, recent threats of norm violations in the federal government are preceded by state governments having already violated the norm—whether it is court packing in Georgia in 2016 and Arizona in 2019,[2] the "lame-duck coups" in North Carolina and Wisconsin in 2016 and 2018,[3] or attacks on labor rights in midwestern states in the 2010s.

In this chapter, I argue that state governments have been leaders in democratic backsliding in the United States in recent years.[4] Although the national

2. Mark Joseph Stern, "Arizona's Governor Is Leading Republicans' Quiet, Radical Takeover of State Supreme Courts," *Slate*, August 29, 2019, https://slate.com/news-and-politics/2019/08/arizona-supreme-court-rigging-doug-ducey-bill-montgomery.html; Kristina Torres, "Expansion of Georgia's Supreme Court Wins Final Approval," *Atlanta Journal-Constitution*, March 22, 2016, https://www.ajc.com/news/state--regional-govt--politics/expansion-georgia-supreme-court-wins-final-approval/skmjVHCCo80HW4hXZKL6rM/.

3. Tara Golshan, "North Carolina Republicans' Shocking Power Grab, Explained," *Vox*, December 16, 2016, https://www.vox.com/policy-and-politics/2016/12/16/13971368/republican-power-grab-north-carolina-explained.

4. Rather than a sharp break in regime type, this investigation asks about more granular changes to American democracy that in some ways parallels comparative analysis of "hybrid"

level may show troubling signs of diminishing democracy, state governments are *the* primary actors who administer democratic backsliding in practice and on the ground. State governments work directly and indirectly with national coalitions to use state institutions—easier to capture than national institutions—to their mutual benefit. Troubling stories abound in recent years of voter suppression, of gerrymandering, of state legislatures taking power from incoming outparty governors, of the use of state police powers to limit dissent. But there has been little effort to systematically trace the dynamics of democratic performance in the states in the contemporary period.[5]

How has democracy in the states expanded and contracted in recent years? I draw upon recent advancements in ideal point modeling to create a measure of democratic health in the fifty states from 2000 to 2018: the State Democracy Index. The measure is based on 61 indicators of democratic performance, such as states' voter registration policies, average wait times for voting,[6] and the extent of partisan gerrymandering in states' legislative districts. While this measure cannot directly tell us what democratic performance would look like in a counterfactual United States with a unitary instead of federalist system, it illuminates important dynamics in American democracy across time and space.

The time-series estimates of state democratic performance show important trends. On average, state-level democracy is mostly stable since 2000—better than one might expect. Such aggregate stability, however, obscures major changes in democratic performance within states. While democracy is static or gradually expanding in many places, in some states, such as North Carolina, I find precipitous drops in democratic performance after 2010. The State Democracy Index, publicly available at jakegrumbach.com, will be of use to scholars and journalists interested in monitoring the front lines in the ongoing battle over American democracy.

Just as slavery and Jim Crow in the U.S. South affected the politics and society of the North, democratic backsliding in states like North Carolina and

---

regimes that combine elements of democracy with those of authoritarianism and oligarchy (e.g., Levitsky and Way 2010).

5. Hasen (2020) provides analysis of the causes of distrust in U.S. elections, voter suppression and "incompetence" in electoral administration, both of which are state-level phenomena. Widespread distrust in the fairness of election outcomes, Hasen argues, could result in an "election meltdown" and constitutional crisis.

6. For more on voting wait times, see the work of Chen et al. (forthcoming), who, using smartphone data, find that Black Americans face significantly longer wait times to vote than white Americans.

Wisconsin affects other states and, more importantly, democracy in the United States as a whole. State authorities administer elections; they are the primary enforcers of laws; they determine in large part who can participate in American politics, and how. The policy and judicial landscapes have grown increasingly favorable for policy variation across states in recent years. As a consequence, states may be increasingly important to trends in democracy across all institutions within American federalism. Political scholars, observers, and participants should pay close attention to dynamics in state democracy.

Federalism as Democracy-Expanding
The Benefits of Decentralization

In recent years, conservative pundits and thinkers have routinely invoked federalism as the solution to troubles in American democracy (e.g., Buckley 2014; Levin 2017). David Brooks is characteristic of this trend, arguing in 2018 that whereas "federal power is impersonal, abstract and rule-oriented, local power is personalistic, relational, affectionate, irregular and based on a shared history of reciprocity and trust."[7]

Mainstream political scientists and legal scholars have often argued the same (Hills 1998; Roe 2003; March and Olsen 2010). Political theorist Samuel Beer (1978) prominently argued that the Founders' *main purpose* in federalism was to create institutions that "closely and actively joined voter and representative" (10). Jenna Bednar (2005, 193) considers "effective representation" to be one of the main objectives of choosing a federalist institutional structure.

Political economists joined in with formal theories of politics as a "marketplace," in which the threat of exit—"voting with your feet"—produces more responsive and effective governance (Tiebout 1956; Oates 1972; Sinn 1992). Although some of these political economists expressed skepticism toward majoritarianism and democracy itself, the theory of the political marketplace, combined with Louis Brandeis's laboratories of democracy discussed earlier in this book, suggested that authority for the states should lead to an improved relationship between citizens and policymakers. Empirical scholars of comparative politics have also suggested that federalism eases the transition into democracy (Stepan 1999; Gibson 2004).

7. David Brooks, "The Localist Revolution," *New York Times,* July 20, 2018, https://www.nytimes.com/2018/07/19/opinion/national-politics-localism-populism.html.

Whereas many scholars of race, as well as William Riker, argue forcefully that federalism has empowered racist coalitions, some mainstream political scientists suggested on the contrary that federalism was a boon for civil rights (Beer 1978, 16–17). The writing of Carl Lawrence Paulus (2019) encapsulates this argument: "Without federalism—or as it is often labeled, states' rights," he argues, "political abolitionism would never have gotten the oxygen needed to light a fire for freedom nationally." This emphasis on federalism's ability to provide national minorities and civil rights proponents one or more states to serve as a springboard is also an important component of a more liberal version of this theoretical tradition: *progressive federalism*.

Progressive Federalism

"Decentralization can produce a healthier democracy in the long term," writes Heather Gerken (2012). Distinct from rational choice and economic theories of federalism, Gerken describes a *progressive federalism* with two major benefits. First, decentralization enables racial, ethnic, and religious minority groups to "rule" in places where they are in the majority. Such a situation, supporters argue, facilitates the "politics of recognition," in which different identities and cultures are respected in a multicultural polity. Second, federalism's decentralization facilitates, protects, and legitimates dissent by providing constitutional authority to subregions of the country, some of which are likely at any given time to dissent against the direction of national policy.

One area of success for progressive federalism, scholars argue, is in the politics of immigration and citizenship. In their book *Citizenship Reimagined*, Allan Colbern and Karthick Ramakrishnan (2020, 4) document the emergence of "progressive state citizenship," in which "states provide rights and protections that exceed those at the national level." While the national government formally determines questions of legal citizenship, immigration policies in states like California have meaningfully affected the legal, economic, and civic inclusion of immigrants. The authors make clear that strong federal enforcement of equal protection under law via the Fourteenth Amendment is critical to avoiding "regressive federalism" but argue that the "current trend in progressive federalism . . . runs counter to the historical narrative of federalism as one that empowers states and localities to block national progress and entrench regressive racial orders" (Colbern and Ramakrishnan 2020, 11).

In the age of Trump, such a theory is alluring. Timothy Egan (2019), writing for the *New York Times*, exclaims that "California, Oregon and Washington are winning the fight against Trump's hateful policies." This is the system working. Federalism is a safety valve that Democrats and liberals, as well as marginalized identity groups, can use while out of national power. Furthermore, if these blue state policy experiments are effective and popular in practice, they serve as examples for voters and officeholders of other states—laboratories of democracy in action.

Proponents of progressive federalism discuss *spillovers*, in which the effects of state policy reverberate outside of its borders (Gerken and Revesz 2012). Although such scholars are well aware of cases of problematic spillovers, such as people who cross state lines to buy easy-to-access guns, they argue that, on balance, these spillovers have been effective at solving social problems. California's large share of the automobile market, for instance, meant that the state's emission standards affected car production across the country.[8]

Overall, progressive federalism shares much with traditional theories of decentralization. However, progressive federalists note that the benefits of federalism may require a more robust national government than would be optimal under the traditional theories. As Gerken (2012) writes:

> The federalism that haunts our history looks quite different from the form of local power that prevails now. Federalism of old involved states' rights, a trump card to protect instances of local oppression. Today's federalism involves a muscular national government that makes policy in virtually every area that was once relegated to state and local governments. The states' rights trump card has all but disappeared, which means that the national government can protect racial minorities and dissenters when it needs to while allowing local forms of power to flourish.

But is the United States truly past "the federalism that haunts our history"? In the next section, I turn to more troubling theories of the role of federalism in democracy.

Federalism as Democracy-Contracting

As Corey Robin (2020) has argued, a silver lining of the 2016 and 2020 presidential elections is that they pushed scholars from the question of "What's the matter with the voters?" to "What's the matter with the institutions?" Indirectly,

---

8. Spillovers, the progressive federalism story goes, also generate new opportunities for bipartisan compromise. Spillovers "force the issue," no longer allowing state politics and policy to exist in isolation. But a unitary system might simply "force the issue" earlier.

this trend has increased scholars' concern about federalism—especially its countermajoritarian functions. But not much of the concern is about federalism directly. Federalism is historically related to, but distinct from, other undemocratic elements of U.S. constitutional design, such as the Electoral College and malapportionment in the U.S. Congress. The Electoral College empowers state legislatures, not voters, to appoint electors, which, if their state government allows, can use the state's Electoral College votes as they wish, potentially ignoring presidential election voters entirely (an institutional feature that became especially concerning in 2020).[9] Also historically related to federalism, the Constitution's two-Senate-seats-per-state design has led to severely unequal say in Congress based on voter geography (Dahl 2003; McAuliffe 2019). It is quite possible that malapportionment in Congress, stemming from a combination of geography and the Three Fifths Clause, delayed the end of slavery in the United States, as the North had more voters but fewer seats until the Republican victories of 1860.[10]

Federalism is also the direct and indirect source of veto points in the American constitutional structure. This may hold back democracy by increasing the number of veto players in the political system, causing more frequent policy stasis and status quo bias. In the words of Edward Gibson and Desmond King (2016, 24), "Fights about federalism are inseparable from fights about democracy in U.S. political history because federalism impedes reform." Rules that make it more difficult for any actor to change laws are asymmetrically problematic for people who are suffering under the status quo.

But here I focus more centrally on federalism's endowment of authority to state governments and how this state-level authority is used to expand or contract democracy in the United States. As I argued earlier, federalism may advantage groups for which money is the primary political resource. Business and the wealthy can more credibly threaten to reduce investment in a state, and they can more effectively influence the politics of states in which they do not live. In this chapter, I focus not on the social and economic policy outcomes that various groups seek, such as taxes or environmental regulation, but rather on the laws and socioeconomic conditions that are conducive to democracy itself.

9. Federalism looms large in legal and theoretical defenses of the Electoral College, as seen, for instance, in legal scholar Robert Hardaway's 1994 book *The Electoral College and the Constitution: The Case for Preserving Federalism.*

10. Judicial perspectives based in federalism may have also contributed to jurisprudence that further entrenched slavery (Maltz 1992).

If states are easier targets for concentrated interests in American society—those groups who stand to benefit most from a weaker American democracy—then it matters greatly that states have authority over areas of law that are critical to democracy. As we saw in chapter 3, state governments have grown in policymaking importance across a wide range of policy areas since the 1970s; policy differences between states are greater than they were a generation ago. But among the most profound policy decisions in the states are those that shape what democracy, itself, looks like in practice. States administer elections, deciding who is eligible and able to vote. And they control the vast majority of policing and the carceral state (Miller 2008), deciding who is free and who is a ward of the state. As Steven Levitsky and Daniel Ziblatt (2018, 2) write in *How Democracies Die*, "American states, which were once praised by the great jurist Louis Brandeis as 'laboratories of democracy,' are in danger of becoming laboratories of authoritarianism as those in power rewrite electoral rules, redraw constituencies, and even rescind voting rights to ensure that they do not lose."

Thus, in the system of American federalism, even when *national* actors are interested in narrowing democracy, they describe strategies involving *state-level* authorities. In 2019, for instance, the Associated Press obtained a recording of an advisor to President Trump outlining a strategy for Wisconsin Republicans in state government to suppress Democratic votes, describing that "it's always been Republicans suppressing votes in places. . . . Let's start protecting our voters. We know where they are. . . . Let's start playing offense a little bit" (quoted in Bauer 2019). The inverse occurs as well. In 2020, Kansas Senate president Susan Wagle implored Republican donors to contribute to state legislative candidates so they could maintain a veto-proof majority that would gerrymander Democrat Sharice Davids out of her federal U.S. House seat.[11] Investigative journalists have chronicled a plethora of similar statements from officials, as well as qualitative evidence of voter suppression on the ground. Studies have begun to look at the electoral effects of democratically important state-level variables, such as gerrymandering (Stephanopoulos and Warshaw 2020) and voter ID laws (Grimmer and Yoder 2019).

Black Americans have historically looked to the federal government for relief from state-level authoritarianism and exclusion. Activists called on federal authorities to take action against states—first to abolish slavery (Fields 1990; Foner 1995) and later to dismantle state and local systems of lynch law (Wells-Barnett 1892), segregation, disenfranchisement, and exclusion during

---

11. Smith, "Kansas Senate President Pushes Redistricting Plan."

the Jim Crow period (Johnson 2010; Mickey 2015). Riker (1964, 155) offers a critical view of federalism in this respect, arguing that "if one disapproves of racism, one should disapprove of federalism. . . . All that federalism ever did was to facilitate the expression of racist beliefs and the perpetuation of racist acts." Gibson and King (2016) argue that the "Second Reconstruction" of the civil rights period was more successful than nineteenth-century Reconstruction primarily because the former occurred in the context of a balance in federalism that had shifted from the state to the national level.

The empirical analysis in this book does not tell us directly whether a unitary rather than federalist United States would produce a healthier democratic republic. The United States is but one case, and it has had federalism (albeit in changing forms) since its founding. What this analysis can speak to, however, are the profoundly important state-level changes in democratic performance in recent years—and their causes.

Measuring Democracy

Conceptualizing Democracy

Democracy is a broad concept, so a helpful way to get conceptual traction is to break its definition into component parts.[12] Mainstream scholars of American politics have tended to conceptualize democracy through the lenses of *elections* and public opinion most prominently. This is the case among quantitative American politics and political economy scholars (e.g., Downs 1957; Lax and Phillips 2012; Gilens and Page 2014; Achen and Bartels 2016), but earlier qualitative Americanists also put their main focus on elections and how they translate into legislative seats (e.g., Dahl 2003).[13]

In this Americanist tradition, electoral policies and outcomes help serve as indicators for how democracy is performing. Some of these are policies and

---

12. Conceptualizing subcomponents of democracy, such as "electoral democracy" or "liberal democracy," is distinct from the conceptualization of "diminished subtypes" of democracy in some comparative research (Collier and Levitsky 1997, 439). Electoral democracy as a diminished subtype implies that a polity has free, fair, and legitimate elections but lacks other necessary components to make it a "full" democracy, such as civil liberties, much like the diminished subtype concept of "male democracy" contrasts with polities that extend democratic citizenship to both men and women. Thus, the conceptualization of electoral democracy as a subcomponent means it takes us "up" the ladder of generality (Sartori 1970), applying to more cases, whereas its conceptualization as a diminished subtype takes us "down" the ladder of generality.

13. A focus on leaders in "competition for votes" is also central to Schumpeter 1942.

procedures that set the rules of the game. Election laws can make it easy and simple, or difficult and costly, for members of the polity to exercise their most important form of political participation, their vote. Districts can be gerrymandered, compacting and diluting votes in ways to make their influence over who serves in office highly unequal.[14] Other indicators of democratic performance are not rules about democratic inputs but rather measures of democratic outputs. Prominently, a bevy of studies has investigated the correspondence between the policy and ideological attitudes of constituents on the one hand and politician behavior and policy outcomes on the other (e.g., Erikson, Wright, and McIver 1993; Gilens 2012; Lax and Phillips 2012; Caughey and Warshaw 2018).

However, other intellectual traditions have relied on broader conceptualizations of democracy. Comparativists, with the help of their cross-national focus, have studied the causes and consequences of democratic transitions across time and space. With a wider geographic and temporal focus, comparativists have put in considerable effort to conceptualize—and measure—democracy and democratic performance. Most prominently, the V-Dem group has conceptualized five different components of democracy: elections, liberalism, participation, deliberation, and egalitarianism. I draw on this conceptual mapping heavily. (As you will see later in the "Measuring Democracy" section, I draw upon their measurement strategy as well.) Such a conceptualization of democracy draws especially on historical institutionalism and democratic theory. Major works from democratic theorists such as Robert Dahl (2008) and Ian Shapiro (2009) reviewed changing understandings of democracy throughout history, such as the deliberative principles of Jürgen Habermas (1992) and John Rawls.

Democracy requires rights, which limit what electoral and legislative majorities can do (Estlund 2009; Brettschneider 2010). This is the *liberalism* component. The most important rights in the liberalism tradition are usually negative rights, that is, freedom from state encroachment in rights to speech, association, belief, and other areas. The democratic component of liberalism is especially concerned that a "tyranny of the majority" would violate the rights of

14. The Mississippi Constitution, for instance, requires that the governor win not only the majority of the statewide popular vote but also a plurality of votes in a majority of the state's legislative districts; if a gubernatorial candidate does not meet these thresholds, the Mississippi State House selects the winner. The purpose of this institutional feature was clear in the 1890 convention that ratified the constitution. Mississippi's constitutional "founding father" James K. Vardaman, who went on to serve as governor and then U.S. senator, proclaimed that "Mississippi's constitutional convention of 1890 was held for no other purpose than to eliminate the n***** from politics."

minorities. Shapiro (2009) suggested that "nondenomination," itself closely related to liberalism, be a key tenet of democracy.[15] Feminist theories of liberal democracy suggest that reproductive rights are necessary for women to be equal democratic citizens (Phillips 1991; Craske, Molyneux, and Afshar 2002).

There have been important critiques of liberalism, however, that it has in practice depended on national prosperity derived from imperialism, racial exploitation, and the exclusion of nonwhite peoples (Mills 2017). To varying degrees, scholars in the liberal tradition have addressed such critiques by emphasizing *equality* of those rights under law—and the realization of rights in practice. Rogers Smith (1993) emphasized that the disconnect between the liberal understandings of American democracy and historical race and gender hierarchies necessitates the tracing of "multiple traditions" in American civic identity. Desmond King (2009) extended this idea, suggesting that dynamics in American democracy could be illuminated by looking at immigration policy and which people it determined to be full members of the polity.

These debates over liberalism help to conceptualize the *egalitarianism* component of democracy. To what extent is egalitarianism integral to democracy, and what kinds of equality are most important? Some, such as the scholars just mentioned, tend to be focused on the realization of equal de jure rights. But democracy may depend on both procedural rules and substantive outcomes (Brettschneider 2010). Scholars of social democracy, including many comparative politics scholars, include positive social and economic rights as central to democracy. V-Dem, for instance, considers the equal distribution of resources, "both tangible and intangible," to be an element of egalitarianism and important for democracy.[16] The egalitarian focus is further related to organizational and relational conceptualizations of democracy (Han 2016, 2017). Voluntarism in civil society organizations has been central to understandings of democracy, and especially American democracy, since at least de Tocqueville. As Theda Skocpol, Marshall Ganz, and Ziad Munson (2000, 527) describe, "associations have provided paths into active citizenship, allowing Americans to build community, pursue shared goals, and influence social and political affairs."

15. More conservative theorists have also suggested that protecting the owners of capital is also an important minority consideration (North 1981; Weingast 2016).

16. A wrinkle, however, is the potential for the rise of the bourgeoisie to be a mechanism toward democratization. It may be that incumbent elites expand democracy to provide concessions not to the poor but to the rising "new money" upper class—whose emergence is associated with higher, not lower, economic inequality (Ansell and Samuels 2014). My focus in this book, however, is on a mature democracy, the United States, with levels of income and wealth inequality larger than those of virtually any society in history (Hacker and Pierson 2010; Piketty 2014).

But perhaps most importantly, the centrality of chattel slavery and racial hierarchy to the history of the United States has led American scholars across a variety of disciplines to focus explicitly on the rights and equities of African Americans as key markers of democratic performance (Foner 1988; Shelby 2005). Such analysis has broadly investigated racial democracy in terms of the right to vote (e.g., Kousser 1974), civil liberties (e.g., Francis 2014), and the distribution of social and economic capital (e.g., DuBois 1935; Glaude 2017). Further research has linked institutional racism and authoritarianism, in both the Jim Crow era of pervasive lynching (Mickey 2015) and the post–civil rights era (Parker and Towler 2019). The continuing political significance of race prompts me to consider *racial equity* a central component of democracy, especially in the American context. In the state democracy measures I create, I include some direct indicators of racial inequality as determinants of state-level democratic performance, though many race-neutral democracy indicators reflect a racialized politics (e.g., gerrymandered district lines).

The multitiered federalist institutional structure of the United States presents an additional conceptual challenge to investigating the democratic performance of states. This idea is related but not identical to what Gibson (2005, 103) has described as the potential for "an authoritarian province in a nationally democratic country" (see also Gibson 2013). Not only are states not separate, atomized polities from each other horizontally; they are embedded in complex relationships with the federal government vertically in a structure resembling more of a "marble cake" than the "layer cake" of classical dual federalism (Weissert 2011). The particular way the cake is marbled is also in flux, changing dynamically based on the preferences of coalitions (Riker 1964, 1975). More specific to this chapter's inquiry into democracy, state governments may act in ways that expand or contract democracy, but only dependent on federal activity. For example, the Supreme Court in *Shelby County v. Holder* (2013) struck down key provisions of the Voting Rights Act, allowing states to implement changes to electoral procedures in ways that threaten the freeness and fairness of elections.[17]

The richest dive into the democratic performance of states in recent years has been that of Michener (2018), who points to individuals' interactions and experiences with state government as central to democratic performance. This book takes a related but distinct route in empirically investigating democracy

---

17. Quantitative studies buttress historical research showing that the Voting Rights Act had profound effects on legislative responsiveness to Black voters (Schuit and Rogowski 2017) and on racial inequality in labor market outcomes (Aneja and Avenancio-León 2019).

in the states, addressing de jure laws (e.g., election law), implementation (e.g., gerrymandering), and observed democratic outcomes (e.g., the correspondence between opinion and policy) over time. The next section discusses in further detail how I operationalize democracy.

Operationalizing Democracy

As the preceding section implies, there is no easy or consensus strategy to operationalize democracy in a quantitative study. I thus created two distinct measures of democratic performance in the states, each of which speaks to a different intellectual tradition of studying American democracy. The first measure, the State Democracy Index, characterizes the health of democracy in the states more narrowly based on the freeness and fairness of their elections and the strength of their civil liberties. A second measure, which I use in the appendix, combines the electoral indicators from the State Democracy Index with a large number of additional indicators that make up other democratic components (e.g., liberalism, egalitarianism, racial equity, and representation).

Importantly, democratic performance is conceptually distinct from "policy liberalism" (Caughey and Warshaw 2016), "size of government" (Garand 1988), and other concepts that capture the left-right orientation of policy outcomes across political systems. One might worry that ideological and partisan considerations influence the definition of democracy, which would lead to a tautological study of the causes of democratic changes. However, the main measure in this and the next chapter, with a focus on electoral and liberal democracy, is narrowly defined around indicators related to the cost of voting, fairness of districting, and basic civil liberties that are considerably more minimal than the definitions often found in comparative democracy research (e.g., V-Dem 2014). Furthermore, defining democracy as to ensure the definition is bipartisan puts democracy research at greater risk of tautology and the "argument from middle ground" fallacy or, in contemporary parlance, "bothsiderism."

Democracy Indicators

These *democracy indicators* are individual variables that we aggregate into the State Democracy Index measure. Forty-seven of these variables are indicators related to electoral democracy, such as felon disenfranchisement and measures of gerrymandering. Felon disenfranchisement and prisoner voting policies were collected from the National Conference of State Legislatures (NCSL). Data on same-day voter registration, early voting, voter ID laws, youth preregistration, no-fault absentee voting, and automatic voter registration are from Grumbach and Hill (forthcoming).[18]

Additional electoral variables, especially indicators of state administrative performance in elections, are from the MIT Election Lab.[19] Gerrymandering data, which feature prominently in the democracy indices, are provided by Stephanopoulos and Warshaw 2020, with an additional district compactness variable from Kaufman, King, and Komisarchik 2021.[20] We also use indicators of policy responsiveness to public opinion (separated into social and economic policy domains) based on the state policy and mass public liberalism measures from Caughey and Warshaw 2018.[21] Importantly, some of these indicators capture de jure electoral policies and procedures, such as voter registration laws, while others measure democratic *outcomes* like policy responsiveness to public opinion and voting wait times.

Indicators covering liberal democracy and freedom from authoritarian control come from additional sources. Indicators related to criminal justice are from the Correlates of State Policy Database (Jordan and Grossmann 2016), as well as the Bureau of Justice Statistics and Institute for Justice. We also include state asset forfeiture ratings by the Institute for Justice "Policing for Profit" data set.[22] We list all 61 indicators and their sources in table 7.1.

18. There has been recent debate about the importance of voter suppression laws in the United States. In particular, there is evidence that voter ID laws might have limited effects on turnout (Cantoni and Pons 2021). High-performing electoral democracies, such as in northern Europe, also require government-issued identification to vote. However, these countries tend to have universal national (often compulsory) identification policies and provide significant exceptions to the ID rule. Voter ID laws' limited effect on turnout might also have been due to counteractive mobilization efforts by organizations (Cantoni and Pons 2021). Additional evidence from Texas suggests that many thousands of voters, disproportionately Black and Latino, would have been disenfranchised if not for a hardship exception in the state's law—a provision that strict ID states do not have (Fraga and Miller, forthcoming). But overall, the criterion for voter ID or any other law to be considered "voter suppression" is whether it increases the individual cost of voting overall or for a subgroup of Americans, not whether its average treatment effect estimate is near-zero (Zhang, forthcoming).

19. Available at electionlab.mit.edu/data.

20. Indicators of gerrymandering that measure one of the two parties' advantage (e.g., efficiency gap) are transformed into their absolute values to measure the extent of partisan advantage in either direction.

21. Specifically, we use the squared residuals from a bivariate regression of state policy liberalism on state opinion liberalism, which capture how "out of step" a state's policy is with its residents' policy attitudes.

22. Available at https://ij.org/report/policing-for-profit-3/policing-for-profit-data/.

TABLE 7.1. Democracy Indicators

Indicator	Source
Asset forfeiture grade	Institute for Justice
Automatic voter registration	Grumbach and Hill, forthcoming
Black incarceration rate	Bureau of Justice Statistics
Criminalization of forms of protest	International Center for Not-for-Profit Law
Determinate sentencing	Grumbach 2018
District compactness	Kaufman, King, and Komisarchik 2019
DNA exoneration	Correlates of State Policy
Early voting	Correlates of State Policy
Election data completeness	MIT Election Lab
Felony disenfranchisement	Correlates of State Policy
Gerrymandering: declination (Cong.)	Stephanopolous and Warshaw 2020
Gerrymandering: declination (Cong.-Pres.)	Stephanopolous and Warshaw 2020
Gerrymandering: declination (state leg.)	Stephanopolous and Warshaw 2020
Gerrymandering: declination (state leg.-pres.)	Stephanopolous and Warshaw 2020
Gerrymandering: efficiency gap (Cong.)	Stephanopolous and Warshaw 2020
Gerrymandering: efficiency gap (Cong.-Pres)	Stephanopolous and Warshaw 2020
Gerrymandering: efficiency gap (state leg.)	Stephanopolous and Warshaw 2020
Gerrymandering: efficiency gap (state leg.-pres.)	Stephanopolous and Warshaw 2020
Gerrymandering: mean-median difference (Cong.)	Stephanopolous and Warshaw 2020
Gerrymandering: mean-median difference (Cong.-Pres.)	Stephanopolous and Warshaw 2020
Gerrymandering: mean-median difference (state leg.)	Stephanopolous and Warshaw 2020
Gerrymandering: mean-median difference (state leg.-pres.)	Stephanopolous and Warshaw 2020
Gerrymandering: partisan symmetry (Cong.)	Stephanopolous and Warshaw 2020
Gerrymandering: partisan symmetry (Cong.-Pres.)	Stephanopolous and Warshaw 2020
Gerrymandering: partisan symmetry (state leg.)	Stephanopolous and Warshaw 2020
Gerrymandering: partisan symmetry (state leg.-pres.)	Stephanopolous and Warshaw 2020
Incarceration rate	Bureau of Justice Statistics
Military and overseas ballots not returned	MIT Election Lab
Military and overseas ballots rejected	MIT Election Lab
No-fault absentee voting	Correlates of State Policy
Number of felons ineligible to vote as percent of state population	Correlates of State Policy
Online registration	MIT Election Lab
Opinion-policy difference (economic)	Caughey and Warshaw 2018
Opinion-policy difference (social)	Caughey and Warshaw 2018
Percent of eligible voters who register	MIT Election Lab
Postelection audit required	MIT Election Lab

(*continued*)

TABLE 7.1. (*continued*)

Indicator	Source
Protections against compelling reporters to disclose sources	Correlates of State Policy
Provisional ballots cast	MIT Election Lab
Provisional ballots rejected	MIT Election Lab
Registration or absentee ballot problems (off-year)	MIT Election Lab
Registration or absentee ballot problems (on-year)	MIT Election Lab
Registrations rejected	MIT Election Lab
Repealed death penalty	Correlates of State Policy
Restrictions on voter reg. drives	Brennan Center
Same-day registration	Grumbach and Hill, forthcoming
State allows currently incarcerated to vote	National Conference of State Legislatures
Three strikes	Grumbach 2018
Truth in sentencing	Grumbach 2018
Turnout of voting-eligible population	MIT Election Lab
Under- and over-votes cast in an election	MIT Election Lab
Voter ID (any)	Grumbach and Hill, forthcoming
Voter ID (strict)	Grumbach and Hill, forthcoming
Voters deterred because of disability or illness (off-year)	MIT Election Lab
Voters deterred because of disability or illness (on-year)	MIT Election Lab
Voting wait times	MIT Election Lab
Website for absentee status	MIT Election Lab
Website for precinct ballot	MIT Election Lab
Website for provisional ballot check	MIT Election Lab
Website for registration status	MIT Election Lab
Website with polling place	MIT Election Lab
Youth preregistration	National Conference of State Legislatures

The State Democracy Index covers the years 2000 through 2018. On the one hand, the shortness of this time period is a limitation. However, there are serious challenges to creating a measure of state democracy that covers both the contemporary period and earlier eras, such as the Jim Crow period, which featured overwhelmingly greater variation in democratic performance across states.[23] By limiting the State Democracy Index to the past two decades, we

23. This challenge is similar to estimating the median legislators' ideal point in the pre—and post–civil rights eras. Post-1960s legislative contestation was over a much smaller range of the ideological space when it comes to civil rights (Caughey and Schickler 2016).

capture an era of important contestation over American democracy while avoiding bridging between time periods for which there is very different data availability and, more importantly, potentially incomparable terms of civil and human rights.

Measurement Models

For our main State Democracy Index measure, we model democracy as a latent variable (Treier and Jackman 2008). This latent variable analysis lets observed relationships between the democracy indicators determine how each indicator should affect states' democracy scores. This strategy uses a model to create an "ideal point" on a latent dimension for each state-year that best predicts the real observed democracy indicators data. In particular, I use Bayesian factor analysis for mixed data because the democracy indicators may be binary (e.g., same-day voter registration), ordinal (e.g., disenfranchisement of all, some, or no felons), or continuous (e.g., legislative district efficiency gap) (Quinn 2004). The model is based on the equation below. In particular, the distribution of democratic performance for state s in year t, y_{st}, is a function of the state's latent democratic performance for that year, θ_{st}, as well as the democracy indicator's discrimination parameter β_j and difficulty parameter α_{jt}.[24] Subscript j denotes different indicators, which are analogous to test questions in the IRT framework. In this equation, N_j is a normal distribution with j dimensions (as there are j democracy indicators). Ψ is a $J \times J$ variance-covariance matrix:

$$y_{st} \sim N_j(\beta_j \theta_{st} - \alpha_j, \Psi)$$

The main benefit of this factor analysis is that the measure requires little in the way of assumptions from me about how any particular indicator should affect democracy scores.[25] However, this comes at the cost of some loss of control; in certain circumstances, the estimated parameters for democracy indicators can be "wrong" in theoretical and substantive terms. Whether or

24. In order to maintain a constant substantive interpretation of how "democratic" a given indicator is across time, I model time-invariant difficulty parameters in contrast to the policy liberalism measure of Caughey and Warshaw (2016).

25. Bayesian latent dimension models like this one require the modeler to constrain the parameter space. I do this by assigning a random set of 10 indicators a positive or negative difficulty parameter based on whether it is theoretically democracy expanding or contracting (for a similar application to state policy liberalism, see Caughey and Warshaw 2016).

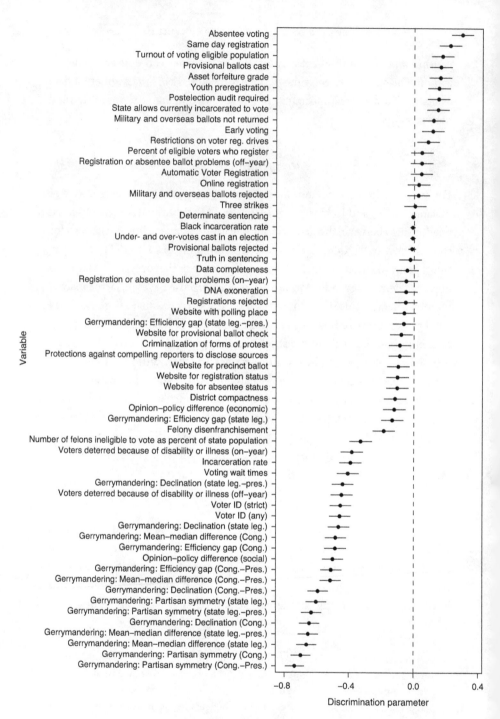

FIGURE 7.1. Factor Loadings of Democracy Indicators.

Note: Discrimination parameter estimates and Bayesian credible intervals for indicators used in the State Democracy Index.

not you consider this a serious problem is dependent on whether you philosophically interpret these "errors" as measurement error or bias.[26]

Figure 7.1 shows the discrimination parameter estimates, β_j for democracy indicator j. In short, the discrimination parameters represent the slope of the relationship between an indicator and a state's latent democracy performance score. Indicators with positive discrimination parameters *increase* a state's democracy score, whereas items with negative parameters *decrease* them.[27]

The discrimination parameters in figure 7.1 suggest that a small number of indicators do not load well onto the latent democracy dimension (discrimination parameters close to zero). Although some indicators related to the carceral state, such as state incarceration rates and asset forfeiture ratings, load onto the democracy index well, others, such as three strikes laws and Black incarceration rates, are orthogonal. This is suggestive evidence that authoritarianism related to policing and incarceration might be a separate dimension of state democracy. A separate carceral authoritarianism dimension would be consistent with the results presented in chapter 3 showing that, in contrast to many other policy areas (e.g., health care or gun control), criminal justice policy in the states has not shown much polarization by party.

The item parameters in figure 7.1 inform us about the dimensionality of state democratic performance. When item parameters do not conform to theory, one solution is to directly impose item parameters on the indicators rather than model them. To do so, in addition to our Bayesian factor analysis measure, we use simple additive indexing to create an alternative democracy measure. In the additive index, we weight each democracy indicator equally by range scaling each to the [0,1] interval and then take the state average across all the indicators. Policies that are democracy contracting, such as felony disenfranchisement, are reverse coded. This is equivalent to adding up all of a state's democracy-expanding policies and then subtracting the sum of democracy-contracting policies (again, similar to the measurement strategy used in chapter 3). The additive measures used in the main analyses weight each indicator equally. We provide robustness checks with this additive

---

26. It is also worth noting that error in these democracy measures will reduce the precision of hypothesis tests, but because I use these democracy measures as dependent variables, this will not induce bias or inconsistency (among many sources, see Angrist and Pischke 2008).

27. Not shown here, difficulty parameters α_j are intercepts that scale the relationships between indicators and democracy scores.

measure in the appendix, and the results are very similar to those with the "data-driven" Bayesian measure.

We test the validity of the State Democracy Index in different ways. We check construct validation by comparing our measure to measures of related concepts. To our knowledge, the closest analogue to our measure is the Cost of Voting Index (COVI) from Li, Pomante, and Schraufnagel 2018, which is based on seven state electoral policy variables in presidential election years. State democracy, as a concept, is related to the cost of voting. We therefore check our measure's convergent validity by estimating its correlation to this previous measure in figure A.2, finding a moderately strong correlation of −0.62 (higher values of COVI indicate greater cost of voting). We also show that our measure is positively correlated with state-level turnout of the voting-eligible public in figure A.2. We unfortunately have little opportunity to test for convergent validation because of the lack of existing measures of overall state-level democratic performance. There is scholarly interest in measuring subnational democratic performance at the (see Giraudy 2015; McMann 2018), and a small number of quantitative measures of democracy within other countries' political subunits (Harbers, Bartman, and van Wingerden 2019), but we have not found such a measure of democratic performance focused on the fifty states.

In the next sections, we investigate descriptive trends in state democratic performance.

Trends in State Democracy

With the State Democracy Index in hand, I first explore variation between states, and within states across time, in democratic performance. Figure 7.2 shows a map of state scores in the year 2000 (left panel) and in the year 2018 (right panel). (For ease of display, I average a state's *State Electoral* score and *State Democracy* score; as each score can be estimated with additive indexing or factor analysis, this means I am averaging four scores for each state in 2000 and again in 2016.)

The maps in figure 7.2 show some clear regional variation, especially in 2018. States on the West Coast and in the Northeast score higher on the democracy measures than states in the South. New Mexico, Colorado, and some midwestern states also have strong democracy scores.

The maps also show within-state change during this time period. States like North Carolina and Wisconsin were among the most democratic states in the

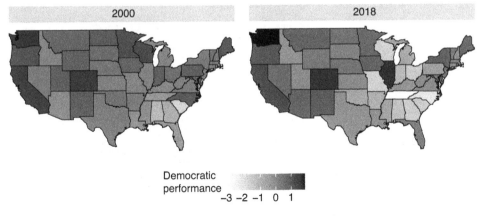

FIGURE 7.2. Democracy in the States, 2000 and 2018.

year 2000, but by 2018 they are close to the bottom. Illinois and Vermont move from the middle of the pack in 2000 to among the top democratic performers in 2018.

Figure 7.3 highlights one case of major change in democratic performance, North Carolina. While the state was notoriously difficult to democratize in the civil rights period (Mickey 2015)—it maintained its Jim Crow literacy tests for voting until the 1970s—North Carolina had become a leader in expanding access to voting during the late 1990s and early 2000s. The state had expanded opportunities for early voting and implemented policies to expand voter registration, such as same-day registration and pre-registration for youth. Voter turnout had increased by over 10 percentage points on average during this time.

But a major shift occurred after the Republican Party won control of both legislative chambers in 2010. Beginning in 2011, North Carolina made a series of changes to its election laws and procedures. The state redrew its legislative district boundaries. The new districts, which received rapid condemnation from Democrats and civil rights groups, clearly advantaged white and Republican voters. In 2018, for example, Republicans won about 49.3 percent of the two-party vote in North Carolina—but this *minority* of votes from the electorate translated to fully 77 percent (10 of 13) of North Carolina's seats in Congress. Gerrymandering experts such as Christopher Warshaw have called North Carolina's districts "the most gerrymandered map in modern history." After electing a Republican governor in 2012, the unified Republican government then implemented a strict voter ID law and curtailed early voting laws

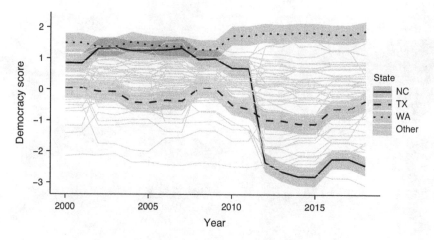

FIGURE 7.3. The Weakening of Democracy in North Carolina.
Note: Lines represent the State Democracy Index scores for states (2000–2018). The solid black line represents North Carolina, the dashed line represents Texas, and the dotted line Washington. Shaded ribbons are Bayesian credible intervals.

in areas with heavier concentrations of Black voters. These changes are reflected in figure 7.3.

Figure 7.4 shows trends in state democracy by party, with the solid line representing unified Republican states, and dotted and dashed lines representing Democratic and divided states, respectively. The states polarize by party over this time period: the average Democratically controlled state becomes more democratic, while the average Republican-controlled state becomes less democratic.

But regardless of the measure, the groups of states controlled by each party change over this time period; we do not know from figure 7.4 whether Republican states are becoming less democratic, or less democratic states are becoming more Republican. The partisan relationships could also be confounded by our other potential causes of democratic changes: competition and polarization. In the next chapter I look to within-state analysis to examine whether these forces influence democratic performance.

Conclusion

Despite their constitutional centrality for democratic institutions, there has been little systematic measurement of how state governments are performing as stewards of democracy. This chapter builds upon a foundation from

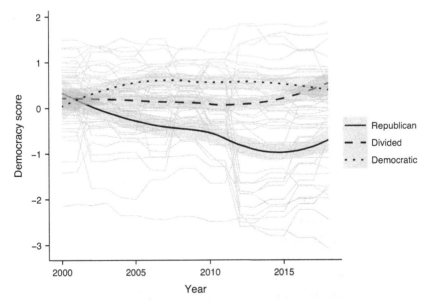

FIGURE 7.4. Democracy in the States by Party Control of Government.
Note: Plot shows average State Democracy Index scores for states under unified Democratic
(dotted line), divided (dashed line), and unified Republican (solid line) control. Shaded
ribbons are 95 percent confidence intervals.

multiple traditions of scholarship—democratic theory, comparative cross-national analysis, historical research on race in the United States, among others—to develop measures of dynamics in American democracy across geography and time.

The resulting State Democracy Index captures the expansion and contraction in state-level democracy between 2000 and 2018. The fifty states have been measured and ranked extensively on concepts such as educational performance, business climate, and libertarian freedom (Sorens, Muedini, and Ruger 2008). Yet they have not been measured in terms of democratic performance. I hope that the State Democracy Index proves useful for scholars seeking answers to questions about the causes and consequences of democracy beyond the scope of this book, such as the microfoundational roles of interest groups or mass attitudes. On a more somber note, the measures may also prove useful in case of impending democratic crisis.

Our measure opens up new opportunities for research on questions related to representation and democracy, as well as federalism and state and local politics. Scholars might be interested in investigating the role of interest groups or money in politics on state democratic performance (Hertel-Fernandez 2016; Anzia and Moe 2016), perhaps by exploiting variation in state campaign finance policy (La Raja and Schaffner 2015) or election timing (Anzia 2011). Others might study how state democracy is affected by declining state and local politics journalism (Moskowitz 2021), or by voters' attitudes toward democratic institutions (Welzel 2007; Ahlquist et al. 2018; Graham and Svolik 2020; Miller and Davis 2021). There is especially great potential for behavioral scholars of race and ethnic politics to investigate the relationship between racial attitudes, attitudes toward democracy, and state democratic performance (e.g., Mutz 2018; Weaver and Prowse 2020; Jefferson 2021). Like comparative and political economy scholarship on whether "democracy causes growth" (Acemoglu et al. 2019), scholars can also use the State Democracy Index as an explanatory variable to study the effect of democratic performance on economic performance, socioeconomic outcomes among residents, and public attitudes such as trust. Comparative scholars can use our measurement strategy to create new measures of democratic performance in subnational units in one or more other countries, potentially constructing comprehensive cross-national measures of subunit democracy in political federations.

In contrast to my measures, cross-national measures of democracy sometimes cover much longer stretches of time. V-Dem, for instance, measures democratic performance for countries as far back as 1789—though this is not without its challenges (e.g., Reconstruction, a period of rapid expansion and then contraction of rights for Black Americans, is barely a blip on the U.S. V-Dem trend). Still, it is a worthy goal to construct a State Democracy Index that covers the transformational changes to the franchise, civil liberties, and other components of democracy that occurred in earlier periods of U.S. history. Alexander Keyssar (2000) and others have engaged in this kind of historical analysis of changes in voting rights but without this kind of systematic measurement strategy.

Perhaps more importantly, a longer time frame would contextualize the magnitude of recent shifts in state-level democracy. This chapter provides clear evidence of important changes in democratic performance, such as the rapid decline of democracy in states such as North Carolina since 2010. But these recent changes have occurred on a narrower range of the democracy dimension than those in earlier periods, when, for example, states differed in terms of the legality of slavery and the female franchise. Despite some troubling examples in state-level democracy in recent years, they do not come close to the profound differences in regime type that existed between states in the eras before the twentieth-century civil rights period. At the same time, true democratic collapse is likely to be presaged by the kinds of democratic backsliding described in this chapter—which can entrench minority rule, curtail dissent, and limit participation in democratic institutions.

The State Democracy Index suggests that there have been dramatic shifts in democratic performance in the American states over this time period. In some states, democracy grew in inclusive ways, expanding access to political participation, reducing the authoritarian use of police powers, and making electoral institutions more fair. In other states, however, democracy narrowed dramatically, as state governments gerrymandered districts and created new barriers to participation and restrictions on the franchise.

As Philip Rocco (2021, 301) writes, "While uneven subnational democracy is preferable to a situation in which territorial governments are evenly undemocratic, the existence of undemocratic outliers nevertheless helps to undermine democracy as a whole." Slavery, Jim Crow, and other forms of subnational authoritarianism affected the political economy of the North and the U.S. as a nation; though less barbaric in form, democratic backsliding in North Carolina and Wisconsin similarly affects democracy in the U.S. as a whole. State authorities administer elections; they are the primary enforcers of laws; they determine in large part who can participate in American politics, and how. The policy and judicial landscapes have grown increasingly favorable for policy variation across states in recent years. As a consequence, states may be increasingly important to trends in democracy across all institutions within American federalism. Political scholars, observers, and participants should pay close attention to dynamics in state democracy.

In the next chapter, I use the State Democracy Index to test the predictions of long-standing theories of the forces that underlie democratic expansion and contraction: (un)competitive party systems, polarization, racial threat, and the interests of groups in party coalitions.

8

Explaining Dynamics in Subnational Democracy

CONCEPTUALIZING AND MEASURING subnational democracy in the United States is a major undertaking. But the payoffs are substantial. The State Democracy Index measure developed in the previous chapter suggests that there have been major shifts in democratic performance within states in recent years. The important question, however, is not simply *how* democracy has changed in the states but *why*. Luckily, the new democracy measures allow me to test the predictions of competing theories of the causes of democratic changes.

What drives democratic expansions and contractions in political systems? Political science offers some potential explanations. They engage with transformative processes in modern American politics: partisan *competition* (Keyssar 2000), ideological *polarization* (Lieberman et al. 2019), *racial threat* (Bobo and Hutchings 1996), and national *party coalitions* (Hacker and Pierson 2020). Strong competition between the parties could expand or contract democracy in the states. On the one hand is a hopeful story of partisan competition, where parties have incentives to expand the electorate in search of more votes, improving democracy in the process by, for example, expanding the franchise (Keyssar 2000; Teele 2018a, 2018b). On the other hand, by incentivizing partisan brinksmanship (Lee 2009), partisan competition can lead a party with a precarious grip on power to diminish democracy by exploiting countermajoritarian institutions and attempting to prevent their opponents' electoral bases from voting. A second theory focuses on polarization—the ideological distance between the parties' agendas. Polarization increases politicians' need to ensure that their opponents do not win office. A party in government in a polarized state will thus have greater incentive to change policies that affect democracy, such as election laws that influence the cost of voting for different groups in the state. A third theory predicts that demographic change will produce racial threat, turning some voters against democracy as they oppose the democratic inclusion of new voters and growing influence of voters of color. Importantly, these theories tend to consider states as separate polities with competition effects that do not spill across borders or levels of government (Teele 2018b; O'Brian 2019b).

Finally, a different theoretical tradition predicts *asymmetry* in the party-democracy relationship because the parties represent different group coalitions in American society. Rather than the symmetric reelection maximizers described in classic American politics textbooks, other theories of democracy point to the importance of conservative parties as historical coalitions of interests with incentives to constrain democracy (Ziblatt 2017). The Republican Party, a coalition of the very wealthy, major industry, and an electoral base motivated in no small part by white identity politics, has incentives to limit the expansion of the electorate with new voters with very different racial attitudes and, to some extent, class interests (Hacker and Pierson 2020). Furthermore, this theory considers party coalitions to be linked horizontally across states and vertically across levels of government—instead of atomized, individual reelection maximizers, these are networks of intense policy demanders with policy goals in support of the groups in their coalition (Bawn et al. 2012).

After developing these theoretical predictions, I describe the empirical relationships between measures of states' partisan competitiveness, elite polarization, and party control, on the one hand, and their democratic performance on the other. I more formally test the predictions of the theories with a difference-in-differences design that estimates whether within-state variation in these variables leads to changes in democratic performance. Across alternative measures and model specifications, the results are remarkably clear: Republican control of state government reduces democratic performance. The magnitude of democratic contraction from Republican control is surprisingly large, over one-half of a standard deviation. Competitive party systems and polarized politicians do little to explain the major changes in subnational democracy in the contemporary period.

The results underscore the importance of understanding what influences the Republican Party's democracy agenda. They also challenge traditional explanations that abstract away from the historical processes that led to the GOP's unique relationship to democracy compared to other mainstream political parties in the developed world.

Theories of Federalism and Democracy

The Role of Competitive Parties

Does a competitive party system help or harm democracy? Schattschneider famously proclaimed that "the political parties created democracy and modern democracy is unthinkable save in terms of the parties." Scholars point to the consolidation of a competitive party system to explain large-scale expansions of democracy in the United States, Africa (Rakner and Van de Walle 2009), Europe (Mares 2015), and around the world (Weiner 1965). Intense competition for control of state legislatures in the late nineteenth and early twentieth centuries may have provided crucial incentives for state governments to expand the franchise to women. As Dawn Teele (2018b) argues, politicians have incentives to "enfranchise a new group if they are insecure in their current posts and looking for new ways to win, and if they believe they have a chance at mobilizing the newly enfranchised voters to support their party" (443). Similarly, the more competitive party system in the North is a potential reason for the region's incorporation of white working-class and immigrant voters into local and state politics (Keyssar 2000). Beyond its state-sanctioned racial hierarchy, the one-party environment of the "Solid South" during Jim Crow was additionally problematic (Key 1949; Bateman, Katznelson, and Lapinski 2018; Olson 2020).

Furthermore, rational choice and quantitative scholars of American politics highlight the issue-bundling role of competitive parties in democratic systems. By aggregating voters and politicians into groups and reducing the dimensionality of politics (Poole and Rosenthal 1997), parties help solve collective action problems for voters and social choice problems for legislators (Aldrich 1995). Translating mass preferences into governmental behavior is much more difficult absent this issue-bundling role of parties.[1] Voters rely on party cues in elections, and legislators rely on parties to avoid the "cycling" problem of choice in environments of multidimensional preferences (Shepsle and Weingast 1981).

On the other hand, party competition might provoke politicians to constrain democracy. The incentives for a party in government to stack the deck in its favor—by violating norms or changing the rules—are greatest when its

---

1. The behavioral analogue of this issue bundling is the concept of "constraint" from Converse 1964.

hold on power is marginal. An important argument from Frances Lee (2009) suggests that these incentives from competition for legislative majorities generate polarization through "partisan brinksmanship." Indeed, much scholarly and journalistic ink has been spilled about this hyperpartisan brinksmanship, in which legislators oppose any proposal from the outparty, no matter how reasonable or minor, using any and all procedural means at their disposal to do so. The precipitous increase in the use of the filibuster in the U.S. Senate over the past two decades might reflect such incentives.

Yet there has been little extension of Lee's theory to dynamics in democratic performance. Not only may parties facing intense competition use procedure to prevent outparty victories, they may have incentives to expand or contract democracy in their polity by manipulating the composition of the electorate or using the power of the state to hamper the ability of groups aligned with the outparty to organize and mobilize. We would not expect, for instance, the same attempts at manipulation in the 2000 presidential election in Florida were preelection polls suggesting George W. Bush would cruise to a landslide in the state.

In recent years, we have seen many examples of competitive elections for state government that may have gone the other way under different levels of democratic performance. The 2018 Florida gubernatorial election between Democrat Andrew Gillum and Republican Ron DeSantis was decided by only about 30,000 votes out of over 8 million cast for the two candidates. In the same election, voters approved a ballot initiative to restore voting rights to previously incarcerated felons after the completion of their sentence—newly enfranchising over one million Floridians.[2] Had such a law been in effect in the 2018 gubernatorial election, and given the predicted partisanship and turnout of the newly enfranchised Floridians, the winner would have plausibly been Gillum instead of DeSantis. Not only would this have installed a Democratic governor; it would have prevented the unified control of government that currently provides Republicans great opportunity to change policy in the state. By contrast, an uncompetitive party system in Florida would have very different incentives. Republicans in government would not have to worry that reinstating the franchise for ex-felons would flip crucial elections. The same could be said of the 2018 Georgia gubernatorial election, where Stacey Abrams lost a close race after a series of potentially consequential polling place closures

---

2. In 2019 the Republican-controlled Florida state legislature later passed legislation to preempt this reenfranchisement; the decision was upheld by the Florida Supreme Court in 2020.

(Niesse and Thieme 2019). With little outparty threat, by contrast, the solidly Democratic California state government is implementing felony enfranchisement after voters approved a 2020 ballot initiative.

North Carolina offers another potential case of competition influencing politicians' democratic incentives. Voter turnout in the state had been increasing throughout the 1990s and 2000s, and state legislative and gubernatorial elections were growing increasingly close as the southern state transitioned from being a member of the "Solid" South toward a more competitive party system and status as a swing state in presidential elections. In a rare sweep in this competitive climate, the state's new unified Republican government began implementing a series of changes to election policy beginning in 2011 that weakened democracy in the state.

The Role of Polarization

While the prospect of the outparty taking power may give politicians incentives to expand or contract democracy, it matters how deep the ideological disagreements are between the parties. As the parties become more polarized, with Democrats becoming more liberal and Republicans more conservative, the partisan stakes of holding power—and the cost of losing it—grow dramatically. Scholars have investigated a number of potential causes of elite polarization, including racial realignment (Schickler 2016), mass polarization (Abramowitz and Webster 2016), and changes in the interest group environment (Hacker and Pierson 2010; Krimmel 2017). But regardless of its origins, the main idea here is that elite polarization, by deepening the divide between the parties' policy agendas, gives parties greater incentive to ensure that they win and their opponents lose. These strong incentives could lead the parties in government to look for new ways to influence the cost of voting in elections for different groups in their states.

As Robert Lieberman and colleagues (2019, 471) argue, "hyperpolarization magnifies tendencies for the partisan capture of institutions that are supposed to exercise checks and balances but may instead be turned into unaccountable instruments of partisan or incumbent advantage." It generates conflict about and within oversight agencies and the judiciary. It "erodes norms" of institutional behavior, such as the judicious use of executive power and fair treatment on issues such as bureaucratic and judicial appointments—and the levers of democracy itself (Levitsky and Ziblatt 2018).

Polarization may be asymmetric or symmetric (Hacker and Pierson 2005; McCarty, Poole, and Rosenthal 2006), but polarization is fundamentally about the *distance between the parties*. This distinction is helpfully illustrated in debates about the political causes of economic inequality. Measures of congressional polarization (e.g., the distance between each party's median legislator), as well as measures of the ideological position of just the median Republican in Congress, are both strongly correlated with economic inequality in the United States. Nolan McCarty, Keith Poole, and Howard Rosenthal (2006) argue that increased ideological distance between the parties produces legislative gridlock, which "in turn can affect the government's capacity to reduce inequality" (172). Neil O'Brian (2019a), on the other hand, suggests a simpler and more direct explanation for rising inequality is the rightward movement of the Republican Party. In this chapter, I similarly adjudicate between a polarization-centered and a Republican-centered explanation in democratic performance in the states.[3]

The Role of Demographics and Racial Threat

A third theoretical tradition suggests that the racial demographics of state populations shape politics and policy (Hero and Tolbert 1996). Of particular importance to this study is the potential for increasing racial diversity to generate "racial threat" and backlash among conservative white voters (Bobo and Hutchings 1996). As states grow more racially diverse due to immigration and internal migration,[4] some voters might demand restrictions on democracy to block the political inclusion and empowerment of new voters of color (Abrajano and Hajnal 2015; Biggers and Hanmer 2017; Myers and Levy 2018). Importantly, not only would racial backlash lead to democratic backsliding on its own; if

---

3. As McCarty (2019, 12) defines them, "polarization generally refers to differences on policy issues, ideological orientations, or value systems, while . . . partisanship can be more general in that it may refer to any partiality one feels toward one's own party regardless of whether polarized preferences and attitudes are the source." Although the competition theory is more consistent with partisan incentives and the polarization theory with true ideological polarization, my analysis does not directly adjudicate between the distinct microfoundations of ideology versus partisanship.

4. During the time period under study in this book, Latino and Asian American population proportions increased in most states. Furthermore, the Black population of southern states increased as part of the "reverse" Great Migration since 1975.

demographic change leads voters to increasingly elect Republicans to state government, this theory predicts that the *interaction* of demographic change and Republican Party control should produce democratic backsliding.

Racial conflict within states, and corresponding conflict over redistribution, public goods, and political power, was central to Jim Crow (Mickey 2015). By contrast, today's racial conflict appears much more national, as observed in the Tea Party (Parker and Barreto 2014) and political rise of Donald Trump. In the next section, I outline a theory that again puts race at the fore but in a national rather than state or regional context. Critically, this nationally oriented theory takes into account the national Republican Party's racial *and* economic agendas.

The Role of Groups and Party Coalitions

The logics behind a competition-democracy relationship, a polarization-democracy relationship, or a demographic-democracy relationship are strong. An additional theory from Gretchen Helmke, Mary Kroeger, and Jack Paine (2021) offers a novel explanation for Republican attacks on democracy. The authors argue that a permissive legal environment that allows many forms of voter suppression and gerrymandering, combined with a highly sorted electorate that makes it easy to "target" suppression on particular constituencies (e.g., based on urban density or the location of African American voters), would lead us to predict that the Republican Party will asymmetrically contribute to democratic backsliding.

These theories so far, of competition and polarization—and especially Helmke, Kroeger, and Paine's (2021) theory of legal leeway and electoral sorting—are compelling. But an alternative theoretical tradition offers an even simpler explanation for dynamics in democratic performance. This tradition focuses on the configuration of *interests* within party coalitions. Some interests in society stand to lose (or at least not win as much) by ceding control over the levers of government to a wider circle of people. Economic elites and large business interests may see greater amounts of wealth or profit redistributed to the masses.[5] Groups in favor of racial or gender hierarchies do not wish to expand voting and other participatory rights to African Americans and women. This theory is historically bounded. In contrast to theories

5. The Founders explicitly cited this protection of "property" as a justification for counter-majoritarian institutions in the Constitution (see, e.g., Beard 1913; Dahl 2003).

that "drop the proper nouns," here our theory leads me to a specific focus on the Republican Party and the historical processes that led to its modern group coalition.

This theory applied to the modern Republican Party is closely related to what Jacob Hacker and Paul Pierson (2020, 19) call "plutocratic populism":

> Plutocrats fear democracy because they see it as imperiling their economic standing and narrowly defined priorities. Right-wing populists fear democracy because they see it as imperiling their electoral standing and their narrowly defined community. These fears would be less consequential if they were not packaged together within one of the nation's two major parties.

Rising economic inequality, which puts the economic interests of plutocrats at odds with those of an increasingly large majority of voters, weakens the wealthy's commitment to democratic institutions. It also means that the plutocratic coalition cannot simply appeal to its electoral base on economic and policy grounds. Instead, it must reach out to right-wing populists with appeals based on ethnoracial, religious, and national identity cleavages. (Indeed, parties that pursue the economic interests of a narrow slice of society in a democratic system need an agenda that is at least somewhat popular, hence right-wing populism.) Donald Trump, himself, provides a clear example of this process. Republican elites dislike many things about Trump, but they very much enjoy that he mobilizes voters and signs high-end tax cuts. Trump, on the other hand, has little in the way of a policy agenda outside of enriching his family, general anti-immigrant rhetoric, and, for lack of a better phrase, "owning the libs";[6] he is a vehicle that allows plutocrats to more effectively partner with voters who enjoy his appeals to right-wing populism.

The most consequential forms of right-wing populism, both historically and in the contemporary United States, are, of course, based in racism. Slave owners and, later, wealthy white landowners and businessmen stood to lose from solidaristic interracial movements and made efforts to attract poorer whites into their political coalitions with the enticement of a "psychological wage" based in their position above Black people in the racial hierarchy (DuBois 1935). On the other side of this struggle, civil rights activists such as Martin Luther King Jr. and Bayard Rustin, as well as labor leaders such as A. Philip Randolph and Walter Reuther, emphasized the linkages between race, class,

---

6. Ahler and Broockman (2017) provide evidence that to the extent Trump support is related to policy views, it is on the issue of immigration.

and democracy, arguing that powerful interests exploit racial divisions for political gain (Frymer and Grumbach 2021).[7] Although psychological racism is pervasive in the American public and historical moments of interracial solidarity have been rare,[8] major *shifts* in how racism affects politics and policy require additional mechanisms, such as entrepreneurial elites who strategically exploit mass racism.

Indeed, political candidates and elites in the contemporary period have made racial appeals that tap racism in the mass public (e.g., Mendelberg 2001; Hutchings and Jardina 2009; Haney-López 2015), and these racist attitudes are associated with reduced support for democratic institutions (Miller and Davis 2021). Elites can similarly "racialize" policy in many contexts, as is especially prominent in the politics of welfare (Gilens 2009; Brown 2013) and health care (Tesler 2016, chap. 5). Republican-aligned elites seized the opportunity presented by the presence of the first Black president. Despite Barack Obama's avoidance of racial discussion and consistent promotion of Black respectability politics (Gillion 2016; Stephens-Dougan 2016), his presidency, rather than signaling the emergence of a "post-racial America," was met with a Republican Party that made gains by radicalizing on issues of race and immigration (Parker and Barreto 2014). In the contemporary period, elite racial appeals and frames are facilitated by a sophisticated conservative media ecosystem that consolidates the mass elements of the Republican Party (Martin and Yurukoglu 2017; Martin and McCrain 2019). Other commentators have focused instead on the forces of "tribalism," a psychological process in which people hunker down into identity groups in a (real or perceived) zero-sum conflict with outgroups (Fukuyama 2018; Chua 2019). The rise of this "tribalism" has also been employed as evidence of the dangers of democracy and the benefits of elite rule (Geltzer 2018). An argument from a very distinct political tradition, but one that is similarly "bottom-up," comes from scholars who consider psychological proclivities toward white supremacy (or, more narrowly, anti-Blackness) to be an existential feature of human civilization. Historical ebbs and flows of

7. As Martin Luther King argued, "The coalition that can have the greatest impact in the struggle for human dignity here in America is that of the Negro and the forces of labor, because their fortunes are so closely intertwined" ("Letter to Amalgamated Laundry Workers," January 1962).

8. The *New York Times'* "1619 Project" surmises that "for the most part" Black Americans "fought alone" in their struggle for justice (available from https://www.nytimes.com/interactive/2019/08/14/magazine/1619-america-slavery.html).

"tribalism," however, are difficult to explain with a primary focus on the evo-lutionarily derived wiring of the Homo sapien brain. While the context of demographic trends and the first Black president may have been necessary conditions, the recent racial radicalization of the GOP appears centrally about the elites who help to activate latent mass racism by stoking racial threat and resentment.[9]

Finally, the plutocratic-populist partnership is viable in the contemporary period because of the institutional and human geography of the United States, where Republican votes "count" more than Democratic votes due to Repub-lican voters' geographic dispersion across legislative districts and prevalence in small states. This long-standing electoral advantage for more geographically dispersed voters is distinct from gerrymandering, where governments redraw district lines to create electoral advantage. Instead, in plurality electoral sys-tems like that of the United States, geographic clustering, or what Jowei Chen, Jonathan Rodden, and colleagues (2013) call "unintentional gerrymandering," creates premiums or penalties by differing rates of "wasted" votes—an issue that became more politically consequential as the Democratic electoral base grew increasingly urban in the late twentieth century (Rodden 2019, chap. 1). Wasted votes are any votes beyond what it takes to win the election, 50 percent plus one in a two-candidate contest. The geographic dispersion of voters by party can be formally modeled to predict the legislative seat premium or pen-alty for a given party (Calvo and Rodden 2015).

The GOP has the geographic opportunity—based in patterns of slave and free state borders, among other deep historical roots—to win state and federal elections with a nearly all-white base.[10] While any party might be theoretically advantaged under an alternative geographic distribution of voters, in the United States, the party more supportive of racial hierarchy has tended to be more geographically dispersed and thus advantaged by electoral geography in a competitive two-party context (Calvo and Rodden 2015). This modern ge-ography is the result of long-term political-economic patterns of Indian re-moval (Frymer 2017), the slave plantation economy (Rothman 2005), and, in

---

9. Indeed, even sophisticated, systematic behavioral studies into the mass public's support for democratic principles in the contemporary period, such as whether beliefs about democracy influence voting decisions (Graham and Svolik 2020), do not disentangle the roots of shifts in democratic outcomes over time.

10. The only Republican presidential candidate since George H. W. Bush to win the popular vote, George W. Bush in 2004 won 44 percent of the Latino vote.

TABLE 8.1. Theories of Democratic Expansion and Contraction in the States

Theory	Measures	Predicted Effect on Democracy
Competition	Competitiveness of elections or legislative majority	+ or −
Polarization	Distance between party legislative chamber medians	−
Racial Threat	Change in state % Black and % Latino	−
Party	Republican control of government	−

the twentieth century, the rise of suburbanization and its interaction with race (Self 2005; Kruse 2013; Trounstine 2018)—which have combined to make white votes more pivotal in recent elections.[11]

Under this theory, the coalitional partnership between plutocrats and voters motivated by white (and related cultural) identity politics,[12] buttressed by electoral geography, leads to a clear prediction: Republican control of government will be democracy-reducing.

Table 8.1 summarizes the predictions of the four major theories of democratic dynamics that I test in this chapter.

Methods

Empirically Testing Competing Theories of Democracy

Which theory best explains the dynamics of democratic performance? Although institutional and partisan changes are very much not assigned randomly, the theories offer distinct predictions—predictions that may be consistent or inconsistent with real-world outcomes in the states. I follow other empiricists who test the competing predictions of major institutional theories in American politics, such as those of the party cartel and ideological pivot models (Schickler 2000, 2001). I collect empirical time-series measures of the inputs for the partisan, ideological, and competition theories.

11. Despite headlines about a "big sort" of Americans into ideologically homogeneous communities (Bishop 2009), there is a large body of evidence that residential choices are constrained and dominated by non-ideological preferences (Mummolo and Nall 2017; Martin and Webster 2020). Current geographic dispersion and "unintentional gerrymandering" are mostly not the result of residential sorting.

12. I do not wish to downplay the importance of gender, sexuality, religion, and even cultural identities such as being a gun owner to mass attitudes. They are important in their own right and in their interaction with beliefs about race (Filindra and Kaplan 2016).

I use a variety of measures of partisan competition and polarization in the states. Some of the competition measures address the share of a state's legislative seats. Specifically, I use data on legislative seat shares from Klarner (2013) to code *lower chamber competition* as $|0.5-D_{lower}|$ where D_{lower} is the two-party share of lower chamber seats held by Democrats, and *upper chamber competition* as $|0.5-D_{upper}|$ where D_{upper} is the two-party share of upper chamber seats held by Democrats. An additional measure from O'Brian (2019b) captures competition for the state electorate as a whole: *electoral competition* is coded as $|0.5-D_{votes}|$ where D_{votes} is the two-party share of votes in the state's U.S. House election(s) that went to Democratic candidates.[13] As is customary, these measures are smoothed into rolling averages across three election cycles (e.g., Ranney 1976; Shufeldt and Flavin 2012), but I lag them in statistical models such that they capture electoral competition in the three previous election cycles prior to the state's democratic performance in year *t*. Legislative polarization measures are from Shor and McCarty 2011. I use the distance in the parties' legislative chamber medians within each state. Party control of government captures whether a state government is under unified Democratic, unified Republican, or divided governmental control. (For clarity, these independent variables are all standardized to have a mean of 0 and a standard deviation 1.)

I test theoretical predictions with a difference-in-differences design that asks whether within-state change in polarization, competition, or party control is associated with within-state change in democratic performance. While the true causal model between competition, polarization, party control, and democratic performance is likely to involve a structure of highly complex feedback relationships, this design eliminates time-invariant differences between states—the main potential source of bias in estimating the relationship between our input measures and democratic performance.

In the next section, I exploit variation within states across time to more rigorously test the hypotheses about dynamics in democracy.

Results

I present the main results in table 8.2. The results of Models 1 through 3 show that, on their own, there is a modest positive relationship between competition and democracy and no relationship between polarization and democracy—but

13. O'Brian (2019b) collected vote-share data from David and Claggett 2008 and CQ Press's Voting and Election Collection.

TABLE 8.2. Explaining Democratic Expansion and Contraction in the States

Outcome: State Democracy Score

	Model 1	Model 2	Model 3	Model 4	Model 5	Model 6	Model 7
Competition	0.187			0.159	0.182	0.157	0.120
	(0.104)			(0.096)	(0.095)	(0.102)	(0.110)
Polarization		0.016		0.023	0.036	0.025	0.027
		(0.125)		(0.112)	(0.104)	(0.120)	(0.114)
Republican			0.443**	−0.427**	−0.417**	−0.426**	−0.459**
			(0.154)	(0.151)	(0.154)	(0.147)	(0.176)
Competition × Polarization					0.081		
					(0.064)		
Polarization × Republican						−0.011	
						(0.187)	
Competition × Republican							0.120
							(0.199)
Constant	−0.785***	−0.762***	−0.617***	−0.620***	−0.629***	−0.619***	−0.617***
	(0.065)	(0.111)	(0.087)	(0.127)	(0.128)	(0.131)	(0.127)
State FEs	Yes	Yes	Yes	Yes	Yes	Yes	Yes
Year FEs	Yes	Yes	Yes	Yes	Yes	Yes	Yes
N	833	833	833	833	833	833	833
R-squared	0.712	0.705	0.727	0.732	0.733	0.732	0.733
Adj. R-squared	0.687	0.680	0.704	0.708	0.709	0.708	0.709

$**p < .01$; $***p < .001$

a large negative relationship between Republican control and democracy in the states. Across the model specifications, the effect of Republican control of government is between 0.4 and 0.5 standard deviations of democratic performance, a substantial amount. The effect of competition, by contrast, is between 0.1 and 0.2 standard deviations, and the effect of polarization is near zero.

I am also interested in the interactions of competition, polarization, and Republican control. Polarized parties (or the Republican Party) might only have an incentive to restrict democracy in competitive political environments. However, the results in table 8.2 suggest that these interactions do little to explain dynamics in state democracy. The interaction of competition and polarization is modestly positive, as is the interaction of competition and Republican control—both contrary to expectations (though all of the interaction coefficients are statistically insignificant).

Due to recent concern about the weighting of treatment estimates in multiperiod difference-in-differences analysis using two-way fixed effects (Goodman-Bacon, forthcoming), I use alternative aggregation procedures to estimate the average treatment effect on the treated (ATT) of Republican control.[14] In figure A.4, I plot the results from three different types of ATT aggregation from Callaway and Sant'Anna (forthcoming): dynamic, group, and simple (group-time). In addition to using different aggregation procedures, the model drops states that were "treated" (i.e., under Republican control) in the first period, the year 2000.[15] The results are robust (and even larger) when using a generalized synthetic control estimator that creates synthetic control units as a weighted average of the "real" control units in order to match the pretreatment democratic performance of states that will later be "treated" by Republican control (Xu 2017). This robustness check relaxes the parallel trends assumption of difference-in-differences analysis and gives me greater confidence that the results are not due to states trending downward in democratic performance before becoming Republican.

14. Specifically, two-way fixed-effects specifications are a weighted average of all possible two-period difference-in-differences estimators, which is vulnerable to bias if treatment effects vary across time in multiperiod designs.

15. In the Callaway and Sant'Anna (forthcoming) setup, treatment cannot switch back off once it is on. In turn, I assign a state that switches to Republican control a new unit fixed effect once it switches back to divided (or Democratic) control. The results are robust to excluding these state-years.

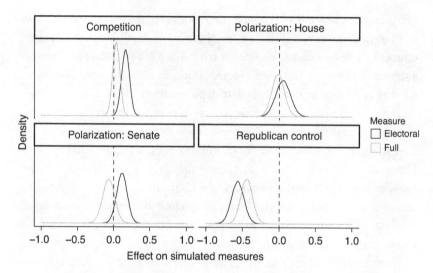

FIGURE 8.1. Effect of Republican Control on Simulated Democracy Measures.

The measures of competition, polarization, and party control that I use in this chapter are generally standard and uncontroversial, but the democracy measure is novel. Readers may be skeptical or have normative and theoretical reasons to weight particular democracy indicators differently than the equal weighting in the additive indices and data-driven weighting in the factor analysis measures. To assuage this concern, I simulate 100,000 measures using randomly generated weights between 0 and infinity for each democracy indicator, each simulation recalculating an additive index and then running the difference-in-differences hypothesis test. Figure 8.1 plots the distribution of coefficient estimates for the tests using each of the 100,000 simulated measures.

Figure 8.1 increases my confidence in the main results presented earlier. Large proportions of coefficients from the hypothesis tests on the simulated measures are close to zero for the competition and polarization measures (an exception is competition's effect on simulated Electoral Democracy measures, which are consistently positive but modest). By contrast, Republican control of government has a large negative effect on democratic performance across the many simulated measures. The results, in other words, are robust to many, many different weighting schemes for the democracy indicators—and many different ways of quantitatively operationalizing the concept of democracy.

Overall, the results point to the importance of the structure of the modern Republican Party coalition. The racial geography of the modern United States allows the GOP to win elections at the state and national level with an

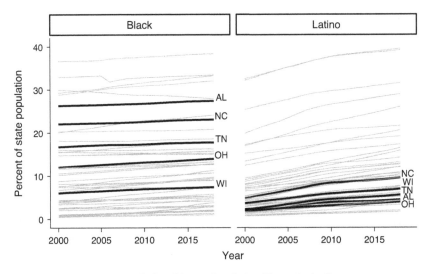

FIGURE 8.2. Black and Latino Population Change in the States.

overwhelmingly white and mostly male base outside of urban areas. This coalition, in most cases, will see potential gains from democratic contraction—from restricting protest activity, from making it more difficult to vote, even from incarcerating greater numbers of people.

Racial Demographic Change and State Democracy

In this section, I turn to the analysis of racial demographic change and its interaction with competition, polarization, and Republican governance. I first assess descriptive trends. Figure 8.2 plots Black and Latino population change in the five states that experience the greatest democratic backsliding over the time period: Alabama, Ohio, North Carolina, Tennessee, and Wisconsin. These states tend to have above-average Black population shares but see little change over time. By contrast, these states have relatively low Latino population shares. Their Latino populations grow gradually over this time period. However, this amount of growth is not out of the ordinary; the trends in these states closely track national averages. This descriptive analysis provides little evidence that local Black or Latino population change matters much for state democratic performance.

Table 8.3 tests theories of demographic threat with my main difference-in-differences design. The results are consistent with the descriptive analysis: trends in racial population proportions have little effect on state democratic

TABLE 8.3. Racial Demographic Change and State Democracy

Outcome: State Democracy Score

	Model 1	Model 2	Model 3	Model 4
Δ % Black	−0.0001	−0.001	0.0005	0.001
	(0.003)	(0.003)	(0.005)	(0.003)
Δ % Latino	−0.001	0.0001	−0.0004	−0.004
	(0.003)	(0.0003)	(0.004)	(0.003)
Competition		0.274		
		(0.140)		
Polarization			0.028	
			(0.177)	
Republican				−0.720**
				(0.221)
Δ % Black × Competition		0.001		
		(0.004)		
Δ % Latino × Competition		−0.002		
		(0.002)		
Δ % Black × Polarization			0.001	
			(0.003)	
Δ % Latino × Polarization			−0.001	
			(0.002)	
Δ % Black × Republican				−0.004
				(0.004)
Δ % Latino × Republican				0.007*
				(0.003)
Constant	−0.747***	−0.757***	−0.757***	−0.388*
	(0.168)	(0.167)	(0.164)	(0.179)
State FEs	Yes	Yes	Yes	Yes
Year FEs	Yes	Yes	Yes	Yes
N	833	833	833	833
R-squared	0.705	0.713	0.705	0.734
Adj. R-squared	0.680	0.687	0.679	0.710

*p < .05; **p < .01; ***p < .001

performance. Furthermore, while Republican control still has a large negative effect on democratic performance, the interaction of Republican control and demographic change matters little. Unexpectedly, the one statistically significant coefficient involving demographic change is the positive coefficient for the interaction of Republican control and Latino population change, meaning that Republican states with greater Latino population growth reduce democratic performance slightly less than other Republican states (though with a coefficient of 0.007, this effect is extremely small in magnitude).

These findings suggest that racial politics *within states* are not central to dynamics in state democracy.[16] This does not mean that race is peripheral to dynamics in state democracy. On the contrary, they highlight the importance of *national* political conflict, which, especially at the mass level, is dominated by conflict over race (Parker and Barreto 2014; Sides, Tesler, and Vavreck 2019). A number of important studies show evidence of racial threat and contestation at highly localized levels (e.g., Enos 2017). But in an era of highly nationalized American politics (Hopkins 2018), when it comes to state governmental choices over democratic institutions, the key question is not about racial politics within a state but whether the state government is part of the national Republican Party.

Conclusion

Despite the national focus of much public discourse about American governance, the states have been a central arena of conflict over democratic contraction and expansion in recent years. Whereas the national government standardized and flattened policies through the New Deal and civil rights periods of the mid-twentieth century, states have more recently become increasingly socioeconomically important policymakers in areas such as health, welfare, and taxes, as we saw in chapter 3. In this chapter, I argue, states are also profoundly shaping the very gears and levers of democracy itself.

This chapter focused on the direct incentives facing elites from competition, polarization, and group coalitions. But these three mechanisms are themselves shaped by forces such as ideology, social movement activity, and the structure of identity in society. Can mass beliefs about democracy be a primary cause of its expansion? Some comparative studies suggest that mass support for democracy can lead to its expansion (Welzel and Inglehart 2006; Welzel 2007), and there is some evidence of policy responsiveness to mass

---

16. This book's focus on within-state change is also the reason its findings about racial demographics differ from those of Biggers and Hanmer (2017), who find that the interaction of Republican control with percent Black or Latino is associated with the implementation of voter ID laws. This chapter's difference-in-differences design suggests that *change* in demographics is not a relevant factor, whether on its own or interacted with Republican control.

ideology at the state level (Erikson, Wright, and McIver 1993; Caughey and Warshaw 2018). One strand of race and ethnic politics research points to racist attitudes in the mass public, which then produce racist violence and hierarchy, as the primary obstacle facing democracy (e.g., Gordon 1995; Douglass and Wilderson 2013), leaving little room for elites or organizations. However, this book leans toward the view of other cross-national research that suggests elites must also accept democracy for it to succeed (e.g., Linz, Stepan, et al. 1996).

A longer historical timeline would allow for the testing of additional mechanisms. In addition to party competition, Keyssar (2000, xxi) points to causes of democratic expansion that were more prominent in the nineteenth and early twentieth centuries, such as "frontier settlement," "the growth of cities and industry," "class tensions," and war.

In the contemporary period, however, the results are overwhelmingly clear—and concerning. The results of this analysis point to the Republican Party as the antidemocracy coalition in American politics and state governments as a key venue in which they are pursuing their goals. Pointing squarely at the GOP—naming names—is not common in American politics research or journalism. (It is easy to find headlines in which "counting votes" and other banal democratic processes are framed as "wins for the Democratic Party.")[17]

The force of Duverger's law has kept the United States a two-party system, and it will continue to do so absent radical change to electoral institutions—all the more concerning that one of the major parties is interested in weakening democracy.

17. "A federal appeals court on Tuesday upheld a six-day extension for counting absentee ballots in Wisconsin's presidential election, handing Democrats a victory in their fight." Scott Bauer, "Court Upholds Wisconsin Ballot Extension, Hands Dems a Win," Associated Press, September 29, 2020, https://apnews.com/article/election-2020-joe-biden-wisconsin-elections -courts-39646260cd6574be6a4d671301c0d7a4.

9

Conclusion

IN THE PRECEDING CHAPTERS, I have argued that the nationalization of the Democratic and Republican party coalitions increased the importance of state-level policymaking in American federalism. The evidence I presented suggests that this state policymaking—whether it is in the area of health policy, the environment, or the rules of American democracy itself—has been driven by national groups with national concerns rather than the localized incentives that animate traditional theories of federalism. The nationalization of the parties has upended the role of states as "laboratories of democracy" that customize policy based on local conditions, converting Republican states in particular to laboratories *against* democracy.

This chapter speaks to the broader implications of this transformation of American federalism. I review the empirical findings presented earlier and consider the still accelerating resurgence of the state level—and what it might mean for the future of American politics. In particular, I discuss whether the recent progress in some states on issues like climate and health policy suggests that the state level can be a viable route to generate positive policy feedbacks and broader change in support of the public interest. I discuss how American federalism's decentralized institutional structure decentralizes accountability, as we saw in the Covid-19 crisis. I conclude that such examples of policy successes should not detract from the broader idea that the state level is disadvantageous for groups seeking policy change on behalf of diffuse interests, including the interests of Americans marginalized by race and class, and leaves the United States vulnerable to democratic backsliding.

I conclude with policy recommendations based on the insights of this research. Groups and policymakers should not neglect the state level when it is the best (and, sometimes, only) viable political venue, and they should be attentive to the potential for policy feedbacks in state policy design. Policy feedbacks, when policy affects future politics, can propel local and state movements and agenda items to the national level. Still, groups and movements that represent diffuse interests should, when possible, pursue institutional changes that centralize policy and reduce the role of lower levels of government over the long term. Specifically, this might involve an expansionary fiscal federalism with greater use of automatic fiscal stabilizers for state and local governments during downturns and greater centralization of public benefits provision. Even more crucially, this would involve centralizing democratic institutions, from election administration to national enforcement against gerrymandering and election subversion.

An Accelerating Shift to the State Level

Florida had long disenfranchised ex-felons. But in 2018, after decades of political pressure, voting rights activists succeeded in putting Amendment 4 on the ballot. As a "tough-on-crime" state in which it is easy to become a felon (releasing helium-inflated balloons is a third-degree felony in Florida), the initiative had the potential to grant voting rights to 1.4 million Floridians—10 percent of the state's adult population, including nearly 22 percent of Black adults. In a massive victory, 65 percent of the Florida electorate voted in favor of Amendment 4 in the November 2018 election.

As the 2020 election approached, however, the state government of Florida took a page from the Jim Crow playbook. In 2019, the Republican-controlled legislature passed a bill requiring felons to pay "all fines and fees" before being granted their voting rights, closely related to southern states' poll taxes in the pre–civil rights period. But the similarities to Jim Crow voting laws went further. Journalists found that hundreds of thousands of ex-felons could not find out how much they owed in fines and fees due to Florida's decentralized and arcane system of administering court fees and sentence-related debts. Many old debt records were written on index cards buried deep within county offices.[1] Ex-felons faced not only a poll tax but one that was so opaque that it was nearly impossible to pay.[2]

1. https://www.cbsnews.com/news/amendment-4-florida-felony-voting-rights-60-minutes-2020-09-27/.

2. State governments across the country took similar steps aimed at reducing voter turnout. A month before the 2020 election, Texas governor Greg Abbott announced that the state would only allow one drop-off location for mail ballots per county, making it more difficult to vote,

Florida's efforts to keep formerly incarcerated people from voting, and so many other attacks on democracy over the past decade, are not simply the result of the emergence of a coalition with antidemocratic interests. Most democracies around the world are home to some group, and probably a powerful one, that would prefer that their society be a bit less democratic, whether the goal is to diminish the power of ethnic or religious minorities or prevent the masses from redistributing their wealth. But in the United States, an antidemocratic coalition took advantage of a decentralized federal institutional structure. This peculiar institutional terrain allowed them to capture a number of states, where they not only made major economic and social policy changes but shifted institutional rules to give them an advantage throughout the American political system.

Indeed, there is a pattern in American history: when state governments have wide policy leeway and there is wide policy variation across states, American democracy tends to suffer. The United States of the 2020s is one of those periods. A conservative majority on the Supreme Court is poised to overturn *Roe v. Wade*, invalidate major national policies like the Affordable Care Act, and make it easier for states to gerrymander their districts and suppress votes. In doing so, they would remove national standards that all states must meet—requirements that health insurers that operate in the state cover preexisting conditions, that a state's coal plants limit their emissions, and much more. If *Roe* is overturned, some states, mostly those controlled by Republicans, could implement state laws that criminalize abortion. Other states, mostly divided or Democratic, will maintain or even expand access to abortion services. These cases will accelerate the trends that are making the state level *the* central policy battleground of American politics.

Some blue state observers may not expect the accelerating resurgence of state politics to affect them. After all, the Supreme Court won't criminalize abortion in California or force New York to allow health insurers to exclude people with preexisting conditions. Moreover, during this period of resurgent state policymaking, liberal states have implemented major policies. Coastal states implemented cap and trade systems and increased vehicle fuel efficiency standards; liberal states raised their minimum wage and taxes on

---

especially in the state's more urban counties. Kaelan Deese, "Texas Governor Orders Only One Mail Ballot Drop-off Location Allowed per County," *The Hill*, October 1, 2020, https://thehill .com/homenews/state-watch/519183-texas-governor-orders-only-one-mail-ballot-drop-off -location-allowed-per.

high earners; more states expanded reproductive rights and protections for LGBT individuals.

The significance of these policy changes shouldn't be understated. But it is easy to overly focus on policy progress in some states while neglecting the question of whether, on average, the country would be freer, fairer, or more just if states had less authority in the American system. The resurgence of the state level as the central institutional battleground of American politics is not so simple. It doesn't mean that politics is simply transferred from the national level into fifty polities. It fundamentally changes the distribution of political advantages and disadvantages. Unlike ordinary voters and mass-based social movements, political actors with geographically mobile resources can strategically search for the most favorable time and place to influence politics. Wealthy individuals and large businesses can threaten to exit states in ways that working people cannot. And with state governments' constitutional authority over election administration, antidemocratic coalitions can establish a beachhead from which they can tilt the rules of the political system in their favor.

In the Trump era, moving authority from the national down to the state level might have sounded like a panacea. But this logic leads to unintended consequences. Indeed, by giving state governments new opportunities to gerrymander, suppress votes, and diminish the power of labor unions, the resurgence of policymaking at the state level may have helped Trump come to power in the first place. When combined with *national* political parties—a Democratic and especially a Republican Party that are nationally coordinated teams of interest groups and politicians—the huge constitutional authority that sits at the *state* level can unleash new threats to American democracy.

National Agenda Setters Turn to the States

State governments are playing a greater role in the lives of their residents. On the economic side, your state of residence matters much more for how much you are paid as a minimum wage worker, how much you pay in taxes as a millionaire, and how generous your welfare state is than it did a generation ago. On the social side, your state now plays a greater role in determining your ability to obtain an abortion, use marijuana, or own a gun.

Today, the correlation between state public opinion and state policy is stronger than it was a generation ago. But that doesn't necessarily mean ordinary voters were behind the major policy action in state governments of recent years. With few exceptions, state governments started to make major economic and social policy changes while state public opinion remained mostly stable over time. It remains a possibility that even with stable opinion, other changes in voter attitudes or behavior helped to produce the resurgence of significant state policymaking. Another possibility, however, is that a more organized set of political actors is behind this transformation.

The new glue that would bind state and national politics, galvanizing and polarizing politicians and policy in the states, was partisan teams of activists, donors, and organizations. These groups' increasingly organized participation can be seen in their campaign contributions to state legislative candidates, as shown in chapter 5. They can also be seen in the growth of organizational networks bankrolled by extremely wealthy individuals (Page, Seawright, and Lacombe 2018, chap. 5; Hertel-Fernandez 2019).

Decentralized Accountability

It is not just that federalism is an advantageous system for concentrated and antidemocratic interests. Across the board, federalism weakens politicians' incentives to perform well. The multiplicity of overlapping political authorities makes it difficult to know which politicians to reward or punish for their performance.[3] With little response from the Trump administration, the Covid-19 crisis provided a test case for whether Democratic state governments could marshal effective pandemic responses on their own.

In the early days of the pandemic, supporters of federalism celebrated state governments' leadership in the face of inaction from the feds. "Governors Leapfrog Feds on Coronavirus Response" (Povich 2020), read a report from the Pew Research Center. And for a moment in the late spring of 2020, Andrew Cuomo, in particular, was America's savior. Liberals eagerly tuned into the New York governor's morning press conferences, where their new hero reassured the country about the Covid-19 crisis and lambasted the federal response from the Trump administration. Cuomo's approval rating shot up to 77 percent in late April as he reached celebrity status.[4] As political scientist Kathleen Hall Jamieson suggested, "a person from Mars observing the rhetoric and actions of our leaders would reasonably assume that Andrew Cuomo is the

---

3. Benedictis-Kessner (2018), for instance, shows that citizens' frequent misattribution of responsibility to the wrong level of government reduces accountability in the policy area of public transit.

4. https://scri.siena.edu/wp-content/uploads/2020/04/SNY0420-Crosstabs.pdf.

president" (quoted in Povich 2020). "My Boyfriend Andrew Cuomo's New Girlfriend Is America," read a *Marie Claire* headline.[5] A viral *NowThis* piece carried the headline, "People Are Thirsting after Gov. Andrew Cuomo Right Now."[6] He would soon receive an International Emmy Award "in recognition of his leadership during the COVID-19 pandemic."[7]

But lurking underneath the performative gravitas of Cuomo's press conferences was the uncomfortable fact that New York State was not doing well. Covid-19 was wreaking havoc in New York City and throughout the state. About 30,000 New Yorkers had lost their lives to Covid-19 by June, more deaths than all but four countries on earth. It's reasonable to say that for much of 2020, New York was not only the American epicenter but the world's pandemic epicenter.

Some of the suffering was due to Cuomo's own mismanagement. The governor was slow to issue a lockdown order for his state, engaging in an antagonistic back-and-forth dithering with New York City mayor Bill de Blasio. He cut public services, including public health through the state's Medicaid program. Cuomo's executive order on nursing homes expanded the pandemic's damage.[8] As late as July 2020, waits for Covid-19 test results were at least a week long, and contact tracing never quite got off the ground. A long-time opponent of criminal justice reform, Cuomo presided over a spreading epidemic in the state's carceral system and resisted clemency cases. A plan to produce hundreds of thousands of gallons of New York State–branded hand sanitizer turned out to be a plan to have prisoners bottle imported hand sanitizer—a plan that had to be halted when the pandemic inevitably spread throughout the Clinton Correctional Facility. The notorious Rikers Island jail complex, where sixteen-year-old Kalief Browder had spent

5. Michelle Collins, "My Boyfriend Andrew Cuomo's New Girlfriend Is America," *Marie Claire*, March 26, 2020, https://www.marieclaire.com/culture/a31945211/andrew-cuomo-hot/.

6. Ashleigh Carter, "People Are Thirsting after Gov. Andrew Cuomo Right Now," *NowThis*, March 27, 2020, https://nowthisnews.com/news/people-are-thirsting-after-gov-andrew-cuomo -right-now.

7. Marta Zielinska, "'He Effectively Created Television Shows': Cuomo to Receive Emmy for Daily Covid Briefings," WCBS News Radio, November 20, 2020, https://www.radio.com /wcbs880/news/local/cuomo-to-receive-emmy-award-for-leadership-amid-pandemic.

8. Joaquin Sapien and Joe Sexton, "Andrew Cuomo's Report on Controversial Nursing Home Policy for COVID Patients Prompts More Controversy," *ProPublica*, July 10, 2020, https://www.propublica.org/article/andrew-cuomos-report-on-controversial-nursing-home -policy-for-covid-patients-prompts-more-controversy.

years in solitary confinement awaiting charges for theft, became the "epicenter of the epicenter."[9]

So why was Cuomo so beloved despite such grand failures of governance? Some of it was the public's justifiable desperation for the kind of clear rhetorical leadership that Trump eschewed. Some of it was just the usual politics of the polarized era: here was a prominent Democrat mincing no words in attacking Trump on a national stage. But some of this disconnect stems from federalism, the multilevel constitutional structure that gives authority to both the national and state governments.

Cuomo was able to deflect blame because federalism decentralizes accountability. This is not to say that his characterization of the federal government's response as calamitous was inaccurate. The Trump administration had slow walked policy actions like securing PPP equipment, politicized disease testing, called for premature ends to state lockdowns, and downplayed the importance of safety measures like wearing masks.[10] But Cuomo's ability to point not only to another branch of his state government but to another entire level of government in a federal system protected him from political accountability. It's hard to know how to distribute blame among the many executives and legislators in your local, state, and national government. When everybody is responsible, nobody is responsible.

Federalism may have also played a part in Cuomo's own poor policy decisions in office. Powerful concentrated interests, such as the fossil fuel industry, have outsized influence in Congress and presidential administrations—but they may distort democracy even more powerfully at the state and local levels. This could be true of Cuomo's New York government, for whom his opposition to criminal justice reform and taxes on the wealthy won praise from police unions and Wall Street.[11] Not only are concentrated interests influential in state politics, but compared to the national politics, voters aren't paying much attention to the state level anyway.

9. Sonia Moghe, "Inside New York's Notorious Rikers Island Jails, 'the Epicenter of the Epicenter' of the Coronavirus Pandemic," CNN, May 18, 2020, https://www.cnn.com/2020/05/16/us/rikers-coronavirus/index.html.

10. The testing program of the Centers for Disease Control (CDC) proved disastrously flawed. Further issues between the CDC and the administration delayed crucial travel restrictions. In a controversial move, the Food and Drug Administration (FDA) approved the malaria drug hydroxychloroquine for Covid-19 treatment but then had to reverse course.

11. Jimmy Vielkind, "The Governor of Wall Street," Politico, October 28, 2014, https://www.politico.com/states/new-york/albany/story/2014/10/the-governor-of-wall-street-000000.

At the same time, federalism tied the hands of Cuomo and the state government of New York. Despite its wealth as a state, New York not only lacked the fiscal and monetary capacity to provide economic aid at an adequate scale but its constitutional balanced budget requirement forced it to make cuts to safety net programs (including Medicaid—again, during a pandemic). The state also faced the negative spillovers from other states' weak pandemic responses. Crowds of spring breakers reveling in unregulated Florida, where the Republican governor Ron DeSantis resisted "draconian" lockdowns through March,[12] soon traveled back north. Viral stories abounded of people crossing state lines to go shopping in areas without mask-wearing requirements. The control that federalism supposedly granted New York and other state governments over the pandemic response was in part illusory.

Give Up on the States?

My argument is not that the supporters of democracy and equality should give up on politics at the state level. Despite the advantages it provides for narrow and antidemocratic interests, it is probably the best institutional option available during periods in which the national government is divided or hostile. Indeed, with a federal government that is likely to be divided for a long while, states should do everything they can to respond to pressing social and economic challenges. States may not have the fiscal capacity to implement Medicare for All, but they can create a viable public insurance option. Many of the policies that fall under the Green New Deal banner, including renewable energy requirements and investments in clean transportation infrastructure, can be accomplished to some degree at the state level. Wealthier states can make their community colleges and public universities free. Universal preschool and pre-K, child allowances, and family leave policies—all are possible in the states. State governments can even establish wage boards to promote sectoral collective bargaining, which is common in European countries. And, of course, groups should continue to work in policy areas where states and cities have near-total authority, such as residential zoning, where restrictions on density and public housing have created a housing crisis in states like California.

But recognizing state governments as sometimes the last best option should not be confused with celebrating them as champions of democracy. If they are

12. Sam Dorman, "Gov. DeSantis Touts Florida's Coronavirus Numbers over Democrat-Led States That Took 'Draconian' Measures," Fox News, May 22, 2020, https://www.foxnews.com /politics/ron-desantis-florida-covid-dem-states.

implemented at the state level, the policies I just described will likely appear as much more constrained versions of what they could be at the federal level. Even very progressive state governments will (rationally) fear the exodus of businesses and wealthy residents if they raise taxes or regulate carbon too aggressively, regardless of what would be best for the long-term health of their economies and residents. Ordinary voters will have a difficult time monitoring state policy in the information-poor environment of state politics, and groups representing working people will be less able to maneuver political resources to the right states at the right time than their counterparts representing more concentrated interests.

Groups that care about democracy and justice should take advantage of the moments when they control the national government. They should, of course, use executive actions and congressional legislation to further their goals. But critically, *they should pursue institutional changes that reduce the role of lower levels of government over the long term.*

Policy Feedbacks

The Obama administration and Democratic congressional supermajority of 2009 and 2010 did not focus especially hard on reducing the role of the states. Their signature policy achievement, the Affordable Care Act, was vulnerable to a Supreme Court ruling that allowed state governments to avoid expanding their Medicaid programs. The Justice Department under Attorney General Eric Holder addressed issues of institutional racism in policing, including investigating the Ferguson Police Department after the killing of Michael Brown, but stopped short of forcing state and local authorities to change their behavior. (By contrast, the 2009 economic stimulus bill tied the hands of state authorities, forcing even oppositional governors to accept the federal funds.)[13]

On labor issues, the Democratic House and Senate never brought the Employee Free Choice Act (EFCA) up for a vote. This piece of legislation that would have allowed union certification upon obtaining signatures from a majority of workers—drastically reducing the effectiveness of right-to-work and other state policies meant to curb labor power. Economic research consistently finds that unions increase wages (Budd and Na 2000), improve working conditions (Ravenswood and Markey 2011), and reduce economic inequality (Farber et al. 2021)—but policies like the EFCA that facilitate

---

13. "South Carolina Governor Trumped, Must Take Stimulus Money," CNN, June 4, 2009. https://www.cnn.com/2009/POLITICS/06/04/south.carolina.sanford.stimulus/index.html.

unions would also produce substantial policy feedbacks. Labor unions organize and turn out working-class voters, disproportionately for Democrats
(Feigenbaum, Hertel-Fernandez, and Williamson 2018), but they have an
even larger role in protecting small-d democracy. The American Postal Workers Union (APWU) and U.S. Postal Service (USPS), for instance, made the
decision to deliver absentee and mail ballots in the 2018 and 2020 elections
even when they were sent without proper postage stamps.[14] More broadly,
Paul Frymer and I (2021) found that labor unions reduce racial resentment
among white workers (Frymer and Grumbach 2021). Labor union decline
since the 1980s has opened up new opportunities for political elites to capital-
ize on racial and cultural conflict.

The story on climate change is nuanced, but federalism still presents a
major obstacle. On the one hand, in her book *Short Circuiting Policy*, Leah
Stokes (2020) has shown the potential for policy feedbacks from state-level
initiatives that help incubate renewable energy firms, which then fight to preserve and expand environmental regulation (see also Trachtman, forthcoming). Yet while Stokes and others illuminate important mechanisms for climate
progress under federalism, such an analysis does not address whether climate
mitigation and adaptation would be farther along under a more nationally
oriented political structure. Climate change activists have long worried not
only that the polluting industry's threat of exit leads to a "race to the bottom,"
putting downward pressure on environmental regulation, but also that, akin
to the "resource curse" in studies of international development, extractive and
high-emission industries can capture state political systems—extracting natural resources, as well as economic rents (Goldberg, Wibbels, and Mvukiyehe
2008; Clay and Portnykh 2018). The challenges inherent in solving climate
change through state-level policy are also related to those of the decentralized
American welfare state.

Expansionary Fiscal Federalism

During the 1970s, Congress's Advisory Commission on Intergovernmental
Relations (ACIR) developed policy proposals for using the federal government to support state and local governments during economic emergencies.

---

14. https://www.theguardian.com/world/live/2020/apr/22/coronavirus-us-live-first
-deaths-weeks-earlier-trump-cuomo-latest-news-updates?page=with:block-5ea0b2e58f
084784dca58330#block-5ea0b2e58f084784dca58330.

During downturns, automatic federal payments would kick in to maintain state-administered public services, like public schools. This and other ACIR plans for a more active federal role in state and local financing never got off the ground. In fact, Congress disbanded the ACIR itself in 1996.

While critical state-administered social programs like unemployment insurance and SNAP have built-in automatic stabilizers, the lack of comprehensive countercyclical federal policy for the states greatly exacerbated the catastrophe of the Great Recession. Nowhere is this clearer than public education, which relies on a combination of state and local property tax revenue. Public school employment was decimated during the recession and *never* fully recovered. In 2019, the year before the Covid-19 economic collapse put public education in an even deeper hole, there were over 300,000 fewer public school employees than there were in 2007.[15]

Because it relies in large part on state-level funding, even Medicaid, which by law contains a built-in federal stabilizer policy, suffers on the budgetary chopping block during economic downturns (precisely the moment when Americans need it most). States are, in many ways, just not set up to provide social programs that alleviate poverty or limit insecurity in any substantial way. Even when their voters might support it, state governments are reluctant to raise taxes for fear that large businesses and wealthy taxpayers will use their exit option. While economists describe the important role of Federal Reserve monetary policy in maintaining growth and limiting unemployment, state governments have no such monetary policy tools. Even more significantly, most state constitutions mandate balanced state budgets—essentially making it illegal for state governments to provide economic stimulus during downturns.

With decentralization of administration being a key tool for keeping the American welfare state hollow and unequally (especially racially unequally) distributed (Pierson 1995; Weir 2005; Katznelson 2013), a first best policy response would be to join other industrialized countries in creating a centralized welfare state. But plans for a more expansionary fiscal federalism, like those of the ACIR in the 1970s, can generate major improvements even while maintaining decentralized administration.

15. Quentin Fottrell, "Public-School Teacher Jobs Haven't Recovered since the Great Recession," *MarketWatch*, October 7, 2018, https://www.marketwatch.com/story/there-are-still-fewer-public-school-teachers-than-there-were-before-the-great-recession-2018-10-05.

Centralizing American Democracy

Even more importantly, those who wish to protect and expand American democracy should work to shift authority over elections and districting to the
national level. There are many potential reforms in this area, such as expanding
federal grants to state election administrators or creating an independent districting commission at the federal level. Lee Drutman and Charlotte Hill offer
a particularly bold and promising reform: the creation of a Federal Elections
Agency.[16] (Currently, the Federal Election Commission regulates campaign
finance, and federal regulation of election administration in the states is mostly
confined to Department of Justice enforcement of the Voting Rights Act.) A
Federal Elections Agency would set and enforce standards for election administration and security in the states through the provision of federal funds, coordination of voter registration data, and sharing of expertise. Like the Federal
Reserve, the Federal Elections Agency would be designed to be politically
independent, with commissioners who are unaffiliated with the parties and
abide by strict conflict of interest policies.

The federal government should also take additional steps to block state laws
that criminalize peaceful forms of political activity. In 2020, Governor DeSantis and Republican legislators in Florida proposed an "anti-mob" law that
would create new felonies for crimes of participating in "disorderly assemblies"
and "criminal mischief," such as blocking traffic during a protest (for more on
state legislation that restricts the rights of protestors, see Suh and Tarrow,
forthcoming).[17]

Likewise, national authority may be necessary to curb institutional racism
in American policing. State and local Democratic administrations have, for the
most part, failed to make substantive reforms to the law enforcement agencies
under their command. Social movements should continue to put pressure on
state and local officials on this issue, but it might be more effective over the
long term to support the U.S. Department of Justice or even Congress in investigating and reforming state and local agencies.

16. Lee Drutman and Charlotte Hill, "America Needs a Federal Elections Agency," New
America, 2020, https://www.newamerica.org/political-reform/reports/america-needs-federal
-elections-agency/.

17. Ana Ceballos and David Ovalle, "DeSantis Pushes Expansion of Stand Your Ground Law
as Part of 'Anti-Mob' Crackdown," *Miami Herald*, November 10, 2020, https://www.miamiherald
.com/news/politics-government/state-politics/article247094007.html.

State Government and American
Democracy at a Crossroads

Any political actor who wishes to influence public policy must incorporate the reality of American federalism into their strategy. This includes, first, recognizing that the Constitution places massive authority at the feet of state governments—especially authority over democratic institutions like elections. In an era of nationally polarized parties, this means that party control of state government is highly consequential.

Before the November 2020 election, former U.S. attorney general Eric Holder lamented that when "Democrats didn't focus on those state legislative races to the extent that we should have in 2010 . . . the 2011 redistricting went well for the Republicans and led to the gerrymandering that we have seen, and that has affected our politics over the course of this last decade." Although it was not as bad as the "shellacking" of 2010, unfortunately for Holder and the Democratic Party, the 2020 election was not a smashing success at the state level. The Democratic Party will have to continue to work to build capacity in gubernatorial and especially state legislative elections. This will involve some of the more well-established strategies that haven't yet been taken, like investing in and sharing national party resources with state and local party organizations (Schlozman and Rosenfeld 2019), the labor movement, and community leaders, and learning the lessons of conservative groups like ALEC (Hertel-Fernandez 2019). But it will also have to involve innovation in how to develop deep and durable—not episodic—engagement with communities that vary racially, economically, and geographically. There are signs of more durable organizing from groups like Indivisible and Sister District, as well as newer, more state-focused organizations like FutureNow.

At the same time, pro-democracy coalitions, whether partisan or nonpartisan, should use the power they gain at the national level to shift authority upward and away from the state level, where budgets are constrained, voters have less information, business and the wealthy can quickly flood political battles with money—and where threats to democracy continue to arise.

Appendix for Chapter 3

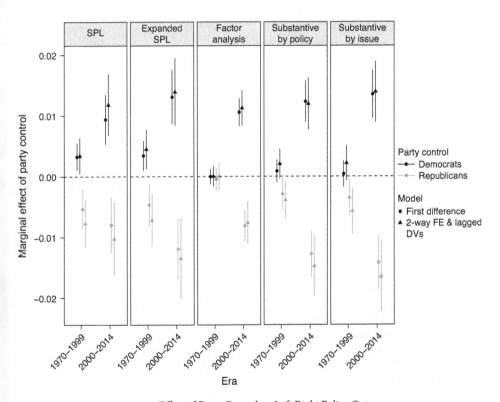

FIGURE A.1. Effect of Party Control on Left-Right Policy Outcomes.

Appendix for Chapter 4

TABLE A.1. Survey Data

Question	Source	Policy Area
Abortion legal	ANES	Abortion
Abortion legal	Gallup	Abortion
Abortion rape exception	GSS	Abortion
Abortion legal	GSS	Abortion
Equal employment for Black people	ANES	Civil Rights & Liberties
Affirmative action	ANES	Civil Rights & Liberties
Aid to Black people	ANES	Civil Rights & Liberties
Women equal role	ANES	Civil Rights & Liberties
Legal rights of accused	ANES	Criminal Justice
Support death penalty	Gallup	Criminal Justice
Support death penalty	GSS	Criminal Justice
Courts too harsh	GSS	Criminal Justice
Spending on public schools	ANES	Education
Environment thermometer	ANES	Environment
Spending to protect environment	ANES	Environment
Support gun ownership	GSS	Guns
Licenses for gun ownership	GSS	Guns
Assault weapon ban	Gallup	Guns
Government health assistance	Gallup	Health & Welfare
Government health insurance	ANES	Health & Welfare
Government spending on services	ANES	Health & Welfare
Spending on the poor	ANES	Health & Welfare
Spending on welfare	ANES	Health & Welfare
Spending on elderly	ANES	Health & Welfare
Childcare assistance	ANES	Health & Welfare
Spending on the poor	GSS	Health & Welfare
Government health assistance	GSS	Health & Welfare
Increase immigration	ANES	Immigration
Undocumented immigrant thermometer	ANES	Immigration
Labor union thermometer	ANES	Labor
Big business thermometer	ANES	Labor
Government support for employment	ANES	Labor
LGBT adoption	ANES	LGBT
LGBT in military	ANES	LGBT
LGBT anti-discrimination	ANES	LGBT
LGBT thermometer	ANES	LGBT
Legalize marijuana	Gallup	Marijuana
Legalize marijuana	GSS	Marijuana
Tax high incomes	GSS	Taxes

TABLE A.2. Myopic Partisan Learning

	1	2	3
Intercept	−5.317***	−5.325***	−5.317***
	(0.242)	(0.243)	(0.242)
Same Party	0.082***	0.077***	0.076***
	(0.009)	(0.009)	(0.009)
Δ Incumbent Legislature Vote Share$_{t-1}$	0.008*		0.008*
	(0.003)		(0.003)
Δ Incumbent Governor Vote Share$_{t-1}$	0.002		0.002
	(0.003)		(0.003)
Same Party × Δ Legislator Vote Share$_{t-1}$	0.032***		0.035***
	(0.008)		(0.008)
Same Party × Δ Governor Vote Share$_{t-1}$	0.019*		0.019*
	(0.008)		(0.008)
Δ Employment$_{t-1}$		0.012*	0.015**
		(0.005)	(0.005)
Δ GSP$_{t-1}$		0.000	−0.002
		(0.004)	(0.004)
Same Party × Δ Employment$_{t-1}$		0.017*	0.022*
		(0.008)	(0.009)
Same Party × Δ GSP$_{t-1}$		0.046***	−0.047***
		(0.001)	(0.001)
σ^2 Policy	2.631	2.640	2.631
σ^2 State$_i$	0.157	0.158	0.157
σ^2 State$_j$	0.133	0.130	0.133
σ^2 Year	0.180	0.181	0.180
N	4,748,959	4,948,509	4,748,959
Log-Likelihood	−460729	−479121	−460710
AIC	921478	958261	921448
Deviance	919865	956632	919827

Note: Multilevel logit coefficients with standard errors in parentheses.
*$p < 0.05$; **$p < 0.01$; ***$p < 0.001$

Appendix for Chapter 6

TABLE A.3. Descriptive Statistics

Variable	Mean	Std. Dev.
Δ unemployment (State j)	−0.020	1.130
Income per cap. in $1000s (State j)	36.020	7.370
Δ GSP in $1000s (State j)	6115.080	26974.810
Δ incumbent gub. vote share (State j)	3.790	13.140
Δ incumbent leg. vote share (State j)	0.420	5.680

Appendix for Chapter 7

TABLE A.4. Correlations between Measures

	Electoral (Additive)	Electoral (Factor)	Full (Additive)	Full (Factor)
Electoral (Additive)	–	0.676	0.678	0.567
Electoral (Factor)	0.676	–	0.633	0.743
Full (Additive)	0.678	0.633	–	0.923
Full (Factor)	0.567	0.743	0.923	–

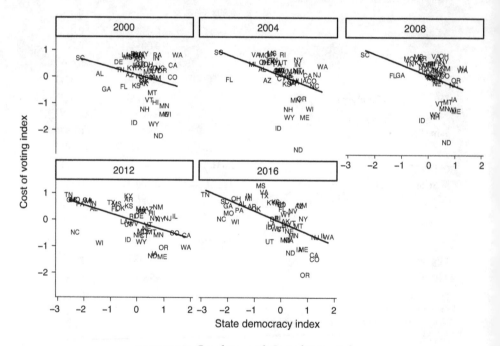

FIGURE A.2. Correlation with Cost of Voting Index.

The resulting measures are correlated with each other, as expected, but some of the relationships are quite moderate. The correlation coefficients between the main State Democracy Index measures and the broader measure range from 0.567 to 0.743, consistent with the idea that these measures tap into similar but somewhat distinct conceptualizations of democracy. In contrast, with the same set of over 100 democracy indicators going into them, the full State Democracy Index measures (additive and factor) are correlated at 0.923.

Appendix for Chapter 8

Descriptive Analysis of State Democracy

As a first cut, figure 8.1 plots the correlations between democratic performance and measures of party competition, polarization, and party control. These are time-series cross-sectional relationships: the model assesses how well the inputs explain variation in democracy across both states and time. Seeing the conditional relationships between the variables is helpful in determining whether, on average, more competitive or polarized states are more democratic (holding constant the other variables). However, because states vary tremendously in their baseline levels of democratic performance, these results should be considered descriptive.

The results of figure 8.1 are based on separate models for each of the four democracy measures, which vary on whether they are *Electoral* or *Full*, and whether they are based on *Additive* indexing or *Factor* measurement models. There is little association between partisan competition or polarization and democratic performance. The *Full* democracy measures show a small but significant negative correlation with competition; states with more competitive elections and narrow legislative majorities are slightly less democratic

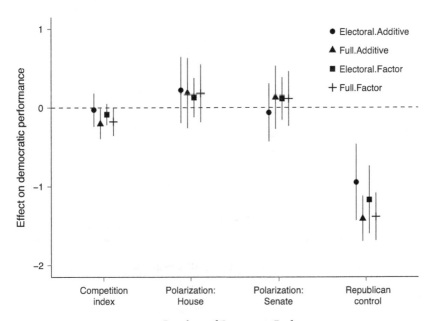

FIGURE A.3. Correlates of Democratic Performance.

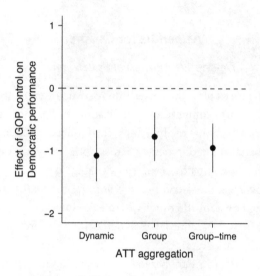

FIGURE A.4. GOP Control Results with Alternative
ATT Aggregation.

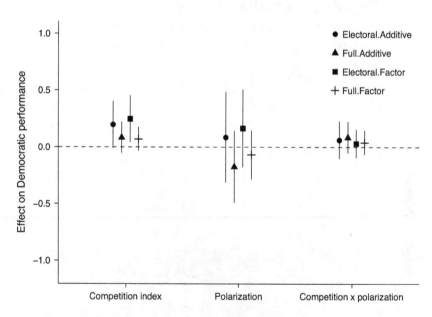

FIGURE A.5. The Interaction of Competition and Polarization with Alternative Democracy
Measures.

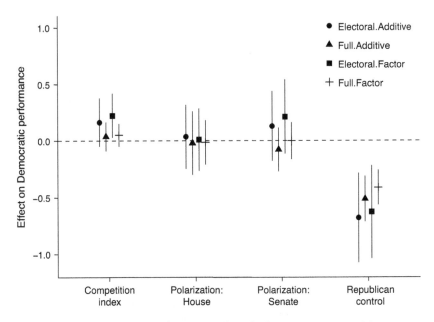

FIGURE A.6. Difference-in-Differences Results with Alternative Democracy Measures.

BIBLIOGRAPHY

Abdul-Razzak, Nour, Carlo Prato, and Stephane Wolton. "After *Citizens United*: How Outside Spending Shapes American Democracy." *Electoral Studies* 67 (2020): 102190.

Abrajano, Marisa, and Zoltan L. Hajnal. *White Backlash: Immigration, Race, and American Politics*. Princeton: Princeton University Press, 2015.

Abramowitz, Alan I. *The Disappearing Center: Engaged Citizens, Polarization, and American Democracy*. New Haven: Yale University Press, 2010.

Abramowitz, Alan I., Brad Alexander, and Matthew Gunning. "Incumbency, Redistricting, and the Decline of Competition in US House Elections." *Journal of Politics* 68, no. 1 (2006): 75–88.

Abramowitz, Alan I., and Kyle L. Saunders. "Is Polarization a Myth?" *Journal of Politics* 70, no. 2 (2008): 542–55.

Abramowitz, Alan I., and Steven Webster. "The Rise of Negative Partisanship and the Nationalization of US Elections in the 21st Century." *Electoral Studies* 41 (2016): 12–22.

Acemoglu, Daron, Suresh Naidu, Pascual Restrepo, and James A. Robinson. "Democracy Does Cause Growth." *Journal of Political Economy* 127, no. 1 (2019): 47–100.

Achen, Christopher H. "Mass Political Attitudes and the Survey Response." *American Political Science Review* 69, no. 4 (1975): 1218–31.

Achen, Christopher H., and Larry M. Bartels. *Democracy for Realists: Why Elections Do Not Produce Responsive Government*. Princeton: Princeton University Press, 2016.

Agan, Amanda Y., and Michael D. Makowsky. "The Minimum Wage, EITC, and Criminal Recidivism." *Journal of Human Resources* (forthcoming).

Ahler, Doug, and David Broockman. "The Delegate Paradox: Why Polarized Politicians Can Represent Citizens Best." Working Paper, 2017.

Ahlquist, John S., Nahomi Ichino, Jason Wittenberg, and Daniel Ziblatt. "How Do Voters Perceive Changes to the Rules of the Game? Evidence from the 2014 Hungarian Elections." *Journal of Comparative Economics* 46, no. 4 (2018): 906–19.

Ahn, T. K., Robert Huckfeldt, Alexander K. Mayer, and John Barry Ryan. "Expertise and Bias in Political Communication Networks." *American Journal of Political Science* 57, no. 2 (2013): 357–73.

Aldrich, John H. *Why Parties? The Origin and Transformation of Party Politics in America*. Chicago: University of Chicago Press, 1995.

Alesina, Alberto, and Edward Glaeser. *Fighting Poverty in the US and Europe: A World of Difference*. New York: Oxford University Press, 2004.

Alexander, Michelle. *The New Jim Crow: Mass Incarceration in the Age of Colorblindness*. New York: The New Press, 2012.

Allen, Mahalley D., Carrie Pettus, and Donald P. Haider-Markel. "Making the National Local: Specifying the Conditions for National Government Influence on State Policymaking." *State Politics & Policy Quarterly* 4, no. 3 (2004): 318–44.

Allen, Robert Sharon. *Our Sovereign State.* New York: Vanguard Press, 1949.

Alt, James E., and Robert C Lowry. "Divided Government, Fiscal Institutions, and Budget Deficits: Evidence from the States." *American Political Science Review* 88, no. 4 (1994): 811–28.

Aneja, Abhay P., and Carlos F. Avenancio-León. "Disenfranchisement and Economic Inequality: Downstream Effects of *Shelby County v. Holder.*" *AEA Papers and Proceedings* 109 (2019): 161–65.

Angrist, Joshua D., and Jörn-Steffen Pischke. *Mostly Harmless Econometrics: An Empiricist's Companion.* Princeton: Princeton University Press, 2008.

Ansell, Ben W., and David J. Samuels. *Inequality and Democratization: An Elite Competition Approach.* New York: Cambridge University Press, 2014.

Ansolabehere, Stephen, John M. de Figueiredo, and James M. Snyder. "Why Is There So Little Money in US Politics?" *Journal of Economic Perspectives* 17, no. 1 (2003): 105–30.

Ansolabehere, Stephen, John Mark Hansen, Shigeo Hirano, and James M. Snyder. "More Democracy: The Direct Primary and Competition in US Elections." *Studies in American Political Development* 24, no. 2 (2010): 190–205.

Ansolabehere, Stephen, and Stephen Pettigrew. *Cumulative CCES Common Content (2006–2012).* Harvard Dataverse, 2014.

Ansolabehere, Stephen, Jonathan Rodden, and James M. Snyder. "The Strength of Issues: Using Multiple Measures to Gauge Preference Stability, Ideological Constraint, and Issue Voting." *American Political Science Review* 102, no. 2 (2008): 215–32.

Anzia, Sarah F. "Election Timing and the Electoral Influence of Interest Groups." *Journal of Politics* 73, no. 2 (2011): 412–27.

Anzia, Sarah F., and Terry M. Moe. "Do Politicians Use Policy to Make Politics? The Case of Public-Sector Labor Laws." *American Political Science Review* 110, no. 4 (2016): 763–77.

———. "Polarization and Policy: The Politics of Public-Sector Pensions." *Legislative Studies Quarterly* 42, no. 1 (2017): 33–62.

Arcelus, Francisco, and Allan H. Meltzer. "The Effect of Aggregate Economic Variables on Congressional Elections." *American Political Science Review* 69, no. 4 (1975): 1232–39.

Arnold, Douglas R. *The Logic of Congressional Action.* New Haven: Yale University Press, 1992.

Bafumi, Joseph, and Michael C. Herron. "Leapfrog Representation and Extremism: A Study of American Voters and Their Members in Congress." *American Political Science Review* 104, no. 3 (2010): 519–42.

Bai, Jushan, and Pierre Perron. "Computation and Analysis of Multiple Structural Change Models." *Journal of Applied Econometrics* 18, no. 1 (2003): 1–22.

Bailey, Michael A. "Comparable Preference Estimates across Time and Institutions for the Court, Congress, and Presidency." *American Journal of Political Science* 51, no. 3 (2007): 433–48.

Baker, Anne E. "Do Interest Group Endorsements Cue Individual Contributions to House Candidates?" *American Politics Research* 44, no. 2 (2015): 197–221.

Banzhaf, H. Spencer, and Randall P. Walsh. "Do People Vote with Their Feet? An Empirical Test of Tiebout." *American Economic Review* 98, no. 3 (2008): 843–63.

Barber, Michael. "Donation Motivations: Testing Theories of Access and Ideology." *Political Research Quarterly* 69, no. 1 (2016a). http://doi.org/10.1177/1065912915624164.

———. "Ideological Donors, Contribution Limits, and the Polarization of State Legislatures" 78, no. 1 (2016b): 296–310.

Barber, Michael J., Brandice Canes-Wrone, and Sharece Thrower. "Sophisticated Donors: Which Candidates Do Individual Contributors Finance?" Working Paper, 2015.

Bardhan, Pranab. "Decentralization of Governance and Development." *Journal of Economic Perspectives* 16, no. 4 (2002): 185–205.

Barrilleaux, Charles, and Michael Berkman. "Do Governors Matter? Budgeting Rules and the Politics of State Policymaking." *Political Research Quarterly* 56, no. 4 (2003): 409–17.

Barrilleaux, Charles, and Carlisle Rainey. "The Politics of Need: Examining Governors' Decisions to Oppose the 'Obamacare' Medicaid Expansion." *State Politics & Policy Quarterly* 14, no. 4 (2014): 437–60.

Bartels, Larry M. "Constituency Opinion and Congressional Policy Making: The Reagan Defense Buildup." *American Political Science Review* 85, no. 2 (1991): 457–74.

———. "Partisanship and Voting Behavior, 1952–1996." *American Journal of Political Science* (2000): 35–50.

———. "The Social Welfare Deficit: Public Opinion, Policy Responsiveness, and Political Inequality in Affluent Democracies." Working Paper, 2015.

———. *Unequal Democracy: The Political Economy of the New Gilded Age.* Princeton: Princeton University Press, 2009.

Bastian, Jacob, and Katherine Michelmore. "The Long-Term Impact of the Earned Income Tax Credit on Children's Education and Employment Outcomes." *Journal of Labor Economics* 36, no. 4 (2018): 1127–63.

Bateman, David A., Ira Katznelson, and John S. Lapinski. *Southern Nation: Congress and White Supremacy after Reconstruction.* Princeton: Princeton University Press, 2018.

Bateman, David A., and John Lapinski. "Ideal Points and American Political Development: Beyond DW-NOMINATE." *Studies in American Political Development* 30, no. 2 (2016): 147–71.

Bauer, Scott. "Trump Adviser: Expect More Aggressive Poll Watching in 2020." Associated Press, December 20, 2019.

Baum, Lawrence. *The Supreme Court.* Washington, DC: CQ Press, 2015.

Baumgartner, Frank R., and Bryan D. Jones. *Agendas and Instability in American Politics.* Chicago: University of Chicago Press, 2010.

Baumgartner, Frank R., and Beth L. Leech. *Basic Interests: The Importance of Groups in Politics and in Political Science.* Princeton: Princeton University Press, 1998.

Bawn, Kathleen, Martin Cohen, David Karol, Seth Masket, Hans Noel, and John Zaller. "A Theory of Political Parties: Groups, Policy Demands and Nominations in American Politics." *Perspectives on Politics* 10, no. 3 (2012): 571–97.

Baybeck, Brady, William D. Berry, and David A. Siegel. "A Strategic Theory of Policy Diffusion via Intergovernmental Competition." *Journal of Politics* 73, no. 1 (2011): 232–47.

Beard, Charles A. *An Economic Interpretation of the Constitution of the United States.* New York: Macmillan, 1913.

Beck, Nathaniel, and Jonathan N. Katz. "Modeling Dynamics in Time-Series–Cross-Section Political Economy Data." *Annual Review of Political Science* 14 (2011): 331–52.

Bednar, Jenna. "Federalism as a Public Good." *Constitutional Political Economy* 16, no. 2 (2005): 189–205.

Beer, Samuel H. "Federalism, Nationalism, and Democracy in America." *American Political Science Review* 72, no. 1 (1978): 9–21.

Beland, Daniel, Philip Rocco, and Alex Waddan. *Obamacare Wars*. Lawrence: University Press of Kansas, 2016.

Benedictis-Kessner, Justin de. "How Attribution Inhibits Accountability: Evidence from Train Delays." *Journal of Politics* 80, no. 4 (2018): 1417–22.

Benedictis-Kessner, Justin de, and Christopher Warshaw. "Mayoral Partisanship and Municipal Fiscal Policy." *Journal of Politics* 78, no. 4 (2016): 1124–38.

———. "Politics in Forgotten Governments: The Partisan Composition of County Legislatures and County Fiscal Policies." *Journal of Politics* 82, no. 2 (2020): 460–75.

Bennett, Colin J. "What Is Policy Convergence and What Causes It?" *British Journal of Political Science* 21, no. 2 (1991): 215–33.

Bensel, Richard. "Lost in Translation: An Epistemological Exploration of the Relation between Historical Analysis and the NOMINATE Algorithm." *Studies in American Political Development* 30, no. 2 (2016): 185–201.

Beramendi, Pablo. "Inequality and the Territorial Fragmentation of Solidarity." *International Organization* 61, no. 4 (2007): 783–820.

Berry, Frances Stokes, and William D. Berry. "State Lottery Adoptions as Policy Innovations: An Event History Analysis." *American Political Science Review* 84, no. 2 (1990): 395–415.

Berry, William D., and Brady Baybeck. "Using Geographic Information Systems to Study Interstate Competition." *American Political Science Review* 99, no. 4 (2005): 505–19.

Berry, William D., Richard C. Fording, and Russell L. Hanson. "Reassessing the 'Race to the Bottom' in State Welfare Policy." *Journal of Politics* 65, no. 2 (2003): 327–49.

Berry, William D., Evan J. Ringquist, and Richard C. Fording. "Measuring Citizen and Government Ideology in the American States, 1960–93." *American Journal of Political Science* 42, no. 1 (1998): 327–48.

Bertrand, Marianne, Matilde Bombardini, Raymond Fisman, and Francesco Trebbi. "Tax-exempt Lobbying: Corporate Philanthropy as a Tool for Political Influence." *American Economic Review* 110, no. 7 (2020): 2065–2102.

Biasi, Barbara, and Heather Sarsons. *Flexible Wages, Bargaining, and the Gender Gap*. No. w27894. National Bureau of Economic Research, 2020.

Biggers, Daniel R., and Michael J. Hanmer. "Understanding the Adoption of Voter Identification Laws in the American States." *American Politics Research* 45, no. 4 (2017): 560–88.

Binder, Sarah A. "The Dynamics of Legislative Gridlock, 1947–96." *American Political Science Review* 93, no. 3 (1999): 519–33.

———. *Stalemate: Causes and Consequences of Legislative Gridlock*. Washington, DC: Brookings Institution Press, 2003.

Bishop, Bill. *The Big Sort: Why the Clustering of Like-Minded America Is Tearing Us Apart*. New York: Houghton Mifflin Harcourt, 2009.

Bobo, Lawrence, and Vincent L. Hutchings. "Perceptions of Racial Group Competition: Extending Blumer's Theory of Group Position to a Multiracial Social Context." *American Sociological Review* (1996): 951–72.

Boehmke, Frederick J. "The Effect of Direct Democracy on the Size and Diversity of State Interest Group Populations." *Journal of Politics* 64, no. 3 (2002): 827–44.

———. "Policy Emulation or Policy Convergence? Potential Ambiguities in the Dyadic Event History Approach to State Policy Emulation." *Journal of Politics* 71, no. 3 (2009): 1125–40.

Boehmke, Frederick J., and Paul Skinner. "State Policy Innovativeness Revisited." *State Politics & Policy Quarterly* 12, no. 3 (2012): 303–29.

Boehmke, Frederick J., and Richard Witmer. "Disentangling Diffusion: The Effects of Social Learning and Economic Competition on State Policy Innovation and Expansion." *Political Research Quarterly* 57, no. 1 (2004): 39–51.

Bonica, Adam. "Avenues of Influence: On the Political Expenditures of Corporations and Their Directors and Executives." Working Paper, 2015.

———. "Ideology and Interests in the Political Marketplace." *American Journal of Political Science* 57, no. 2 (2013): 294–311.

———. "Mapping the Ideological Marketplace." *American Journal of Political Science* 58, no. 2 (2014): 367–86.

Bonica, Adam, Nolan McCarty, Keith T. Poole, and Howard Rosenthal. "Why Hasn't Democracy Slowed Rising Inequality?" *Journal of Economic Perspectives* 27, no. 3 (2013): 103–23.

Boushey, Graeme. *Policy Diffusion Dynamics in America.* Cambridge: Cambridge University Press, 2010.

———. "Targeted for Diffusion? How the Use and Acceptance of Stereotypes Shape the Diffusion of Criminal Justice Policy Innovations in the American States." *American Political Science Review* 110, no. 1 (2016): 198–214.

Bowler, Shaun, and Todd Donovan. *Demanding Choices: Opinion, Voting, and Direct Democracy.* Ann Arbor: University of Michigan Press, 2000.

Brace, Paul, and Aubrey Jewett. "The State of State Politics Research." *Political Research Quarterly* 48, no. 3 (1995): 643–81.

Brady, Henry E., and David Collier. *Rethinking Social Inquiry: Diverse Tools, Shared Standards.* Lanham, MD: Rowman & Littlefield, 2010.

Brady, Henry E., Kay Lehman Schlozman, and Sidney Verba. "Prospecting for Participants: Rational Expectations and the Recruitment of Political Activists." *American Political Science Review* 93, no. 1 (1999): 153–68.

Bratton, Kathleen A., and Kerry L. Haynie. "Agenda Setting and Legislative Success in State Legislatures: The Effects of Gender and Race." *Journal of Politics* 61, no. 3 (1999): 658–79.

Breen, Richard. "Beliefs, Rational Choice and Bayesian Learning." *Rationality and Society* 11, no. 4 (1999): 463–79.

Breiman, Leo, et al. "Statistical Modeling: The Two Cultures (with Comments and a Rejoinder by the Author)." *Statistical Science* 16, no. 3 (2001): 199–231.

Bremer, Stuart A. "Dangerous Dyads: Conditions Affecting the Likelihood of Interstate War, 1816–1965." *Journal of Conflict Resolution* 36, no. 2 (1992): 309–41.

Brettschneider, Corey. *Democratic Rights: The Substance of Self-Government.* Princeton: Princeton University Press, 2010.

Brinkley, Alan. *The End of Reform: New Deal Liberalism in Recession and War.* New York: Vintage, 2011.

Brinkley, Alan. "The Problem of American Conservatism." *American Historical Review* 99, no. 2 (1994): 409–29.

Bromley-Trujillo, Rebecca, Mirya Holman, and Andres Sandoval. "Hot Districts, Cool Legislation: Evaluating Agenda Setting in Climate Change Bill Sponsorship in US States." *State Politics & Policy Quarterly* 19, no. 3 (2019): 375–95.

Broockman, David E. "Approaches to Studying Policy Representation." *Legislative Studies Quarterly* 41, no. 1 (2016): 181–215.

Broockman, David E., and Daniel M. Butler. "The Causal Effects of Elite Position-Taking on Voter Attitudes: Field Experiments with Elite Communication." *American Journal of Political Science* 61, no. 1 (2017): 208–21.

Broockman, David E., Nicholas Carnes, Melody Crowder-Meyer, and Christopher Skovron. "Having Their Cake and Eating It, Too: Why Local Party Leaders Don't Support Nominating Centrists." *British Journal of Political Science* 51, no. 2 (2021): 724–49.

Broockman, David E., and Christopher Skovron. "Bias in Perceptions of Public Opinion among Political Elites." *American Political Science Review* 112, no. 3 (2018): 542–63.

Brooks, Clem, and Jeff Manza. *Why Welfare States Persist: The Importance of Public Opinion in Democracies.* Chicago: University of Chicago Press, 2008.

Brown, Hana E. "Racialized Conflict and Policy Spillover Effects: The Role of Race in the Contemporary US Welfare State." *American Journal of Sociology* 119, no. 2 (2013): 394–443.

Brueckner, Jan K. "A Test for Allocative Efficiency in the Local Public Sector." *Journal of Public Economics* 19, no. 3 (1982): 311–31.

Bucci, Laura C., and Joshua M. Jansa. "Who Passes Restrictive Labour Policy? A View from the States." *Journal of Public Policy* 41, no. 3 (2021): 409–39.

Bucci, Laura C., and Kevin Reuning. "The State of Labor in the Democratic Party Coalition." *Party Politics* (August 2020).

Buchanan, James M. "Federalism as an Ideal Political Order and an Objective for Constitutional Reform." *Publius: The Journal of Federalism* 25, no. 2 (1995a): 19–28.

———. "Federalism and Individual Sovereignty." *Cato Journal* 15 (1995b): 259.

Buchanan, James M., and Gordon Tullock. *The Calculus of Consent: Logical Foundations of Constitutional Democracy.* Ann Arbor: University of Michigan Press, 1962.

Buckley, James L. *Saving Congress from Itself: Emancipating the States and Empowering Their People.* New York: Encounter Books, 2014.

Budd, John W., and In-Gang Na. "The Union Membership Wage Premium for Employees Covered by Collective Bargaining Agreements." *Journal of Labor Economics* 18, no. 4 (2000): 783–807.

Bulman-Pozen, Jessica. "Federalism as a Safeguard of the Separation of Powers." *Columbia Law Review* 112 (2012): 459–506.

———. "Partisan Federalism." *Harvard Law Review* 127 (2014): 1077–1146.

———. "States of the Union." Harvard Law Review blog. 2018. https://blog.harvardlawreview.org/states-of-the-union/.

Burke, Lindsey. *Keep the Federal Government Out of School Choice.* Heritage Foundation, 2017. https://www.heritage.org/education/commentary/keep-the-federal-government-out-school-choice.

Bushouse, Brenda K., and Jennifer E. Mosley. "The Intermediary Roles of Foundations in the Policy Process: Building Coalitions of Interest." *Interest Groups & Advocacy* 7, no. 3 (2018): 289–311.

Butler, Daniel M., and Eleanor Neff Powell. "Understanding the Party Brand: Experimental Evidence on the Role of Valence." *Journal of Politics* 76, no. 2 (2014): 492–505.

Butler, Daniel M., Craig Volden, Adam M. Dynes, and Boris Shor. "Ideology, Learning, and Policy Diffusion: Experimental Evidence." *American Journal of Political Science* 61, no. 1 (2017): 37–49.

Calabresi, Steven G., and Lucy D. Bickford. "Federalism and Subsidiarity: Perspectives from US Constitutional Law." *NOMOS* 55 (2014): 123–89.

Callander, Steven, and Gregory J. Martin. "Dynamic Policymaking with Decay." *American Journal of Political Science* 61, no. 1 (2017): 50–67.

Callaway, Brantly, and Pedro H. C. Sant'Anna. "Difference-in-Differences with Multiple Time Periods." *Journal of Econometrics* (forthcoming).

Calvo, Ernesto, and Jonathan Rodden. "The Achilles Heel of Plurality Systems: Geography and Representation in Multiparty Democracies." *American Journal of Political Science* 59, no. 4 (2015): 789–805.

Campbell, Ballard C. *The Growth of American Government: Governance from the Cleveland Era to the Present*. Bloomington: Indiana University Press, 2014.

Campbell, John L., and Ove K. Pedersen. *The National Origins of Policy Ideas: Knowledge Regimes in the United States, France, Germany, and Denmark*. Princeton: Princeton University Press, 2014.

Canes-Wrone, Brandice, David W. Brady, and John F. Cogan. "Out of Step, Out of Office: Electoral Accountability and House Members' Voting." *American Political Science Review* 96, no. 1 (2002): 127–40.

Canes-Wrone, Brandice, and Kenneth W. Shotts. "The Conditional Nature of Presidential Responsiveness to Public Opinion." *American Journal of Political Science* 48, no. 4 (2004).

Cantoni, Enrico, and Vincent Pons. "Strict ID Laws Don't Stop Voters: Evidence from a US Nationwide Panel, 2008–2018." *Quarterly Journal of Economics* 136, no. 4 (2021): 2615–60.

Carey, John M., Richard G. Niemi, and Lynda W. Powell. "The Effects of Term Limits on State Legislatures." *Legislative Studies Quarterly* (1998): 271–300.

Carnes, Nicholas. *The Cash Ceiling: Why Only the Rich Run for Office—and What We Can Do about It*. Princeton: Princeton University Press, 2020.

———. *White-Collar Government: The Hidden Role of Class in Economic Policy Making*. Chicago: University of Chicago Press, 2013.

Carroll, Royce, Jeffrey B. Lewis, James Lo, Keith T. Poole, and Howard Rosenthal. "Measuring Bias and Uncertainty in DW-NOMINATE Ideal Point Estimates via the Parametric Bootstrap." *Political Analysis* 17, no. 3 (2009): 261–75.

Case, Anne C., Harvey S. Rosen, and James R. Hines. "Budget Spillovers and Fiscal Policy Interdependence: Evidence from the States." *Journal of Public Economics* 52, no. 3 (1993): 285–307.

Caughey, Devin, James Dunham, and Christopher Warshaw. "The Ideological Nationalization of Partisan Subconstituencies in the American States." *Public Choice* 176, no. 1 (2018): 133–51.

Caughey, Devin, and Eric Schickler. "Substance and Change in Congressional Ideology: NOMINATE and Its Alternatives." *Studies in American Political Development* 30, (October 2016): 128–46.

Caughey, Devin, and Christopher Warshaw. *Dynamic Democracy: Citizens, Politicians, and Policymaking in the American States*. Chicago: University of Chicago Press (forthcoming).

Caughey, Devin, and Christopher Warshaw. "Dynamic Estimation of Latent Opinion Using a Hierarchical Group-Level IRT Model." *Political Analysis* 23, no. 2 (2015): 197–211.

———. "The Dynamics of State Policy Liberalism, 1936–2012." *American Journal of Political Science* 60, no. 4 (2016): 899–913.

———. "Policy Preferences and Policy Change: Dynamic Responsiveness in the American States, 1936–2014." *American Political Science Review* 112, no. 2 (2018): 249–66.

Caughey, Devin, Christopher Warshaw, and Yiqing Xu. "Incremental Democracy: The Policy Effects of Partisan Control of State Government." *Journal of Politics* 79, no. 4 (2017): 1342–58.

Chatfield, Sara, and Philip Rocco. "Is Federalism a Political Safety Valve? Evidence from Congressional Decision Making, 1960–2005." *Publius: The Journal of Federalism* 44, no. 1 (2014): 1–23.

Chen, Jowei, Jonathan Rodden, et al. "Unintentional Gerrymandering: Political Geography and Electoral Bias in Legislatures." *Quarterly Journal of Political Science* 8, no. 3 (2013): 239–69.

Chen, M. Keith, Kareem Haggag, Devin G. Pope, and Ryne Rohla. "Racial Disparities in Voting Wait Times: Evidence from Smartphone Data." *Review of Economics and Statistics* (forthcoming).

Chua, Amy. *Political Tribes: Group Instinct and the Fate of Nations*. New York: Penguin Books, 2019.

Chubb, John E. "Institutions, the Economy, and the Dynamics of State Elections." *American Political Science Review* 82, no. 1 (1988): 133–54.

Clay, Karen, and Margarita Portnykh. "The Short-Run and Long-Run Effects of Resources on Economic Outcomes: Evidence from the United States, 1936–2015." National Bureau of Economic Research, 2018.

Clayton, Cornell W. "Law, Politics and the New Federalism: State Attorneys General as National Policymakers." *Review of Politics* 56, no. 3 (1994): 525–53.

Clingermayer, James C., and Dan B. Wood. "Disentangling Patterns of State Debt Financing." *American Political Science Review* 89, no. 1 (1995): 108–20.

Clinton, Joshua D. "Representation in Congress: Constituents and Roll Calls in the 106th House." *Journal of Politics* 68, no. 2 (2006): 397–409.

———. "Using Roll Call Estimates to Test Models of Politics." *Annual Review of Political Science* 15 (2012): 79–99.

Clinton, Joshua, Simon Jackman, and Douglas Rivers. "The Statistical Analysis of Roll Call Data." *American Political Science Review* 98, no. 2 (2004): 355–70.

Cohen, Cathy J. *Democracy Remixed: Black Youth and the Future of American Politics*. New York: Oxford University Press, 2010.

Colbern, Allan, and S. Karthick Ramakrishnan. *Citizenship Reimagined: A New Framework for State Rights in the United States*. New York: Cambridge University Press, 2020.

Collier, David, and Steven Levitsky. "Democracy with Adjectives: Conceptual Innovation in Comparative Research." *World Politics* 49, no. 3 (1997): 430–51.

Conlan, Timothy J. *New Federalism: Intergovernmental Reform from Nixon to Reagan*. Washington, DC: Brookings Institution Press, 1988.

Constantelos, John. "Playing the Field: Federalism and the Politics of Venue Shopping in the United States and Canada." *Publius: The Journal of Federalism* 40, no. 3 (2010): 460–83.

Converse, Philip. "The Nature of Belief Systems in Mass Publics." In *Ideology and Discontent*, edited by David Apter, 206–61. New York: Free Press, 1964.

Conway, Karen Smith, and Andrew J. Houtenville. "Do the Elderly 'Vote with Their Feet?'" *Public Choice* 97, no. 4 (1998): 663–85.

Cooper, Ryan. "The Case against the American Constitution." *The Week*, February 1, 2017. https://theweek.com/articles/677164/case-against-american-constitution.

Courtemanche, Charles, James Marton, Benjamin Ukert, Aaron Yelowitz, and Daniela Zapata. "Early Impacts of the Affordable Care Act on Health Insurance Coverage in Medicaid Expansion and Non-Expansion States." *Journal of Policy Analysis and Management* 36, no. 1 (2017): 178–210.

Cox, Gary W., and Mathew D. McCubbins. *Legislative Leviathan: Party Government in the House.* New York: Cambridge University Press, 1993.

Craske, Nikki, Maxine Molyneux, and Haleh Afshar. *Gender and the Politics of Rights and Democracy in Latin America.* New York: Springer, 2002.

Culpepper, Pepper D. *Quiet Politics and Business Power: Corporate Control in Europe and Japan.* Cambridge: Cambridge University Press, 2010.

———. "Structural Power and Political Science in the Post-crisis Era." *Business and Politics* 17, no. 3 (2015): 391–409.

Cunningham, David E., Kristian Skrede Gleditsch, and Idean Salehyan. "It Takes Two: A Dyadic Analysis of Civil War Duration and Outcome." *Journal of Conflict Resolution* 53, no. 4 (2009): 570–97.

Dahl, Robert A. *How Democratic Is the American Constitution?* New Haven: Yale University Press, 2003.

———. *On Democracy.* New Haven: Yale University Press, 2008.

Dahl, Robert A. *Who Governs?: Democracy and Power in an American City.* New Haven: Yale University Press, 1960.

David, Paul T., and William Claggett. "Party Strength in the United States: 1872–1996." Inter-university Consortium for Political and Social Research, 2008.

DeBray, Elizabeth H. *Politics, Ideology, and Education.* New York: Teachers College Press, 2006.

Derthick, Martha. *Keeping the Compound Republic. Essays on American Federalism.* Washington, DC: Brookings Institution Press, 2004.

Desmarais, Bruce A., Jeffrey J. Harden, and Frederick J. Boehmke. "Persistent Policy Pathways: Inferring Diffusion Networks in the American States." *American Political Science Review* 109, no. 2 (2015): 392–406.

Devine, Pat J., Yannis S. Katsoulacos, and Roger Sugden. *Competitiveness, Subsidiarity and Industrial Policy.* New York: Routledge, 2005.

Dickman, Sam, David Himmelstein, Danny McCormick, and Steffie Woolhandler. "Opting Out of Medicaid Expansion: The Health and Financial Impacts." *Health Affairs Blog* 30 (January 2014).

Dionne, E. J., Jr., Norman J. Ornstein, and Thomas E. Mann. *One Nation after Trump: A Guide for the Perplexed, the Disillusioned, the Desperate, and the Not-yet Deported.* New York: St. Martin's Press, 2017.

Dorroh, Jennifer. "Statehouse Exodus." *American Journalism Review* 31 (2009): 20–35.

Douglass, Patrice, and Frank Wilderson. "The Violence of Presence: Metaphysics in a Blackened World." *Black Scholar* 43, no. 4 (2013): 117–23.

Downs, Anthony. "An Economic Theory of Political Action in a Democracy." *Journal of Political Economy* 65, no. 2 (1957): 135–50.

Drutman, Lee. "America Has Local Political Institutions but Nationalized Politics. This Is a Problem." *Vox*, May 31, 2018a.

———. "The Best Way to Fix Gerrymandering Is to Make It Useless." *New York Times*, June 19, 2018b.

DuBois, W.E.B. *Black Reconstruction in America: An Essay toward a History of the Part Which Black Folk Played in the Attempt to Reconstruct Democracy in America, 1860–1880*. New York: Harcourt Brace, 1935.

Duxbury, Scott W. "Who Controls Criminal Law? Racial Threat and the Adoption of State Sentencing Law, 1975 to 2012." *American Sociological Review* 86, no. 1 (2021): 123–53.

Dye, Thomas R. *American Federalism: Competition among Governments*. New York: Free Press, 1990.

Dynes, Adam M., and John B. Holbein. "Noisy Retrospection: The Effect of Party Control on Policy Outcomes." *American Political Science Review* 114, no. 1 (2020): 237–57.

Eckhouse, Laurel. "Race, Party, and Representation in Criminal Justice Politics." *Journal of Politics* 81, no. 3 (2019): 1143–52.

Egan, Timothy. "Revenge of the Coastal Elites." *New York Times*, May 10, 2019.

Einstein, Katherine Levine, David M. Glick, and Maxwell Palmer. "City Learning: Evidence of Policy Information Diffusion from a Survey of US Mayors." *Political Research Quarterly* 72, no. 1 (2019): 243–58.

Elazar, Daniel J. *American Federalism: A View from the States*. 2nd ed. New York: Thomas Y. Crowell Company, 1972.

———. "Opening the Third Century of American Federalism: Issues and Prospects." *Annals of the American Academy of Political and Social Science* 509, no. 1 (1990): 11–21.

Enda, Jodi, Katerina Eva Masta, and Jan Lauren Boyles. "America's Shifting Statehouse Press." Pew Research Center, July 10, 2014.

Enos, Ryan D. *The Space between Us: Social Geography and Politics*. New York: Cambridge University Press, 2017.

Enns, Peter K. *Incarceration Nation*. New York: Cambridge University Press, 2016.

Enns, Peter K., and Julianna Koch. "Public Opinion in the US States, 1956 to 2010." *State Politics & Policy Quarterly* 13, no. 3 (2013): 349–72.

Ensley, Michael J., Michael W. Tofias, and Scott de Marchi. "Are These Boots Made for Walking? Polarization and Ideological Change Among U.S. House Members." In *The State of the Parties: The Changing Role of Contemporary American Parties*, edited by John C. Green, Daniel J. Coffey, and David B. Cohen, 107–20. Lanham, MD: Rowman & Littlefield, 2014.

Epstein, David, and Sharyn O'Halloran. *Delegating Powers: A Transaction Cost Politics Approach to Policy Making under Separate Powers*. New York: Cambridge University Press, 1999.

Erikson, Robert S. "Economic Conditions and the Presidential Vote." *American Political Science Review* 83, no. 2 (1989): 567–73.

Erikson, Robert S., Michael B. MacKuen, and James A. Stimson. *The Macro Polity*. New York: Cambridge University Press, 2002.

Erikson, Robert S., Gerald C. Wright, and John P. McIver. "Public Opinion in the States: A Quarter Century of Change and Stability." In *Public Opinion in State Politics*, edited by Jeffrey E. Cohen, 229–53. Stanford: Stanford University Press, 2006.

———. *Statehouse Democracy: Public Opinion and Policy in the American States*. New York: Cambridge University Press, 1993.

Estlund, David. *Democratic Authority: A Philosophical Framework*. Princeton: Princeton University Press, 2009.

Fallon, Richard H., Jr. "The 'Conservative' Paths of the Rehnquist Court's Federalism Decisions." *University of Chicago Law Review* (2002): 429–94.

Farber, Henry S., Daniel Herbst, Ilyana Kuziemko, and Suresh Naidu. "Unions and Inequality over the Twentieth Century: New Evidence from Survey Data." *Quarterly Journal of Economics* 136, no. 3 (2021): 1325–85.

Feeley, Malcolm, and Edward Rubin. *Federalism: Political Identity and Tragic Compromise*. Ann Arbor: University of Michigan Press, 2009.

Fehrman, Craig. "All Politics Is National." *FiveThirtyEight*, November 7, 2016.

Feigenbaum, James, Alexander Hertel-Fernandez, and Vanessa Williamson. "From the Bargaining Table to the Ballot Box: Political Effects of Right to Work Laws." National Bureau of Economic Research, 2018. https://www.nber.org/papers/w24259.

Feld, Lars P. "James Buchanan's Theory of Federalism: From Fiscal Equity to the Ideal Political Order." *Constitutional Political Economy* 25, no. 3 (2014): 231–52.

Fellowes, Matthew C., and Gretchen Rowe. "Politics and the New American Welfare States." *American Journal of Political Science* 48, no. 2 (2004): 362–73.

Fenno, Richard F. *Home Style: House Members in Their Districts*. New York: Pearson College Division, 1978.

Fields, Barbara Jeanne. "Slavery, Race and Ideology in the United States of America." *New Left Review* 181, no. 1 (1990): 95–118.

Filindra, Alexandra, and Noah J. Kaplan. "Racial Resentment and Whites' Gun Policy Preferences in Contemporary America." *Political Behavior* 38, no. 2 (2016): 255–75.

Finger, Leslie K., and Michael T. Hartney. "Financial Solidarity: The Future of Unions in the Post-Janus Era." *Perspectives on Politics* (2019): 1–17.

Fiorina, Morris P. "Economic Retrospective Voting in American National Elections: A Micro-Analysis." *American Journal of Political Science* 22, no. 2 (1978): 426–43.

Fischman, Joshua B., and David S. Law. "What Is Judicial Ideology, and How Should We Measure It." *Washington University Journal of Law & Policy* 29, no. 133 (2009): 133–214.

Flavin, Patrick. "Campaign Finance Laws, Policy Outcomes, and Political Equality in the American States." *Political Research Quarterly* 68, no. 1 (2015): 77–88.

Florida, Richard. "Shift Power Back to the Local Level." *Politico* (2019). https://www.politico.com/interactives/2019/how-to-fix-politics-in-america/polarization/shift-power-back-to-the-local-level/.

Foner, Eric. *Free Soil, Free Labor, Free Men: The Ideology of the Republican Party before the Civil War: With a New Introductory Essay*. New York: Oxford University Press, 1995.

———. *Reconstruction: America's Unfinished Revolution, 1863–1877*. New York: Harper & Row, 1988.

———. "Why Is There No Socialism in the United States?" *History Workshop* 17 (Spring 1984): 57–80.

Fording, Richard C., Sanford F. Schram, and Joe Soss. "Do Welfare Sanctions Help or Hurt the Poor? Estimating the Causal Effect of Sanctioning on Client Earnings." *Social Service Review* 87, no. 4 (2013): 641–76.

Forman, James, Jr. "Community Policing and Youth as Assets." *Journal of Criminal Law & Criminology* 95 (2004): 1.

Fortner, Michael Javen. *Black Silent Majority: The Rockefeller Drug Laws and the Politics of Punishment*. Cambridge, MA: Harvard University Press, 2015.

Fouirnaies, Alexander, and Andrew B. Hall. "The Exposure Theory of Access: Why Some Firms Seek More Access to Incumbents than Others." Working Paper, 2015.

———. "How Do Interest Groups Seek Access to Committees?" Working Paper, 2016.

Fraga, Bernard L., and Michael G. Miller. "Who Does Voter ID Keep from Voting?" *Journal of Politics* (forthcoming). https://www.journals.uchicago.edu/doi/abs/10.1086/716282.

Francia, Peter L., Paul S. Herrnson, John C. Green, and Lynda W. Powell. *The Financiers of Congressional Elections: Investors, Ideologues, and Intimates*. New York: Columbia University Press, 2003.

Francis, Megan Ming. *Civil Rights and the Making of the Modern American State*. New York: Cambridge University Press, 2014.

Franko, William W., Caroline J. Tolbert, and Christopher Witko. "Inequality, Self-Interest, and Public Support for 'Robin Hood' Tax Policies." *Political Research Quarterly* 66, no. 4 (2013): 923–37.

Franko, William W., and Christopher Witko. *The New Economic Populism: How States Respond to Economic Inequality*. New York: Oxford University Press, 2018.

Franks, Mary Anne. *The Cult of the Constitution*. Stanford: Stanford University Press, 2019.

Frymer, Paul. *Building an American Empire: The Era of Territorial and Political Expansion*. Princeton: Princeton University Press, 2017.

Frymer, Paul, and Jacob M. Grumbach. "Labor Unions and White Racial Politics." *American Journal of Political Science* 65, no. 1 (2021): 225–40.

Fukuyama, Francis. "Against Identity Politics: The New Tribalism and the Crisis of Democracy." *Foreign Affairs* 97, no. 5 (September/October 2018): 90–114.

Gadarian, Shana Kushner. "The Politics of Threat: How Terrorism News Shapes Foreign Policy Attitudes." *Journal of Politics* 72, no. 2 (2010): 469–83.

Gamm, Gerald, and Thad Kousser. "Broad Bills or Particularistic Policy? Historical Patterns in American State Legislatures." *American Political Science Review* 104, no. 1 (2010): 151–70.

Garand, James C. "Explaining Government Growth in the US States." *American Political Science Review* 82, no. 3 (1988): 837–49.

Gelernter, David. "Back to Federalism." *Washington Examiner*, April 10, 2006. https://www.washingtonexaminer.com/weekly-standard/back-to-federalism.

Gelman, Andrew. *Red State, Blue State, Rich State, Poor State: Why Americans Vote the Way They Do*. Princeton: Princeton University Press, 2009.

Gelman, Andrew, and Jennifer Hill. *Data Analysis Using Regression and Multilevel/Hierarchical Models*. New York: Cambridge University Press, 2007.

Geltzer, Joshua. "America's Problem Isn't Too Little Democracy. It's Too Much." *Politico*, June 26, 2018.

Gerber, Alan S., Donald P. Green, and Christopher W. Larimer. "Social Pressure and Voter Turnout: Evidence from a Large-Scale Field Experiment." *American Political Science Review* 102, no. 1 (2008): 33–48.

Gerber, Elisabeth R. "Legislative Response to the Threat of Popular Initiatives." *American Journal of Political Science* 40, no. 1 (1996): 99–128.

Gerhardt, Michael. "Madison's Nightmare Has Come to America." *Atlantic*, February 2020. https://www.theatlantic.com/ideas/archive/2020/02/constitution-flawed/606208/.

Gerken, Heather K. "A New Progressive Federalism." *Democracy* 24 (2012).

Gerken, Heather K., and Joshua Revesz. "Progressive Federalism: A User's Guide." *Democracy* 24 (2012).

Gessen, Masha. "Autocracy: Rules for Survival." *New York Review of Books*, November 10, 2016.

Gibson, Edward L. "Boundary Control: Subnational Authoritarianism in Democratic Countries." *World Politics* 58, no. 1 (2005): 101–32.

———. *Boundary Control: Subnational Authoritarianism in Federal Democracies*. New York: Cambridge University Press, 2013.

———. *Federalism and Democracy in Latin America*. Baltimore: Johns Hopkins University Press, 2004.

Gibson, Edward L., and Desmond King. "Parties in State Politics." In *Illiberal Practices: Territorial Variance within Large Federal Democracies*, edited by Jacqueline Behrend and Laurence Whitehead, 23–48. Baltimore: Johns Hopkins University Press, 2016.

Gilardi, Fabrizio. "Who Learns from What in Policy Diffusion Processes?" *American Journal of Political Science* 54, no. 3 (2010): 650–66.

Gilardi, Fabrizio, and Katharina Füglister. "Empirical Modeling of Policy Diffusion in Federal States: The Dyadic Approach." *Swiss Political Science Review* 14, no. 3 (2008): 413–50.

Gilardi, Fabrizio, Katharina Füglister, and Stéphane Luyet. "Learning from Others: The Diffusion of Hospital Financing Reforms in OECD Countries." *Comparative Political Studies* 42, no. 4 (2009): 549–73.

Gilens, Martin. *Affluence and Influence: Economic Inequality and Political Power in America*. Princeton: Princeton University Press, 2012.

———. *Why Americans Hate Welfare: Race, Media, and the Politics of Antipoverty Policy*. Chicago: University of Chicago Press, 2009.

Gilens, Martin, and Benjamin I. Page. "Testing Theories of American Politics: Elites, Interest Groups, and Average Citizens." *Perspectives on Politics* 12, no. 3 (2014): 564–81.

Gilens, Martin, Shawn Patterson, and Pavielle Haines. "Campaign Finance Regulations and Public Policy." *American Political Science Review* 115, no. 3 (2021): 1074–81.

Gillion, Daniel Q. *Governing with Words: The Political Dialogue on Race, Public Policy, and Inequality in America*. New York: Cambridge University Press, 2016.

Gimpel, James G., Frances E. Lee, and Joshua Kaminski. "The Political Geography of Campaign Contributions in American Politics." *Journal of Politics* 68, no. 3 (2006): 626–39.

Giraudy, Agustina. *Democrats and Autocrats: Pathways of Subnational Undemocratic Regime Continuity within Democratic Countries*. New York: Oxford University Press, 2015.

Gius, Mark. "The Effects of State and Federal Gun Control Laws on School Shootings." *Applied Economics Letters* 25, no. 5 (2018): 317–20.

Glaude, Eddie S., Jr. *Democracy in Black: How Race Still Enslaves the American Soul*. New York: Broadway Books, 2017.

Glick, David M., and Zoe Friedland. "How Often Do States Study Each Other? Evidence of Policy Knowledge Diffusion." *American Politics Research* 42, no. 6 (2014): 956–85.

Goldberg, Ellis, Erik Wibbels, and Eric Mvukiyehe. "Lessons from Strange Cases: Democracy, Development, and the Resource Curse in the US States." *Comparative Political Studies* 41, no. 4–5 (2008): 477–514.

Goldberg, Jonah. "To Beat Trumpism, Denationalize Our Politics." *Los Angeles Times*, May 3, 2016. https://www.latimes.com/opinion/op-ed/la-oe-0503-goldberg-federalism-levin -20160503-column.html.

Goodman-Bacon, Andrew. "Difference-in-Differences with Variation in Treatment Timing." *Journal of Econometrics* (forthcoming).

Goodyear-Grant, Elizabeth, Richard Johnston, Will Kymlicka, and John Myles. *Federalism and the Welfare State in a Multicultural World*. Vol. 198. Queen's School of Policy Studies. Toronto: McGill-Queen's University Press, 2019.

Gordon, L. R. *Bad Faith and Antiblack Racism*. New York: Humanity Books, 1995.

Gordon, Sanford C., and Dimitri Landa. "National Conflict in a Federal System." Working Paper, 2019.

Graham, Matthew H., and Milan W. Svolik. "Democracy in America? Partisanship, Polarization, and the Robustness of Support for Democracy in the United States." *American Political Science Review* 114, no. 2 (2020): 392–409.

Granger, Clive W. J. "Some Recent Development in a Concept of Causality." *Journal of Econometrics* 39, no. 1 (1988): 199–211.

Granger, Clive W. J., and Paul Newbold. "Spurious Regressions in Econometrics." *Journal of Econometrics* 2, no. 2 (1974): 111–20.

Grattet, Ryken, Valerie Jenness, and Theodore R. Curry. "The Homogenization and Differentiation of Hate Crime Law in the United States, 1978 to 1995: Innovation and Diffusion in the Criminalization of Bigotry." *American Sociological Review* 63, no. 2 (1998): 286–307.

Gray, Virginia, and David Lowery. "Interest Group Politics and Economic Growth in the US States." *American Political Science Review* 82, no. 1 (1988): 109–31.

Gray, Virginia, David Lowery, Matthew Fellowes, and Andrea McAtee. "Public Opinion, Public Policy, and Organized Interests in the American States." *Political Research Quarterly* 57, no. 3 (2004): 411–20.

Green, Donald P., Bradley Palmquist, and Eric Schickler. *Partisan Hearts and Minds: Political Parties and the Social Identities of Voters*. New Haven: Yale University Press, 2002.

Greenacre, Michael. *Correspondence Analysis in Practice*. Boca Raton, FL: CRC Press, 2007.

Greve, Michael S. "The State of Our Federalism." *American Enterprise Institute*, 2011. https://www .aei.org/wp-content/uploads/2011/10/State-of-Federalism-Greve.pdf.

Grimmer, Justin, and Eleanor Neff Powell. "Money in Exile: Campaign Contributions and Committee Access." *Journal of Politics* 78, no. 4 (2016): 974–88.

Grimmer, Justin, and Jesse Yoder. "The Durable Differential Deterrent Effects of Strict Photo Identification Laws." Working Paper, 2019.

Grogan, Colleen M., and Elizabeth Rigby. "Federalism, Partisan Politics, and Shifting Support for State Flexibility: The Case of the US State Children's Health Insurance Program." *Publius: The Journal of Federalism* 39, no. 1 (2008): 47–69.

Grossback, Lawrence J., Sean Nicholson-Crotty, and David A. M. Peterson. "Ideology and Learning in Policy Diffusion." *American Politics Research* 32, no. 5 (2004): 521–45.

Grossmann, Matt. *Artists of the Possible: Governing Networks and American Policy Change since 1945*. New York: Oxford University Press, 2014.

———. *Red State Blues: How the Conservative Revolution Stalled in the States*. New York: Cambridge University Press, 2019.

Grossmann, Matt, and David A. Hopkins. "Ideological Republicans and Group Interest Demo-crats: The Asymmetry of American Party Politics." *Perspectives on Politics* 13, no. 1 (2015): 119–39.

Grumbach, Jacob M. "Does the American Dream Matter for Members of Congress? Social-Class Backgrounds and Roll-Call Votes." *Political Research Quarterly* 68, no. 2 (2015): 306–23.

———. "From Backwaters to Major Policymakers: Policy Polarization in the States, 1970–2014." *Perspectives on Politics* 16, no. 2 (2018): 416–35.

———. "Interest Group Activists and the Polarization of State Legislatures." *Legislative Studies Quarterly* 45, no. 1 (2020): 5–34.

———. "The Public or the Party? Significant Policies and Responsiveness in the U.S. States." Working Paper, 2016.

Grumbach, Jacob M., and Charlotte Hill. "Rock the Registration: Same Day Registration In-creases Turnout of Young Voters." *Journal of Politics* (forthcoming).

Grumbach, Jacob M., and Paul Pierson. "Are Large Corporations Politically Moderate?" Paper presented at Annual Meeting of the American Political Science Association, 2016.

Grumbach, Jacob M., and Alexander Sahn. "Race and Representation in Campaign Finance." *American Political Science Review* 114, no. 1 (2020): 206–21.

Grumbach, Jacob M., Alexander Sahn, and Sarah Staszak. "Gender, Race, and Intersectionality in Campaign Finance." *Political Behavior* (2020): 1–22.

Habermas, Jürgen. *Between Facts and Norms: Contributions to a Discourse Theory of Law and Democracy.* New York: John Wiley & Sons, 1992.

Hacker, Jacob S. "Privatizing Risk without Privatizing the Welfare State: The Hidden Politics of Social Policy Retrenchment in the United States." *American Political Science Review* 98, no. 2 (2004): 243–60.

Hacker, Jacob S., and Paul Pierson. "After the 'Master Theory': Downs, Schattschneider, and the Rebirth of Policy-Focused Analysis." *Perspectives on Politics* 12, no. 3 (2014): 643–62.

———. "Business Power and Social Policy: Employers and the Formation of the American Welfare State." *Politics & Society* 30, no. 2 (2002): 277 325.

———. *Let Them Eat Tweets: How the Right Rules in an Age of Extreme Inequality.* New York: Liveright, 2020.

———. *Off Center: The Republican Revolution and the Erosion of American Democracy.* New Haven: Yale University Press, 2005.

———. "The Path to Prosperity Is Blue." *New York Times*, July 31, 2016.

———. "Winner-Take-All Politics: Public Policy, Political Organization, and the Precipitous Rise of Top Incomes in the United States." *Politics & Society* 38, no. 2 (2010): 152–204.

Hafer, Catherine, and Dimitri Landa. "Public Goods in Federal Systems." *Quarterly Journal of Political Science* 2, no. 3 (2007): 253–76.

Haidt, Jonathan. *The Righteous Mind: Why Good People Are Divided by Politics and Religion.* New York: Vintage, 2012.

Hajnal, Zoltan L. *America's Uneven Democracy: Race, Turnout, and Representation in City Politics.* New York: Cambridge University Press, 2009.

Hajnal, Zoltan, and Jessica Trounstine. "Identifying and Understanding Perceived Inequities in Local Politics." *Political Research Quarterly* 67, no. 1 (2014): 56–70.

Hajnal, Zoltan, and Jessica Trounstine. "Where Turnout Matters: The Consequences of Uneven Turnout in City Politics." *Journal of Politics* 67, no. 2 (2005): 515–35.

Hall, Richard L., and Alan V. Deardorff. "Lobbying as Legislative Subsidy." *American Political Science Review* 100, no. 1 (2006): 69–84.

Halley, Janet E. "Reasoning about Sodomy: Act and Identity in and after *Bowers v. Hardwick.*" *Virginia Law Review* 79, no. 7 (1993): 1721–80.

Hamilton, Alexander, and James Madison. "The Structure of the Government Must Furnish the Proper Checks and Balances between the Different Departments." *Federalist Papers* 51 (1788).

Han, Hahrie. "The Organizational Roots of Political Activism: Field Experiments on Creating a Relational Context." *American Political Science Review* 110, no. 2 (2016): 296–307.

———. "Teaching the Skills of Citizenship." *Democracy Journal* 45 (2017).

Haney-López, Ian. *Dog Whistle Politics: How Coded Racial Appeals Have Reinvented Racism and Wrecked the Middle Class.* New York: Oxford University Press, 2015.

Harbers, Imke, Jos Bartman, and Enrike van Wingerden. "Conceptualizing and Measuring Subnational Democracy across Indian States." *Democratization* 26, no. 7 (2019): 1154–75.

Hardaway, Robert M. *The Electoral College and the Constitution: The Case for Preserving Federalism.* New York: Praeger, 1994.

Harden, Jeffrey J., and Justin H. Kirkland. "Do Campaign Donors Influence Polarization? Evidence from Public Financing in the American States." *Legislative Studies Quarterly* 41, no. 1 (2016): 119–52.

Harris, Alexes. *A Pound of Flesh: Monetary Sanctions as Punishment for the Poor.* New York: Russell Sage Foundation, 2016.

Harvey, Anna, and Taylor Mattia. "Does Money Have a Conservative Bias? Estimating the Causal Impact of *Citizens United* on State Legislative Preferences." *Public Choice* (forthcoming).

Harvey, David. *A Brief History of Neoliberalism.* New York: Oxford University Press, 2007.

Hasen, Richard L. *Election Meltdown: Dirty Tricks, Distrust, and the Threat to American Democracy.* New Haven: Yale University Press, 2020.

Hassell, Hans J. G. "Party Control of Party Primaries: Party Influence in Nominations for the US Senate." *Journal of Politics* 78, no. 1 (2016): 75–87.

———. "Party Elite Engagement and Coordination in House Primary Elections: A Test of Theories of Parties." *American Journal of Political Science* (forthcoming).

———. "Principled Moderation: Understanding Parties' Support of Moderate Candidates." *Legislative Studies Quarterly* 43, no. 2 (2018): 343–69.

Hassell, Hans J. G., and J. Quin Monson. "Campaign Targets and Messages in Direct Mail Fundraising." *Political Behavior* 36, no. 2 (2014): 359–76.

Hawkins, Andrew J. "Lyft Joins Uber in Threatening to Pull out of California over Driver Status." *The Verge*, August 12, 2020. https://www.theverge.com/2020/8/12/21365518/lyft-threatens-shut-down-california-q2-2020.

Helmke, Gretchen, Mary Kroeger, and Jack Paine. "Democracy by Deterrence: Strategic Self-Entrenchment in US Elections." Working Paper, 2021. https://www.gretchenhelmke.com/uploads/7/0/3/2/70329843/helmke_kroeger_paine_2021.pdf.

Hero, Rodney E., and Robert R. Preuhs. "Immigration and the Evolving American Welfare State: Examining Policies in the US States." *American Journal of Political Science* 51, no. 3 (2007): 498–517.

Hero, Rodney E., and Caroline J. Tolbert. "A Racial/Ethnic Diversity Interpretation of Politics and Policy in the States of the US." *American Journal of Political Science* 40, no. 3 (1996): 851.

Hertel-Fernandez, Alexander. "Explaining Liberal Policy Woes in the States: The Role of Donors." *PS: Political Science & Politics* 49, no. 3 (2016): 461–65.

———. *State Capture: How Conservative Activists, Big Businesses, and Wealthy Donors Reshaped the American States—and the Nation.* New York: Oxford University Press, 2019.

———. "Who Passes Business's 'Model Bills'? Policy Capacity and Corporate Influence in US State Politics." *Perspectives on Politics* 12, no. 3 (2014): 582–602.

Hertel-Fernandez, Alexander, and Theda Skocpol. "How the Right Trounced Liberals in the States." *Democracy: A Journal of Ideas*, no. 39 (Winter 2016): 46–59.

Hertel-Fernandez, Alexander, Theda Skocpol, and Daniel Lynch. "Business Associations, Conservative Networks, and the Ongoing Republican War over Medicaid Expansion." *Journal of Health Politics, Policy and Law* 41, no. 2 (2016): 239–86.

Hill, Kim Quaile, and Jan E. Leighley. "The Policy Consequences of Class Bias in State Electorates." *American Journal of Political Science* 36, no. 2 (1992): 351–65.

Hills, Roderick M. "The Political Economy of Cooperative Federalism: Why State Autonomy Makes Sense and 'Dual Sovereignty' Doesn't." *Michigan Law Review* 96, no. 4 (1998): 813–944.

Himmelstein, Jerome L. *To the Right: The Transformation of American Conservatism.* Berkeley: University of California Press, 1992.

Ho, Daniel E., and Kevin M. Quinn. "Measuring Explicit Political Positions of Media." *Quarterly Journal of Political Science* 3, no. 4 (2008): 353–77.

Hood, Roger, and Carolyn Hoyle. *The Death Penalty: A Worldwide Perspective.* New York: Oxford University Press, 2015.

Hopkins, Daniel J. *The Increasingly United States.* Chicago: University of Chicago Press, 2018.

Hopkins, David A. *Red Fighting Blue: How Geography and Electoral Rules Polarize American Politics.* New York: Cambridge University Press, 2017.

Huber, Evelyne, and John D. Stephens. "Welfare State and Production Regimes in the Era of Retrenchment." In *The New Politics of the Welfare State*, edited by Paul Pierson. New York: Oxford University Press, 2001.

Huber, John D., and Charles R. Shipan. *Deliberate Discretion?: The Institutional Foundations of Bureaucratic Autonomy.* New York: Cambridge University Press, 2002.

Hursh, David. "Assessing No Child Left Behind and the Rise of Neoliberal Education Policies." *American Educational Research Journal* 44, no. 3 (2007): 493–518.

Hutchings, Vincent L., and Ashley E. Jardina. "Experiments on Racial Priming in Political Campaigns." *Annual Review of Political Science* 12 (2009): 397–402.

Imai, Kosuke, Luke Keele, and Dustin Tingley. "A General Approach to Causal Mediation Analysis." *Psychological Methods* 15, no. 4 (2010): 309.

Jacobs, David, and Jason T. Carmichael. "The Political Sociology of the Death Penalty: A Pooled Time-Series Analysis." *American Sociological Review* 67, no. 1 (2002): 109–31.

Jacobs, Lawrence R. "Right vs. Left in the Midwest." *New York Times*, November 23, 2013.

Jacobson, Gary C. *The Politics of Congressional Elections.* New York: HarperCollins, 1992.

Jefferson, Hakeem. "Storming the U.S. Capitol Was about Maintaining White Power in America." *FiveThirtyEight*, January 8, 2021.

Jensen, Jennifer M. *The Governors' Lobbyists: Federal-State Relations Offices and Governors Associations in Washington*. Ann Arbor: University of Michigan Press, 2016.

Johnson, Kimberley. *Reforming Jim Crow: Southern Politics and State in the Age before Brown*. New York: Oxford University Press, 2010.

Jones-Correa, Michael. "The Origins and Diffusion of Racial Restrictive Covenants." *Political Science Quarterly* 115, no. 4 (2000): 541–68.

Jordan, Marty P., and Matt Grossmann. *The Correlates of State Policy Project v.1.5*. East Lansing, MI: Institute for Public Policy and Social Research (IPPSR), 2016.

Kahn, Matthew E. "Smog Reduction's Impact on California County Growth." *Journal of Regional Science* 40, no. 3 (2000): 565–82.

Kalla, Joshua L., and David E. Broockman. "Campaign Contributions Facilitate Access to Congressional Officials: A Randomized Field Experiment." *American Journal of Political Science* 60, no. 3 (2016): 545–58.

Kappeler, Andreas, and Timo Välilä. "Fiscal Federalism and the Composition of Public Investment in Europe." *European Journal of Political Economy* 24, no. 3 (2008): 562–70.

Kapsos, Steven. "Employment Intensity of Growth: The Trends and Macroeconomic Determinants." *International Labour Organization* Employment Strategy Papers 2005/12 (2005). http://www.ilo.org/public/english/employment/strat/download/esp2005- 12.pdf.

Karch, Andrew, and Shanna Rose. *Responsive States: Federalism and American Public Policy*. New York: Cambridge University Press, 2019.

Karol, David. *Party Position Change in American Politics: Coalition Management*. New York: Cambridge University Press, 2009.

Katznelson, Ira. *Fear Itself: The New Deal and the Origins of Our Time*. New York: W. W. Norton, 2013.

Kaufman, Aaron R., Gary King, and Mayya Komisarchik. "How to Measure Legislative District Compactness If You Only Know It When You See It." *American Journal of Political Science* 65, no. 3 (2021): 533–50.

Kellstedt, Paul M., and Guy D. Whitten. *The Fundamentals of Political Science Research*. Cambridge: Cambridge University Press, 2013.

Kelly, Nathan J., and Christopher Witko. "Federalism and American Inequality." *Journal of Politics* 74, no. 2 (2012): 414–26.

Kersten, Andrew E. *The Battle for Wisconsin: Scott Walker and the Attack on the Progressive Tradition*. New York: Macmillan, 2011.

Kessler-Harris, Alice. *In Pursuit of Equity: Women, Men, and the Quest for Economic Citizenship in 20th-Century America*. New York: Oxford University Press, 2001.

Kettl, Donald F. *The Divided States of America: Why Federalism Doesn't Work*. Princeton: Princeton University Press, 2020.

Key, V. O. *Politics, Parties, and Pressure Groups*. New York: Thomas Y. Crowell, 1947.

———. *Southern Politics in State and Nation*. New York: Thomas Y. Crowell, 1949.

Keyssar, Alexander. *The Right to Vote: The Contested History of Democracy in the United States*. New York: Basic Books, 2000.

Kincaid, John. "From Cooperative to Coercive Federalism." *Annals of the American Academy of Political and Social Science* 509, no. 1 (1990): 139–52.

King, Desmond. "Forceful Federalism against American Racial Inequality." *Government and Opposition* 52, no. 2 (2017): 356–82.

———. *Making Americans: Immigration, Race, and the Origins of the Diverse Democracy*. Cambridge, MA: Harvard University Press, 2009.

Kingdon, John W. *Agendas, Alternatives, and Public Policies*. Boston: Little Brown, 1984.

Klarner, Carl. "Democracy in Decline: The Collapse of the 'Close Race' in State Legislatures." *Ballotpedia*, 2015. https://ballotpedia.org/Competitiveness_in_State_Legislative_Elections:_1972-2014.

———. "State Partisan Balance Data, 1937–2011 [Computer File]." *Harvard Dataverse*, 2013. https://dataverse.harvard.edu/dataset.xhtml?persistentId=hdl:1902.1/20403.

Klarner, Carl E., William D. Berry, Thomas M. Carsey, Malcolm Jewell, Richard G. Niemi, Lynda W. Powell, and James Snyder. "State Legislative Election Returns, (1967–2010) [Computer File]." *ICPSR*, 2013. https://www.icpsr.umich.edu/web/ICPSR/studies/34297.

Kollman, Kelly, and Matthew Waites. "The Global Politics of Lesbian, Gay, Bisexual and Transgender Human Rights: An Introduction." *Contemporary Politics* 15, no. 1 (2009): 1–17.

Konczal, Mike. "The Forgotten State." *Boston Review*, 2016. https://bostonreview.net/books-ideas/mike-konczal-yuval-levin-fractured-republic-jacob-hacker-paul-pierson-american-amnesia.

Konisky, David M. "Regulatory Competition and Environmental Enforcement: Is There a Race to the Bottom?" *American Journal of Political Science* 51, no. 4 (2007): 853–72.

Kousser, J. Morgan. *The Shaping of Southern Politics: Suffrage Restriction and the Establishment of the One-Party South, 1880–1910*. New Haven: Yale University Press, 1974.

Kousser, Thad. "The Politics of Discretionary Medicaid Spending, 1980–1993." *Journal of Health Politics, Policy and Law* 27, no. 4 (2002): 639–72.

———. *Term Limits and the Dismantling of State Legislative Professionalism*. New York: Cambridge University Press, 2005.

Krehbiel, Keith. *Pivotal Politics: A Theory of US Lawmaking*. Chicago: University of Chicago Press, 1998.

Krimmel, Katherine. "The Efficiencies and Pathologies of Special Interest Partisanship." *Studies in American Political Development* 31, no. 2 (2017): 149–69. Krueger, Brian S., and Ping Xu. "Trade Exposure and the Polarization of Government Spending in the American States." *American Politics Research* 43, no. 5 (2015): 793–820.

Krugman, Paul. "Revenge of the Optimum Currency Area." *NBER Macroeconomics Annual* 27, no. 1 (2013): 439–48.

Kruse, Kevin M. *White Flight: Atlanta and the Making of Modern Conservatism*. Princeton: Princeton University Press, 2013.

La Raja, Raymond J., and Brian F. Schaffner. *Campaign Finance and Political Polarization: When Purists Prevail*. Ann Arbor: University of Michigan Press, 2015.

Lacey, Nicola. *The Prisoners' Dilemma: Political Economy and Punishment in Contemporary Democracies*. Cambridge: Cambridge University Press, 2008.

Lacey, Nicola, and David Soskice. "Crime, Punishment and Segregation in the United States: The Paradox of Local Democracy." *Punishment & Society* 17, no. 4 (2015): 454–81.

Landau, David, Hannah J. Wiseman, and Samuel R. Wiseman. "Federalism for the Worst Case." *Iowa Law Review* 105 (2019): 1187–1255.

Lascher, Edward L., Jr., Michael G. Hagen, and Steven A. Rochlin. "Gun behind the Door? Ballot Initiatives, State Policies and Public Opinion." *Journal of Politics* 58, no. 3 (1996): 760–75.

Lau, Richard R., and David P. Redlawsk. "Advantages and Disadvantages of Cognitive Heuristics in Political Decision Making." *American Journal of Political Science* 45, no. 4 (2001): 951–71.

Lauderdale, Benjamin E. "Unpredictable Voters in Ideal Point Estimation." *Political Analysis* 18, no. 2 (2010): 151–71.

Lave, Tamara Rice. "Shoot to Kill: A Critical Look at Stand Your Ground Laws." *University of Miami Law Review* 67 (2012): 827.

Laver, Michael, and John Garry. "Estimating Policy Positions from Political Texts." *American Journal of Political Science* 44, no. 3 (2000): 619–34.

Lax, Jeffrey R., and Justin H. Phillips. "The Democratic Deficit in the States." *American Journal of Political Science* 56, no. 1 (2012): 148–66.

———. "Gay Rights in the States: Public Opinion and Policy Responsiveness." *American Political Science Review* 103, no. 3 (2009): 367–86.

Lee, Frances E. *Beyond Ideology: Politics, Principles, and Partisanship in the US Senate*. Chicago: University of Chicago Press, 2009.

Lenz, Gabriel S. *Follow the Leader?: How Voters Respond to Politicians' Policies and Performance*. Chicago: University of Chicago Press, 2013.

Lerner, Max. "Constitution and Court as Symbols." *Yale Law Journal* 46, no. 8 (1937): 1290–1319.

Levendusky, Matthew. *The Partisan Sort: How Liberals Became Democrats and Conservatives Became Republicans*. Chicago: University of Chicago Press, 2009.

Levin, Andrew, Chien-Fu Lin, and Chia-Shang James Chu. "Unit Root Tests in Panel Data: Asymptotic and Finite-Sample Properties." *Journal of Econometrics* 108, no. 1 (2002): 1–24.

Levin, Yuval. *The Fractured Republic: Renewing America's Social Contract in the Age of Individualism*. New York: Basic Books, 2017.

———. "How Conservatives Lost the GOP." *Politico*, September/October 2016. https://www.politico.com/magazine/story/2016/09/conservatives-lost-republican-party-yuval-levin-2016-214228.

Levinson, Sanford. *Constitutional Faith*. Princeton: Princeton University Press, 2011.

Levitsky, Steven, and Lucan A. Way. *Competitive Authoritarianism: Hybrid Regimes after the Cold War*. New York: Cambridge University Press, 2010.

Levitsky, Steven, and Daniel Ziblatt. *How Democracies Die*. New York: Broadway Books, 2018.

Levitt, Steven D. "Using Repeat Challengers to Estimate the Effect of Campaign Spending on Election Outcomes in the US House." *Journal of Political Economy* 102, no. 4 (1994): 777–98.

Lewis, Daniel C., and Matthew L. Jacobsmeier. "Direct Democracy and Dynamic Policy Responsiveness: Gay Rights in the US." Paper presented at Annual Meetings of the American Political Science Association, 2012.

Lewis, Daniel C., Frederick S. Wood, and Matthew L. Jacobsmeier. "Public Opinion and Judicial Behavior in Direct Democracy Systems: Gay Rights in the American States." *State Politics & Policy Quarterly* 14, no. 4 (2014): 367–88.

Lewis-Beck, Michael S., and Mary Stegmaier. "Economic Determinants of Electoral Outcomes." *Annual Review of Political Science* 3, no. 1 (2000): 183–219.

Li, Quan, Michael J. Pomante, and Scot Schraufnagel. "Cost of Voting in the American States." *Election Law Journal* 17, no. 3 (2018): 234–47.

Lieberman, Robert C., and John S. Lapinski. "American Federalism, Race and the Administration of Welfare." *British Journal of Political Science* 31, no. 2 (2001): 303–29.

Lieberman, Robert C., Suzanne Mettler, Thomas B. Pepinsky, Kenneth M. Roberts, and Richard Valelly. "The Trump Presidency and American Democracy: A Historical and Comparative Analysis." *Perspectives on Politics* 17, no. 2 (2019): 470–79.

Lindblom, Charles E. "The Market as Prison." *Journal of Politics* 44, no. 2 (1982): 323–36.

———. *Politics and Markets: The World's Political-Economic Systems.* New York: Basic Books, 1977.

Linz, Juan J., Alfred Stepan, et al. *Problems of Democratic Transition and Consolidation: Southern Europe, South America, and Post-Communist Europe.* Baltimore: Johns Hopkins University Press, 1996.

Lowery, David, Virginia Gray, and Gregory Hager. "Public Opinion and Policy Change in the American States." *American Politics Research* 17, no. 1 (1989): 3–31.

Lowi, Theodore. "The Public Philosophy: Interest-Group Liberalism." *American Political Science Review* 61, no. 1 (1967): 5–24.

Lowry, Robert C., James E. Alt, and Karen E. Ferree. "Fiscal Policy Outcomes and Electoral Accountability in American States." *American Political Science Review* 92, no. 4 (1998): 759–74.

Lundin, Martin, PerOla Öberg, and Cecilia Josefsson. "Learning from Success: Are Successful Governments Role Models?" *Public Administration* 93, no. 3 (2015): 733–52.

MacLean, Nancy. *Democracy in Chains: The Deep History of the Radical Right's Stealth Plan for America.* New York: Penguin, 2017.

Maestas, Cherie. "Professional Legislatures and Ambitious Politicians: Policy Responsiveness of State Institutions." *Legislative Studies Quarterly* 25, no. 4 (2000): 663–90.

Majumdar, Sumon, and Sharun W. Mukand. "Policy Gambles." *American Economic Review* 94, no. 4 (2004): 1207–22.

Makse, Todd, and Craig Volden. "The Role of Policy Attributes in the Diffusion of Innovations." *Journal of Politics* 73, no. 1 (2011): 108–24.

Malbin, Michael J. "Three Policy Paths after *Citizens United*: A Critical Review Essay." *Tulsa Law Review* 52, no. 3 (2017): 537–52.

Maltz, Earl M. "Slavery, Federalism, and the Structure of the Constitution." *American Journal of Legal History* 36, no. 4 (1992): 466–98.

Maltzman, Forrest, and Charles R. Shipan. "Change, Continuity, and the Evolution of the Law." *American Journal of Political Science* 52, no. 2 (2008): 252–67.

Mann, Thomas E., and Norman J. Ornstein. *It's Even Worse than It Looks: How the American Constitutional System Collided with the New Politics of Extremism.* New York: Basic Books, 2013.

Manza, Jeff, and Christopher Uggen. *Locked Out: Felon Disenfranchisement and American Democracy.* New York: Oxford University Press, 2008.

March, James G., and Johan P. Olsen. *Rediscovering Institutions.* New York: Simon and Schuster, 2010.

Mares, Isabela. *From Open Secrets to Secret Voting: Democratic Electoral Reforms and Voter Autonomy.* New York: Cambridge University Press, 2015.

Marshall, Monty G., and Keith Jaggers. "Polity IV Project: Political Regime Characteristics and Transitions, 1800–2002." 2002. https://www.systemicpeace.org/inscr/p4manualv2016.pdf.

Martin, Andrew D., and Kevin M. Quinn. "Dynamic Ideal Point Estimation via Markov Chain Monte Carlo for the US Supreme Court, 1953–1999." *Political Analysis* 10, no. 2 (2002): 134–53.

Martin, Gregory J., and Joshua McCrain. "Local News and National Politics." *American Political Science Review* 113, no. 2 (2019): 372–84.

Martin, Gregory J., and Steven W. Webster. "Does Residential Sorting Explain Geographic Polarization?" *Political Science Research and Methods* 8, no. 2 (2020): 215–31. Martin, Gregory J., and Ali Yurukoglu. "Bias in Cable News: Persuasion and Polarization." *American Economic Review* 107, no. 9 (2017): 2565–99.

Martin, Isaac William. *The Permanent Tax Revolt: How the Property Tax Transformed American Politics.* Palo Alto, CA: Stanford University Press, 2008.

Masket, Seth. *No Middle Ground: How Informal Party Organizations Control Nominations and Polarize Legislatures.* Ann Arbor: University of Michigan Press, 2009.

Masket, Seth E., and Michael G. Miller. "Does Public Election Funding Create More Extreme Legislators? Evidence from Arizona and Maine." *State Politics & Policy Quarterly* 15, no. 1 (2015): 24–40.

Mason, Lilliana. *Uncivil Agreement: How Politics Became Our Identity.* Chicago: University of Chicago Press, 2018.

Matsusaka, John G. "Popular Control of Public Policy: A Quantitative Approach." *Quarterly Journal of Political Science* 5, no. 2 (2010): 133–67.

Mayhew, David R. *Congress: The Electoral Connection.* New Haven: Yale University Press, 1974.

———. *Divided We Govern: Party Control, Lawmaking, and Investigations, 1946–1990.* New Haven: Yale University Press, 1991.

———. *Placing Parties in American Politics: Organization, Electoral Settings, and Government Activity in the Twentieth Century.* Princeton: Princeton University Press, 2014.

McAuliffe, Colin. "The Senate Is an Irredeemable Institution." *Data for Progress,* December 17, 2019. https://www.dataforprogress.org/memos/the-senate-is-an-irredeemable-institution.

McCarthy, John D., and Mayer N. Zald. "Resource Mobilization and Social Movements: A Partial Theory." *American Journal of Sociology* 82, no. 6 (1977): 1212–41.

McCarthy, Justin. "Americans Still More Trusting of Local than State Government." *Gallup.com,* October 8, 2018. https://news.gallup.com/poll/243563/americans-trusting-local-state-government.aspx.

McCarty, Nolan. *Polarization: What Everyone Needs to Know®.* New York: Oxford University Press, 2019.

McCarty, Nolan, Keith T. Poole, and Howard Rosenthal. *Polarized America: The Dance of Ideology and Unequal Riches.* Cambridge, MA: MIT Press, 2006.

McConnell, Grant. *Private Power & American Democracy.* New York: Knopf, 1966.

McMann, Kelly M. "Measuring Subnational Democracy: Toward Improved Regime Typologies and Theories of Regime Change." *Democratization* 25, no. 1 (2018): 19–37.

Medoff, Marshall H., and Christopher Dennis. "TRAP Abortion Laws and Partisan Political Party Control of State Government." *American Journal of Economics and Sociology* 70, no. 4 (2011): 951–73.

Melnick, R. Shep. "Federalism and the New Rights." *Yale Law & Policy Review* 14, no. 2 (1996): 325–54.

Mendelberg, Tali. *The Race Card: Campaign Strategy, Implicit Messages, and the Norm of Equality.* Princeton: Princeton University Press, 2001.

Merriman, Ben. *Conservative Innovators: How States Are Challenging Federal Power.* Chicago: University of Chicago Press, 2019.

Meseguer, Covadonga. "Learning and Economic Policy Choices: A Bayesian Approach." *EUI Working Papers* 2003/05 (2003). https://cadmus.eui.eu/handle/1814/1847.

———. "Rational Learning and Bounded Learning in the Diffusion of Policy Innovations." *Rationality and Society* 18, no. 1 (2006): 35–66.

Mettler, Suzanne. *Dividing Citizens: Gender and Federalism in New Deal Public Policy.* Ithaca: Cornell University Press, 1998.

———. *The Submerged State: How Invisible Government Policies Undermine American Democracy.* Chicago: University of Chicago Press, 2011.

Meyerson, Harold. "The Seeds of a New Labor Movement." *American Prospect* (Fall 2014).

Michener, Jamila. *Fragmented Democracy: Medicaid, Federalism, and Unequal Politics.* New York: Cambridge University Press, 2018.

Mickey, Robert. *Paths Out of Dixie: The Democratization of Authoritarian Enclaves in America's Deep South, 1944–1972.* Princeton: Princeton University Press, 2015.

Miller, Lisa L. *The Myth of Mob Rule: Violent Crime and Democratic Politics.* New York: Oxford University Press, 2016.

———. *The Perils of Federalism: Race, Poverty, and the Politics of Crime Control.* New York: Oxford University Press, 2008.

———. "The Representational Biases of Federalism: Scope and Bias in the Political Process, Revisited." *Perspectives on Politics* 5, no. 2 (2007): 305–21.

———. "What's the Matter with American Politics? On Collective Action, Competition and Constraint." Working Paper, 2012.

Miller, Steven V., and Nicholas T. Davis. "The Effect of White Social Prejudice on Support for American Democracy." *Journal of Race, Ethnicity, and Politics* 6, no. 2 (2021): 334–51.

Miller, Wakken E., and Donald E. Stokes. "Constituency Influence in Congress." *American Political Science Review* 57, no. 1 (1963): 45–56.

Mills, Charles. *The Power Elite.* New York: Oxford University Press, 1956.

Mills, Charles W. *Black Rights/White Wrongs: The Critique of Racial Liberalism.* New York: Oxford University Press, 2017.

Mintrom, Michael. "Policy Entrepreneurs and the Diffusion of Innovation." *American Journal of Political Science* 41, no. 3 (1997): 738–70.

Mooney, Christopher Z. "The Decline of Federalism and the Rise of Morality-Policy Conflict in the United States." *Publius: The Journal of Federalism* 30, no. 1 (2000): 171–88.

Morley, Felix. *Freedom and Federalism.* New York: Liberty Press, 1959.

Moskowitz, Daniel J. "Local News, Information, and the Nationalization of US Elections." *American Political Science Review* 115, no. 1 (2021): 114–29.

Mummolo, Jonathan, and Clayton Nall. "Why Partisans Do Not Sort: The Constraints on Political Segregation." *Journal of Politics* 79, no. 1 (2017): 45–59.

Mutz, Diana C. "Status Threat, Not Economic Hardship, Explains the 2016 Presidential Vote." *Proceedings of the National Academy of Sciences* 115, no. 19 (2018): 4330–39.

Myers, Dowell, and Morris Levy. "Racial Population Projections and Reactions to Alternative News Accounts of Growing Diversity." *ANNALS of the American Academy of Political and Social Science* 677, no. 1 (2018): 215–28.

Newell, Jim. "Gov. Scott Walker's Amazing Prank Call with 'David Koch.'" *Gawker*, February 23, 2011.

Nicholson-Crotty, Sean. "The Politics of Diffusion: Public Policy in the American States." *Journal of Politics* 71, no. 1 (2009): 192–205.

Niesse, Mark, and Nick Thieme. "Closures Accelerated after Supreme Court Invalidated Voting Rights Act Provision, Putting Thousands Farther from the Polls." *Atlanta Journal-Constitution*, December 13, 2019.

Nivola, Pietro S. "Why Federalism Matters." *Brookings* (blog), October 1, 2005. https://www .brookings.edu/research/why-federalism-matters/.

Norrander, Barbara, and Clyde Wilcox. "Public Opinion and Policymaking in the States: The Case of Post-*Roe* Abortion Policy." *Policy Studies Journal* 27, no. 4 (1999): 707–22.

North, Douglass C. *Structure and Change in Economic History*. New York: W. W. Norton, 1981.

Oates, Wallace E. "An Essay on Fiscal Federalism." *Journal of Economic Literature* 37, no. 3 (1999): 1120–49.

———. *Fiscal Federalism*. New York: Harcourt Brace, 1972.

O'Brian, Neil A. "Income Inequality and Congressional Republican Position Taking, 1913–2013." *Journal of Politics* 81, no. 4 (2019a): 1533–38.

———. "One-Party States and Legislator Extremism in the US House, 1876–2012." *Journal of Politics* 81, no. 4 (2019b).

Olson, Mancur. *The Logic of Collective Action*. Cambridge, MA: Harvard University Press, 1965.

Olson, Michael. "Party System Competitiveness and Roll Call Voting: Evidence from State Legislatures in the U.S. South, 1880–1920." Working Paper, 2020.

Overby, L. Marvin, Thomas A. Kazee, and David W. Prince. "Committee Outliers in State Legislatures." *Legislative Studies Quarterly* 29, no. 1 (2004): 81–107.

Pacheco, Julianna. "The Social Contagion Model: Exploring the Role of Public Opinion on the Diffusion of Antismoking Legislation across the American States." *Journal of Politics* 74, no. 1 (2012): 187–202.

Paddock, Joel. *State & National Parties & American Democracy*. New York: Peter Lang, 2005.

Page, Benjamin I., Larry M. Bartels, and Jason Seawright. "Democracy and the Policy Preferences of Wealthy Americans." *Perspectives on Politics* 11, no. 1 (2013): 51–73.

Page, Benjamin I., Jason Seawright, and Matthew J. Lacombe. *Billionaires and Stealth Politics*. Chicago: University of Chicago Press, 2018.

Page, Benjamin I., and Robert Y. Shapiro. "Effects of Public Opinion on Policy." *American Political Science Review* 77, no. 1 (1983): 175–90.

———. *The Rational Public: Fifty Years of Trends in Americans' Policy Preferences*. Chicago: University of Chicago Press, 2010.

Park, David K., Andrew Gelman, and Joseph Bafumi. "Bayesian Multilevel Estimation with Poststratification: State-Level Estimates from National Polls." *Political Analysis* 12, no. 4 (2004): 375–85.

Parker, Christopher S., and Matt A. Barreto. *Change They Can't Believe In: The Tea Party and Reactionary Politics in America*. Updated edition. Princeton: Princeton University Press, 2014.

Parker, Christopher Sebastian, and Christopher C. Towler. "Race and Authoritarianism in American Politics." *Annual Review of Political Science* 22 (2019): 503–19.

Patterson, Samuel C., and Gregory A. Caldeira. "Getting Out the Vote: Participation in Gubernatorial Elections." *American Political Science Review* 77, no. 3 (1983): 675–89.

Paulus, Carl Lawrence. "Federalism against the Slave Power." *Kirk Center*, November 10, 2019. https://kirkcenter.org/reviews/federalism-against-the-slave-power/.

Perez-Truglia, Ricardo, and Guillermo Cruces. "Partisan Interactions: Evidence from a Field Experiment in the United States." *Journal of Political Economy* 125, no. 4 (2017): 1208–43.

Peterson, Paul E. *City Limits*. Chicago: University of Chicago Press, 1981.

Peterson, Paul E., and Mark C. Rom. *Welfare Magnets: A New Case for a National Standard*. Washington, DC: Brookings Institution Press, 2010.

Petrocik, John R. "Issue Ownership in Presidential Elections, with a 1980 Case Study." *American Journal of Political Science* 40, no. 3 (1996): 825–50.

Phillips, Anne. *Engendering Democracy*. State College: Penn State Press, 1991.

Picheta, Rob, and Henrik Pettersson. "The US Shoots, Kills and Imprisons More People than Other Developed Countries. Here's the Data." CNN, June 8, 2020. https://www.cnn.com /2020/06/08/us/us-police-floyd-protests-country-comparisons-intl/index.html.

Pierson, Paul. "The Costs of Marginalization: Qualitative Methods in the Study of American Politics." *Comparative Political Studies* 40, no. 2 (2007): 146–69.

———. *Dismantling the Welfare State?: Reagan, Thatcher and the Politics of Retrenchment*. New York: Cambridge University Press, 1994.

———. "Fragmented Welfare States: Federal Institutions and the Development of Social Policy." *Governance* 8, no. 4 (1995): 449–78.

———. *Politics in Time: History, Institutions, and Social Analysis*. Princeton: Princeton University Press, 2004.

Pierson, Paul, and Eric Schickler. "Madison's Constitution under Stress: A Developmental Analysis of Political Polarization." *Annual Review of Political Science* 23 (2020): 37–58.

Pierson, Paul, and Theda Skocpol. "Historical Institutionalism in Contemporary Political Science." *Political Science: The State of the Discipline* 3 (2002): 693–721.

Piketty, Thomas. *Capital in the Twenty-First Century*. Cambridge, MA: Harvard University Press, 2014.

Pilling, David. *The Growth Delusion: Wealth, Poverty, and the Well-Being of Nations*. New York: Tim Duggan Books, 2018.

Poole, Keith T., and Howard Rosenthal. *Congress: A Political-Economic History of Roll Call Voting*. New York: Oxford University Press, 1997.

Porter, Eduardo. "Unleashing the Campaign Contributions of Corporations." *New York Times*, August 28, 2012.

Posner, Paul. "The Politics of Coercive Federalism in the Bush Era." *Publius: The Journal of Federalism* 37, no. 3 (2007): 390–412.

Poterba, James M. "Balanced Budget Rules and Fiscal Policy: Evidence from the States." *National Tax Journal* 48, no. 3 (1995): 329–36.

Povich, Elaine S. "Governors Leapfrog Feds on Coronavirus Response." Pew Research Center, March 20, 2020. https://pew.org/2WE1pBx.

Prasad, Monica, and Steven Munch. "State-Level Renewable Electricity Policies and Reductions in Carbon Emissions." *Energy Policy* 45 (2012): 237–42.

Price, Byron E., and Norma M. Riccucci. "Exploring the Determinants of Decisions to Privatize State Prisons." *American Review of Public Administration* 35, no. 3 (2005): 223–35.

Qian, Yingyi, and Barry R. Weingast. "Federalism as a Commitment to Preserving Market Incentives." *Journal of Economic Perspectives* 11, no. 4 (1997): 83–92.

Quinn, Kevin M. "Bayesian Factor Analysis for Mixed Ordinal and Continuous Responses." *Political Analysis* 12, no. 4 (2004): 338–53.

Rabe, Barry G. *Statehouse and Greenhouse: The Emerging Politics of American Climate Change Policy.* Washington, DC: Brookings Institution Press, 2004.

Rakner, Lise, and Nicolas Van de Walle. "Democratization by Elections? Opposition Weakness in Africa." *Journal of Democracy* 20, no. 3 (2009): 108–21.

Ranney, Austin. "Parties in State Politics." In *Politics in the American States: A Comparative Analysis,* edited by Herbert Jacob and Kenneth N. Vines. Boston: Little, Brown, 1976.

Rapaczynski, Andrzej. "From Sovereignty to Process: The Jurisprudence of Federalism after *Garcia.*" *Supreme Court Review* (1985): 341–419.

Rauch, Jonathan. "A Separate Peace." *Atlantic,* April 1, 2007. https://www.theatlantic.com /magazine/archive/2007/04/a-separate-peace/305679/.

Ravenswood, Katherine, and Raymond Markey. "The Role of Unions in Achieving a Family-Friendly Workplace." *Journal of Industrial Relations* 53, no. 4 (2011): 486–503.

Rawls, John. *A Theory of Justice.* Cambridge, MA: Harvard University Press, 1971.

Reckhow, Sarah, and Megan Tompkins-Stange. "Financing the Education Policy Discourse: Philanthropic Funders as Entrepreneurs in Policy Networks." *Interest Groups & Advocacy* 7, no. 3 (2018): 258–88.

Redlawsk, David P. "Hot Cognition or Cool Consideration? Testing the Effects of Motivated Reasoning on Political Decision Making." *Journal of Politics* 64, no. 4 (2002): 1021–44.

Reich, Rob. *Just Giving: Why Philanthropy Is Failing Democracy and How It Can Do Better.* Princeton: Princeton University Press, 2018.

Rhodes, Jesse H., Brian F. Schaffner, and Raymond J. La Raja. "Detecting and Understanding Donor Strategies in Midterm Elections." *Political Research Quarterly* 71, no. 3 (2018): 503–16.

Rigby, Elizabeth, and Gerald C. Wright. "Political Parties and Representation of the Poor in the American States." *American Journal of Political Science* 57, no. 3 (2013): 552–65.

Riker, William H. "Federalism." In *Handbook of Political Science: Governmental Institutions and Processes,* edited by Fred I. Greenstein and Nelson W. Polsby, 93–172. Reading, MA: Addison-Wesley, 1975.

———. *Federalism: Origin, Operation, Significance.* Boston: Little, Brown, 1964.

Riverstone-Newell, Lori. "The Rise of State Preemption Laws in Response to Local Policy Innovation." *Publius: The Journal of Federalism* 47, no. 3 (2017): 403–25.

Roberts, David. "Tech Nerds Are Smart. But They Can't Seem to Get Their Heads around Politics." *Vox,* August 27, 2015. https://www.vox.com/2015/8/27/9214015/tech-nerds-politics.

Robertson, David Brian. *Federalism and the Making of America.* New York: Routledge, 2017.

Robin, Corey. "The Gonzo Constitutionalism of the American Right." *New York Review of Books*, October 21, 2020. http://www.nybooks.com/daily/2020/10/21/the-gonzo-constitutionalism -of-the-american-right/.

Rocco, Philip. "Ending Federalism as We Know It." *Jacobin*, November 9, 2020.

———. "Laboratories of What? American Federalism and the Politics of Democratic Subversion." In *Democratic Resilience: Can the United States Withstand Rising Polarization?*, edited by Suzanne Mettler, Robert Lieberman, and Ken Roberts, 297–319. New York: Cambridge University Press, 2021.

Rodden, Jonathan A. *Why Cities Lose: The Deep Roots of the Urban-Rural Political Divide*. New York: Basic Books, 2019.

Roe, Mark J. "Delaware's Competition." *Harvard Law Review* 117 (2003): 588.

Rogers, Steven. "Electoral Accountability for State Legislative Roll Calls and Ideological Representation." *American Political Science Review* 111, no. 3 (2017): 555–71.

———. "National Forces in State Legislative Elections." *ANNALS of the American Academy of Political and Social Science* 667, no. 1 (2016): 207–25.

Roh, Jongho, and Donald P. Haider-Markel. "All Politics Is Not Local: National Forces in State Abortion Initiatives." *Social Science Quarterly* 84, no. 1 (2003): 15–31.

Romano, Roberta. *The Advantage of Competitive Federalism for Securities Regulation*. Washington, DC: American Enterprise Institute, 2002.

Rose, Shanna, and Cynthia J. Bowling. "The State of American Federalism, 2014–15: Pathways to Policy in an Era of Party Polarization." *Publius: The Journal of Federalism* 45, no. 3 (2015): 351–79.

Rothman, Adam. *Slave Country: American Expansion and the Origins of the Deep South*. Cambridge, MA: Harvard University Press, 2005.

Sanbonmatsu, Kira. "Political Parties and the Recruitment of Women to State Legislatures." *Journal of Politics* 64, no. 3 (2002): 791–809.

Sances, Michael W. "The Distributional Impact of Greater Responsiveness: Evidence from New York Towns." *Journal of Politics* 78, no. 1 (2016): 105–19.

Sartori, Giovanni. "Concept Misformation in Comparative Politics." *American Political Science Review* 64, no. 4 (1970): 1033–53.

Schaffner, Brian F., Jesse H. Rhodes, and Raymond J. La Raja. *Hometown Inequality: Race, Class, and Representation in American Local Politics*. New York: Cambridge University Press, 2020.

Schattschneider, Elmer Eric. *Party Government*. New York: Transaction Publishers, 1942.

———. *Politics, Pressures and the Tariff: A Study of Free Private Enterprise in Pressure Politics, as Shown in the 1929–1930 Revision of the Tariff*. New York: Prentice-Hall, 1935.

———. *The Semisovereign People*. New York: Holt, Rinehart and Winston, 1960.

Schickler, Eric. *Disjointed Pluralism: Institutional Innovation and the Development of the US Congress*. Princeton: Princeton University Press, 2001.

———. "Institutional Change in the House of Representatives, 1867–1998: A Test of Partisan and Ideological Power Balance Models." *American Political Science Review* 94, no. 2 (2000): 269–88.

———. "New Deal Liberalism and Racial Liberalism in the Mass Public, 1937–1968." *Perspectives on Politics* 11, no. 1 (2013): 75–98.

Schickler, Eric. *Racial Realignment: The Transformation of American Liberalism, 1932–1965*. Princeton: Princeton University Press, 2016.

Schleicher, David. "Federalism and State Democracy." *Texas Law Review* 95 (2016): 763.

———. "Federalism Is in a Bad State." Harvard Law Review blog, October 12, 2018. https://blog .harvardlawreview.org/federalism-is-in-a-bad-state/.

Schlozman, Daniel. *When Movements Anchor Parties: Electoral Alignments in American History*. Princeton: Princeton University Press, 2015.

Schlozman, Daniel, and Sam Rosenfeld. "The Hollow Parties." In *Can America Govern Itself*, edited by Frances E. Lee and Nolan McCarty, 154–210. New York: Cambridge University Press, 2019.

Schlozman, Kay Lehman, and John T. Tierney. *Organized Interests and American Democracy*. New York: Harper Collins, 1986.

Schlozman, Kay Lehman, Sidney Verba, and Henry E. Brady. *The Unheavenly Chorus: Unequal Political Voice and the Broken Promise of American Democracy*. Princeton: Princeton University Press, 2012.

Schuck, Peter H. "Money Won't Buy You Votes." *Los Angeles Times*, April 20, 2014.

Schuit, Sophie, and Jon C. Rogowski. "Race, Representation, and the Voting Rights Act." *American Journal of Political Science* 61, no. 3 (2017): 513–26.

Schumpeter, Joseph A. *Capitalism, Socialism and Democracy*. New York: Harper & Brothers, 1942.

Self, Robert O. *American Babylon: Race and the Struggle for Postwar Oakland*. Princeton: Princeton University Press, 2005.

Shapiro, David. "Banking on Bondage: Private Prisons and Mass Incarceration." American Civil Liberties Union, 2011. https://www.aclu.org/banking-bondage-private-prisons-and-mass -incarceration.

Shapiro, Ian. *The State of Democratic Theory*. Princeton: Princeton University Press, 2009.

Sharkansky, Ira. "Economic Development, Regionalism and State Political Systems." *Midwest Journal of Political Science* 12, no. 1 (1968): 41–61.

Shelby, Tommie. *We Who Are Dark: The Philosophical Foundations of Black Solidarity*. Cambridge, MA: Harvard University Press, 2005.

Shepsle, Kenneth A., and Barry R. Weingast. "Structure-Induced Equilibrium and Legislative Choice." *Public Choice* 37, no. 3 (1981): 503–19.

Shipan, Charles R., and Craig Volden. "Policy Diffusion: Seven Lessons for Scholars and Practitioners." *Public Administration Review* 72, no. 6 (2012): 788–96.

———. "When the Smoke Clears: Expertise, Learning and Policy Diffusion." *Journal of Public Policy* 34, no. 3 (2014): 357–87.

Shirley, Kenneth E., and Andrew Gelman. "Hierarchical Models for Estimating State and Demographic Trends in US Death Penalty Public Opinion." *Journal of the Royal Statistical Society* 178, no. 1 (2015): 1–28.

Shor, Boris, Joseph Bafumi, Luke Keele, and David Park. "A Bayesian Multilevel Modeling Approach to Time-Series Cross-Sectional Data." *Political Analysis* 15, no. 2 (2007): 165–81.

Shor, Boris, and Nolan McCarty. "The Ideological Mapping of American Legislatures." *American Political Science Review* 105, no. 3 (2011): 530–51.

Shufeldt, Gregory, and Patrick Flavin. "Two Distinct Concepts: Party Competition in Government and Electoral Competition in the American States." *State Politics & Policy Quarterly* 12, no. 3 (2012): 330–42.

Sides, John, Michael Tesler, and Lynn Vavreck. *Identity Crisis: The 2016 Presidential Campaign and the Battle for the Meaning of America.* Princeton: Princeton University Press, 2019.

Simmons, Beth A., and Zachary Elkins. "The Globalization of Liberalization: Policy Diffusion in the International Political Economy." *American Political Science Review* 98, no. 1 (2004): 171–89.

Simon, Herbert A. "Human Nature in Politics: The Dialogue of Psychology with Political Science." *American Political Science Review* 79, no. 2 (1985): 293–304.

Simon, Jonathan. *Governing through Crime: How the War on Crime Transformed American Democracy and Created a Culture of Fear.* New York: Oxford University Press, 2007.

Simonovits, Gabor, Andrew M. Guess, and Jonathan Nagler. "Responsiveness without Representation: Evidence from Minimum Wage Laws in U.S. States." *American Journal of Political Science* 63, no. 2 (2019): 401–10.

Sinclair, Betsy. *The Social Citizen: Peer Networks and Political Behavior.* Chicago: University of Chicago Press, 2012.

Sinn, Stefan. "The Taming of Leviathan: Competition among Governments." *Constitutional Political Economy* 3, no. 2 (1992): 177–96.

Skocpol, Theda. *Diminished Democracy: From Membership to Management in American Civic Life.* Norman: University of Oklahoma Press, 2013a.

———. "Naming the Problem: What It Will Take to Counter Extremism and Engage Americans in the Fight against Global Warming." Prepared for the symposium "The Politics of America's Fight against Global Warming," February 14, 2013b. https://scholars.org/sites/scholars/files/skocpol_captrade_report_january_2013_0.pdf.

Skocpol, Theda, Marshall Ganz, and Ziad Munson. "A Nation of Organizers: The Institutional Origins of Civic Voluntarism in the United States." *American Political Science Review* 94, no. 3 (2000): 527–46.

Skocpol, Theda, and Alexander Hertel Fernandez. "The Koch Network and Republican Party Extremism." *Perspectives on Politics* 14, no. 3 (2016): 681–99.

Smith, Bradley A. "The Case for Corporate Political Spending." *Wall Street Journal*, February 27, 2010.

———. "The Power of Political Money Is Overrated." *New York Times*, February 29, 2016.

Smith, Jason Scott. *Building New Deal Liberalism: The Political Economy of Public Works, 1933–1956.* New York: Cambridge University Press, 2006.

Smith, Mark A. "The Nature of Party Governance: Connecting Conceptualization and Measurement." *American Journal of Political Science* 41, no. 3 (1997): 1042–56.

Smith, Rogers M. "Beyond Tocqueville, Myrdal, and Hartz: The Multiple Traditions in America." *American Political Science Review* 87, no. 3 (1993): 549–66.

Sorens, Jason, Fait Muedini, and William P. Ruger. "US State and Local Public Policies in 2006: A New Database." *State Politics & Policy Quarterly* 8, no. 3 (2008): 309–26.

Soroka, Stuart N., and Christopher Wlezien. *Degrees of Democracy: Politics, Public Opinion, and Policy.* New York: Cambridge University Press, 2010.

Soss, Joe, Sanford F. Schram, Thomas P. Vartanian, and Erin O'Brien. "Setting the Terms of Relief: Explaining State Policy Choices in the Devolution Revolution." *American Journal of Political Science* 45, no. 2 (2001): 378–95.

Soss, Joe, and Vesla Weaver. "Police Are Our Government: Politics, Political Science, and the Policing of Race–Class Subjugated Communities." *Annual Review of Political Science* 20 (2017): 565–91.

Stegmueller, Daniel. "How Many Countries for Multilevel Modeling? A Comparison of Frequentist and Bayesian Approaches." *American Journal of Political Science* 57, no. 3 (2013): 748–61.

Stein, Jason. "Right to Work Latest Move in GOP Transformation of State." *Milwaukee Journal Sentinel*, February 25, 2015.

Stein, Jeff. "GOP Senators Are Rushing to Pass Graham-Cassidy. We Asked 9 to Explain What It Does." *Vox*, September 20, 2018.

Stepan, Alfred C. "Federalism and Democracy: Beyond the US Model." *Journal of Democracy* 10, no. 4 (1999): 19–34.

Stephanopoulos, Nicholas, and Christopher Warshaw. "The Impact of Partisan Gerrymandering on Political Parties." *Legislative Studies Quarterly* 45, no. 4 (2020): 609–43.

Stephens-Dougan, LaFleur. "Priming Racial Resentment without Stereotypic Cues." *Journal of Politics* 78, no. 3 (2016): 687–704.

Stiglitz, Joseph E. "GDP Fetishism." *Economists' Voice* 6, no. 8 (2009). https://www.degruyter.com/document/doi/10.2202/1553-3832.1651/html.

Stimson, James A. *Public Opinion in America: Moods, Cycles, and Swings*. New York: Westview, 1991.

Stimson, James A., Michael B. MacKuen, and Robert S. Erikson. "Dynamic Representation." *American Political Science Review* 89, no. 3 (1995): 543–65.

Stokes, Leah Cardamore. *Short Circuiting Policy: Interest Groups and the Battle over Clean Energy and Climate Policy in the American States*. New York: Oxford University Press, 2020.

Stollwerk, Alissa F. "Estimating Subnational Opinion with Cluster-Sampled Polls: Challenges and Suggestions." Paper presented at APSA Annual Meeting, 2012.

Stuart, Forrest. *Down, Out, and Under Arrest: Policing and Everyday Life in Skid Row*. Chicago: University of Chicago Press, 2016.

Stuckatz, Jan. "How the Workplace Affects Employee Political Contributions." *American Political Science Review* (forthcoming).

Suh, Chan S., and Sidney G. Tarrow. "Suppression by Stealth: The Partisan Response to Protest in State Legislatures." *Politics & Society* (forthcoming).

Sundqvist, Sanna, Lauri Frank, and Kaisu Puumalainen. "The Effects of Country Characteristics, Cultural Similarity and Adoption Timing on the Diffusion of Wireless Communications." *Journal of Business Research* 58, no. 1 (2005): 107–10.

Sussell, Jesse, and James A. Thomson. *Are Changing Constituencies Driving Rising Polarization in the US House of Representatives?* Santa Monica, CA: Rand Corporation, 2015.

Tatalovich, Raymond. *The Politics of Abortion in the United States and Canada: A Comparative Study*. New York: M. E. Sharpe, 2015.

Tausanovitch, Chris, and Christopher Warshaw. "Representation in Municipal Government." *American Political Science Review* 108, no. 3 (2014): 605–41.

Teaford, Jon C. *The Rise of the States: Evolution of American State Government.* Baltimore: Johns Hopkins University Press, 2002.

Teele, Dawn Langan. *Forging the Franchise: The Political Origins of the Women's Vote.* Princeton: Princeton University Press, 2018a.

———. "How the West Was Won: Competition, Mobilization, and Women's Enfranchisement in the United States." *Journal of Politics* 80, no. 2 (2018b): 442–61.

Terwee, Caroline B., Sandra D. M. Bot, Michael R. de Boer, Daniëlle A.W.M. van der Windt, Dirk L. Knol, Joost Dekker, Lex M. Bouter, and Henrica C. W. de Vet. "Quality Criteria Were Proposed for Measurement Properties of Health Status Questionnaires." *Journal of Clinical Epidemiology* 60, no. 1 (2007): 34–42.

Tesler, Michael. *Post-Racial or Most-Racial?: Race and Politics in the Obama Era.* Chicago: University of Chicago Press, 2016.

Thomsen, Danielle M., and Michele L. Swers. "Which Women Can Run? Gender, Partisanship, and Candidate Donor Networks." *Political Research Quarterly* 70, no. 2 (2017): 449–63.

Tiebout, Charles M. "A Pure Theory of Local Expenditures." *Journal of Political Economy* 64, no. 5 (1956): 416–24.

Tolbert, Caroline J., Karen Mossberger, and Ramona McNeal. "Institutions, Policy Innovation, and E-Government in the American States." *Public Administration Review* 68, no. 3 (2008): 549–63.

Trachtman, Samuel. "Public Policy, Organized Interests, and Interdependency in American Federalism: The Case of Rooftop Solar Policy." *Perspectives on Politics* (forthcoming).

———. "When State Policy Makes National Politics: The Case of 'Obamacare' Marketplace Implementation." *Journal of Health Politics, Policy and Law* 45, no. 1 (2020): 111–41.

Travis, Jeremy, Bruce Western, and Steve Redburn. *The Growth of Incarceration in the United States: Exploring Causes and Consequences.* Washington, DC: National Academies Press, 2014.

Treier, Shawn, and D. Sunshine Hillygus. "The Nature of Political Ideology in the Contemporary Electorate." *Public Opinion Quarterly* 73, no. 4 (2009): 679–703.

Treier, Shawn, and Simon Jackman. "Democracy as a Latent Variable." *American Journal of Political Science* 52, no. 1 (2008): 201–17.

Trounstine, Jessica. *Segregation by Design: Local Politics and Inequality in American Cities.* New York: Cambridge University Press, 2018.

Truman, David Bicknell. *The Governmental Process: Political Interests and Public Opinion.* New York: Alfred A. Knopf, 1951.

Victor, Jennifer. "Campaign Fund Raising Is an Arms Race with Limited Impact." *New York Times*, February 25, 2016.

Volden, Craig. "The Politics of Competitive Federalism: A Race to the Bottom in Welfare Benefits?" *American Journal of Political Science* 46, no. 2 (2002): 352–63.

———. "States as Policy Laboratories: Emulating Success in the Children's Health Insurance Program." *American Journal of Political Science* 50, no. 2 (2006): 294–312.

Volden, Craig, Michael M. Ting, and Daniel P. Carpenter. "A Formal Model of Learning and Policy Diffusion." *American Political Science Review* 102, no. 3 (2008): 319–32.

Voorheis, John, Nolan McCarty, and Boris Shor. "Unequal Incomes, Ideology and Gridlock: How Rising Inequality Increases Political Polarization." Working Paper, 2015.

Wacquant, Loic. "From Slavery to Mass Incarceration." *New Left Review* 13 (January–February 2002): 41–60.

———. *Punishing the Poor: The Neoliberal Government of Social Insecurity*. Durham: Duke University Press, 2009.

Wakiyama, Takako, and Eric Zusman. "The Impact of Electricity Market Reform and Subnational Climate Policy on Carbon Dioxide Emissions across the United States: A Path Analysis." *Renewable and Sustainable Energy Reviews* 149 (2021): 111337.

Walker, Edward T. *Grassroots for Hire: Public Affairs Consultants in American Democracy*. New York: Cambridge University Press, 2014.

Walker, Jack L. "The Diffusion of Innovations among the American States." *American Political Science Review* 63, no. 3 (1969): 880–99.

———. *Mobilizing Interest Groups in America: Patrons, Professions, and Social Movements*. Ann Arbor: University of Michigan Press, 1991.

Waltenburg, E. N., and B. Swinford. *Litigating Federalism: The States before the U.S. Supreme Court*. New York: Greenwood, 1999.

Wang, Jessica. "Imagining the Administrative State: Legal Pragmatism, Securities Regulation, and New Deal Liberalism." *Journal of Policy History* 17, no. 3 (2005): 257–93.

Wawro, Gregory. "A Panel Probit Analysis of Campaign Contributions and Roll-Call Votes." *American Journal of Political Science* 45, no. 3 (2001): 563–79.

Wawro, Gregory J., and Ira Katznelson. "Designing Historical Social Scientific Inquiry: How Parameter Heterogeneity Can Bridge the Methodological Divide between Quantitative and Qualitative Approaches." *American Journal of Political Science* 58, no. 2 (2014): 526–46.

Weaver, R. Kent. *Ending Welfare as We Know It*. Washington, DC: Brookings Institution Press, 2000.

Weaver, Vesla M. "Frontlash: Race and the Development of Punitive Crime Policy." *Studies in American Political Development* 21, no. 2 (2007): 230–65.

Weaver, Vesla M., and Amy E. Lerman. "Political Consequences of the Carceral State." *American Political Science Review* 104, no. 4 (2010): 817–33.

Weaver, Vesla M., and Gwen Prowse. "Racial Authoritarianism in U.S. Democracy." *Science* 369, no. 6508 (September 4, 2020): 1176–78. https://doi.org/10.1126/science.abd7669.

Weden, Margaret M., Christine E. Peterson, Jeremy N. Miles, and Regina A. Shih. "Evaluating Linearly Interpolated Intercensal Estimates of Demographic and Socioeconomic Characteristics of US Counties and Census Tracts, 2001–2009." *Population Research and Policy Review* 34, no. 4 (2015): 541–59.

Weiner, Myron. "Political Integration and Political Development." *Annals of the American Academy of Political and Social Science* 358, no. 1 (1965): 52–64.

Weingast, Barry R. "Capitalism, Democracy, and Countermajoritarian Institutions." *Supreme Court Economic Review* 23, no. 1 (2016): 255–77.

Weir, Margaret. "States, Race, and the Decline of New Deal Liberalism." *Studies in American Political Development* 19, no. 2 (2005): 157–72.

Weissert, Carol S. "Beyond Marble Cakes and Picket Fences: What US Federalism Scholars Can Learn from Comparative Work." *Journal of Politics* 73, no. 4 (2011): 965–79.

Wells-Barnett, Ida B. *Southern Horrors: Lynch Law in All Its Phases*. New York: Floating Press, 1892.

Welzel, Christian. "Are Levels of Democracy Affected by Mass Attitudes? Testing Attainment and Sustainment Effects on Democracy." *International Political Science Review* 28, no. 4 (2007): 397–424.

Welzel, Christian, and Ronald Inglehart. "Emancipative Values and Democracy: Response to Hadenius and Teorell." *Studies in Comparative International Development* 41, no. 3 (2006): 74–94.

Western, Bruce. *Punishment and Inequality in America.* New York: Russell Sage Foundation, 2006.

Weyland, Kurt. *Bounded Rationality and Policy Diffusion: Social Sector Reform in Latin America.* Princeton: Princeton University Press, 2009.

———. "Theories of Policy Diffusion Lessons from Latin American Pension Reform." *World Politics* 57, no. 2 (2005): 262–95.

Whittington, Keith E. "Taking What They Give Us: Explaining the Court's Federalism Offensive." *Duke Law Journal* 51, no. 1 (2001): 477–520.

Wilcox, Clyde. "Organizational Variables and Contribution Behavior of Large PACs: A Longitudinal Analysis." *Political Behavior* 11, no. 2 (1989): 157–73.

Wildavsky, Aaron. *Speaking Truth to Power: Art and Craft of Policy Analysis.* New York: Routledge, 2017.

Wilk, Eric M., and Charles M. Lamb. "Federalism, Efficiency, and Civil Rights Enforcement." *Political Research Quarterly* 64, no. 2 (2011): 392–404.

Willbern, York. "Professionalization in the Public Service: Too Little or Too Much?" *Public Administration Review* 14, no. 1 (1954): 13–21.

Wilson, Reid. "The Precipitous Decline of State Political Coverage." *Washington Post*, July 10, 2014. https://www.washingtonpost.com/blogs/govbeat/wp/2014/07/10/the-precipitous-decline-of-state-political-coverage/.

Wingersky, Marilyn S., and Frederic M. Lord. "An Investigation of Methods for Reducing Sampling Error in Certain IRT Procedures." *Applied Psychological Measurement* 8, no. 3 (1984): 347–64.

Winston, Pamela. *Welfare Policymaking in the States: The Devil in Devolution.* Washington, DC: Georgetown University Press, 2002.

Wolbrecht, Christina, and Michael T. Hartney. "'Ideas about Interests': Explaining the Changing Partisan Politics of Education." *Perspectives on Politics* 12, no. 3 (2014): 603–30.

Wright, Gerald C., Robert S. Erikson, and John P. McIver. "Measuring State Partisanship and Ideology with Survey Data." *Journal of Politics* 47, no. 2 (1985): 469–89.

Xu, Yiqing. "Generalized Synthetic Control Method: Causal Inference with Interactive Fixed Effects Models." *Political Analysis* 25, no. 1 (2017): 57–76.

Yarbrough, Jean. "Madison and Modern Federalism." In *James Madison*, edited by Terence Ball, 313–37. New York: Routledge, 2017.

Yates, Jeff, and Richard Fording. "Politics and State Punitiveness in Black and White." *Journal of Politics* 67, no. 4 (2005): 1099–1121.

Yglesias, Matthew. "American Democracy Is Doomed." *Vox*, October 8, 2015.

Yoder, Jesse. "Does Property Ownership Lead to Participation in Local Politics? Evidence from Property Records and Meeting Minutes." *American Political Science Review* 114, no. 4 (2020a): 1213–29.

Yoder, Jesse. "How Wealthy Are Local Elected Officials? Evidence from Candidates' Housing Wealth." Working Paper, 2020b. http://stanford.edu/~yoderj/candidate_home_values.pdf.

Young, Kevin A., Tarun Banerjee, and Michael Schwartz. "Capital Strikes as a Corporate Political Strategy: The Structural Power of Business in the Obama Era." *Politics & Society* 46, no. 1 (2018): 3–28.

Zahariadis, Nikolaos. "The Multiple Streams Framework: Structure, Limitations, Prospects." In *Theories of the Policy Process*, edited by Paul A. Sabatier and Christopher M. Weible. 3rd ed. Boulder, CO: Westview Press, 2014.

Zaller, John. *The Nature and Origins of Mass Opinion.* New York: Cambridge University Press, 1992.

Zhang, Emily Rong. "Questioning Questions in the Law of Democracy: What the Debate over Voter ID Laws' Effects Teaches about Asking the Right Questions." *UCLA Law Review* (forthcoming). https://papers.ssrn.com/sol3/papers.cfm?abstract_id=3942940.

Ziblatt, Daniel. *Conservative Political Parties and the Birth of Modern Democracy in Europe.* New York: Cambridge University Press, 2017.

Ziegler, Mary. "Beyond Backlash: Legal History, Polarization, and *Roe v. Wade.*" *Washington & Lee Law Review* 71 (2014): 969.

Zimmerman, Joseph F. *Contemporary American Federalism: The Growth of National Power.* Albany: SUNY Press, 2009.

INDEX

Page numbers in *italics* refer to figures and tables.

PRINCETON STUDIES IN
AMERICAN POLITICS

Historical, International, and Comparative Perspectives

Suzanne Mettler, Eric Schickler, and
Theda Skocpol, Series Editors

Ira Katznelson, Martin Shefter, Founding
Series Editors (Emeritus)

A NOTE ON THE TYPE

This book has been composed in Arno, an Old-style serif typeface in the
classic Venetian tradition, designed by Robert Slimbach at Adobe.

CPSIA information can be obtained
at www.ICGtesting.com
Printed in the USA
JSHW021348230623
43610JS00006B/4